The

Elements

of

Typographic

Style

POETRY:

The Shipwright's Log · 1972
Cadastre · 1973
Eight Objects · 1975
Bergschrund · 1975
Tzuhalem's Mountain · 1982
The Beauty of the Weapons: Selected Poems 1972–82 · 1982
Tending the Fire · 1985
The Blue Roofs of Japan · 1986
Pieces of Map, Pieces of Music · 1986
Conversations with a Toad · 1987
The Calling: Selected Poems 1970–1995 · 1995
Elements (with drawings by Ulf Nilsen) · 1995
The Book of Silences · 2001

PROSE:

Visions: Contemporary Art in Canada
    (with Geoffrey James, Russell Keziere & Doris Shadbolt) · 1983
Ocean/Paper/Stone · 1984
The Raven Steals the Light (with Bill Reid) · 1984
Shovels, Shoes and the Slow Rotation of Letters · 1986
The Black Canoe (with photographs by Ulli Steltzer) · 1991
Boats Is Saintlier than Captains:
    Thirteen Ways of Looking at Morality, Language and Design · 1997
Native American Oral Literatures and the Unity of the Humanities · 1998
A Short History of the Printed Word (with Warren Chappell) · 1999
A Story as Sharp as a Knife:
    The Classical Haida Mythtellers and Their World · 1999

TRANSLATION:

Ghandl of the Qayahl Llaanas, *Nine Visits to the Mythworld* · 2000
Skaay of the Qquuna Qiighawaay, *Being in Being* · 2001
The Fragments of Parmenides · 2001

¶ THE ELEMENTS *of*

TYPOGRAPHIC STYLE

version 2.4

Robert Bringhurst

¶ HARTLEY & MARKS, *Publishers*

HARTLEY & MARKS, PUBLISHERS

• PO Box 147
  Point Roberts, WA 98281
  USA
• 3661 West Broadway
  Vancouver, BC V6R 2B8
  Canada

Typeset in Canada;
printed & bound in Canada.
∞

This printing of the second edition
incorporates additions and
corrections to the following pages:
2, 21, 43, 73, 87, 91, 113, 121, 137,
140, 142, 147, 181, 186, 188, 193,
207, 214, 215, 224, 227, 228, 230,
231, 232, 233, 236, 240, 247, 252,
254, 256, 264, 270, 277, 279, 281,
284, 300, 301, 302, 306, 309, 313,
315, 316, 317, 327, 331, 332, 333, 335,
336, 340, 343, 345, 347.

*Library of Congress Cataloging in
Publication Data:*

Bringhurst, Robert.
    The elements of typographic style
    /   Robert Bringhurst. –
    2nd ed.   p.   cm.
    Includes index.
    ISBN 0-88179-133-4 (cloth) –
    ISBN 0-88179-132-6 (pbk)
    1. Layout (Printing)
    2. Type and type-founding.
    3. Book design.
    I. Title.
Z246.B74   1996
686.2'24 – dc20   96-3124
                                      CIP

*Canadian Cataloguing in Publication
Data:*

Bringhurst, Robert, 1946–
    The elements of typographic style
    Includes index.
    ISBN 0-88179-133-4 (bound) –
    ISBN 0-88179-132-6 (pbk.)
    1. Layout (Printing)
    2. Type and type-founding.
    3. Book design.
    4. Printing – Specimens.
    I. Title.
Z246.B74   1996   686.2'24
C96-910471-5

for my colleagues & friends

in the worlds of letters:

writers & editors,

type designers, typographers,

printers & publishers,

shepherding words and books

on their lethal and innocent ways

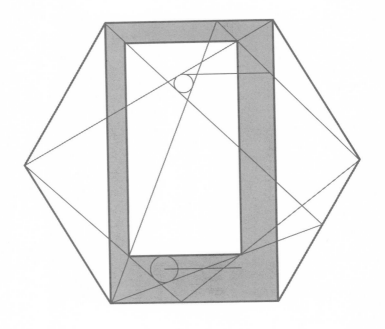

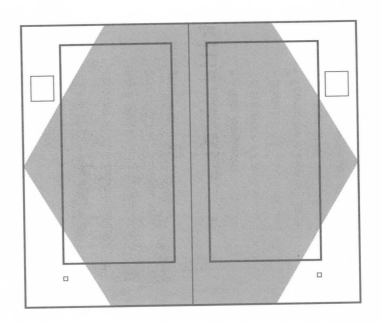

CONTENTS

—Everything written symbols can say has already passed by. They are like tracks left by animals. That is why the masters of meditation refuse to accept that writings are final. The aim is to reach true being by means of those tracks, those letters, those signs – but reality itself is not a sign, and it leaves no tracks. It doesn't come to us by way of letters or words. We can go toward it, by following those words and letters back to what they came from. But so long as we are preoccupied with symbols, theories and opinions, we will fail to reach the principle.

—But when we give up symbols and opinions, aren't we left in the utter nothingness of being?

—Yes.

KIMURA KYŪHO, *Kenjutsu Fushigi Hen*
[*On the Mysteries of Swordsmanship*],
1768

A true revelation, it seems to me, will only emerge from stubborn concentration on a solitary problem. I am not in league with inventors or adventurers, nor with travellers to exotic destinations. The surest – also the quickest – way to awake the sense of wonder in ourselves is to look intently, undeterred, at a single object. Suddenly, miraculously, it will reveal itself as something we have never seen before.

CESARE PAVESE, *Dialoghi con Leucò*,
1947

There are many books about typography, and some of them are models of the art they teach. But when I set myself to compile a simple list of working principles, one of the benchmarks I first thought of was William Strunk and E.B. White's small masterpiece, *The Elements of Style.* Brevity, however, is the essence of Strunk & White's manual of literary technique. This book is longer than theirs, and for that there is a cause.

Typography makes at least two kinds of sense, if it makes any sense at all. It makes visual sense and historical sense. The visual side of typography is always on display, and materials for the study of its visual form are many and widespread. The history of letterforms and their usage is visible too, to those with access to manuscripts, inscriptions and old books, but from others it is largely hidden. This book has therefore grown into something more than a short manual of typographic etiquette. It is the fruit of a lot of long walks in the wilderness of letters: in part a pocket field guide to the living wonders that are found there, and in part a meditation on the ecological principles, survival techniques and ethics that apply. The principles of typography as I understand them are not a set of dead conventions but the tribal customs of the magic forest, where ancient voices speak from all directions and new ones move to unremembered forms.

One question, nevertheless, has been often in my mind. When all right-thinking human beings are struggling to remember that other men and women are free to be different, and free to become more different still, how can one honestly write a rulebook? What reason and authority exist for these commandments, suggestions and instructions? Surely typographers, like others, ought to be at liberty to follow or to blaze the trails they choose.

Typography thrives as a shared concern – and there are no paths at all where there are no shared desires and directions. A typographer determined to forge new routes must move, like other solitary travellers, through uninhabited country and against the grain of the land, crossing common thoroughfares in the silence before dawn. The subject of this book is not typographic solitude, but the old, well-travelled roads at the core of the tradition: paths that each of us is free to follow or not, and to enter and leave when we choose – if only we know the paths are there and have a sense of where they lead. That freedom is denied us if the tradition is concealed or left for dead. Originality is everywhere, but much originality is blocked if the way back to earlier discoveries is cut or overgrown.

If you use this book as a guide, by all means leave the road when you wish. That is precisely the use of a road: to reach individually chosen points of departure. By all means break the rules, and break them beautifully, deliberately and well. That is one of the ends for which they exist.

Letterforms change constantly, yet differ very little, because they are alive. The principles of typographic clarity have also scarcely altered since the second half of the fifteenth century, when the first books were printed in roman type. Indeed, most of the principles of legibility and design explored in this book were known and used by Egyptian scribes writing hieratic script with reed pens on papyrus in 1000 BC. Samples of their work sit now in museums in Cairo, London and New York, still lively, subtle and perfectly legible thirty centuries after they were made.

Writing systems vary, but a good page is not hard to learn to recognize, whether it comes from Táng Dynasty China, the Egyptian New Kingdom or Renaissance Italy. The principles that unite these distant schools of design are based on the structure and scale of the human body – the eye, the hand and the forearm in particular – and on the invisible but no less real, no less demanding, no less sensuous anatomy of the human mind. I don't like to call these principles universals, because they are largely unique to our species. Dogs and ants, for example, read and write by more chemical means. But the underlying principles of typography are, at any rate, stable enough to weather any number of human fashions and fads.

It is true that typographers' tools are presently changing with considerable force and speed, but this is not a manual in the use of any particular typesetting system or medium. I suppose that most readers of this book will set most of their type in digital form, using computers, but I have no preconceptions about which brands of computers, or which versions of which proprietary software, they may use. The essential elements of style have more to do with the goals typographers set for themselves than with the mutable eccentricities of their tools. Typography itself, in other words, is far more device-independent than PostScript, which is the computer language used to render these particular letters, and the design of these pages, into typographic code. If I have succeeded in my task, this book should be as useful to artists and antiquarians setting foundry metal by hand and pulling proofs on a flat-bed press, as to those who check their work on a screen or laser printer, then ship it to high-resolution digital output devices by optical disk or long-distance telephone line.

Typography is the craft of endowing human language with a durable visual form, and thus with an independent existence. Its heartwood is calligraphy – the dance, on a tiny stage, of the living, speaking hand – and its roots reach into living soil, though its branches may be hung each year with new machines. So long as the root lives, typography remains a source of true delight, true knowledge, true surprise.

As a craft, typography shares a long common boundary and many common concerns with writing and editing on the one side and with graphic design on the other; yet typography itself belongs to neither. This book in its turn is neither a manual of editorial style nor a textbook on design, though it overlaps with both of these concerns. The perspective throughout is first and foremost typographic – and I hope the book will be useful for that very reason to those whose work or interests may be centered in adjacent fields.

This book owes much to the conversation and example, over the years, of several friends and master craftsmen – Kay Amert, Stan Bevington, Crispin Elsted, Glenn Goluska, Vic Marks and George Payerle – and to the practice of two artists and exemplars: the late Adrian Wilson, and Hermann Zapf. It owes as much, in other ways, to another friend and colleague, E.M. Ginger. Artists and scholars around the world have shared their knowledge freely. James Mosley and his staff at the St Bride Printing Library, London, have been particularly helpful. I am grateful to them all.

I have many others to thank as well for their contributions to this second edition of the book. Their names appear in the afterword, page 333.

R.B.

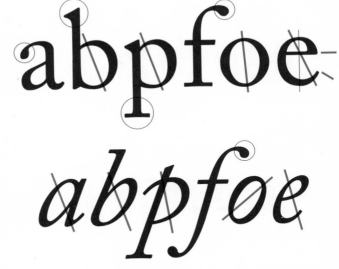

aperture: the
opening in letters
such as a, c, e, s

RENAISSANCE (15th & 16th centuries): modulated stroke; humanist [oblique] axis; crisp, pen-formed terminals; large aperture; italic equal to and independent of roman.

These charts
show first and
foremost the axis
of the *stroke*,
which is the axis
of *the pen that
makes the letter*. It
is often very
different from the
axis of the
lettershape itself.
A pen that points
northwest can
make an upright
letter or a letter
that slopes to the
northeast.

BAROQUE (17th century): modulated stroke; variable axis; modelled serifs and terminals; moderate aperture; italic subsidiary to roman and closely linked with it. A secondary vertical axis often develops in Baroque letters – but the *primary* axis of the penstroke is normally oblique.

12

NEOCLASSICAL (18th century): modulated stroke; rationalist [vertical] axis; refined, adnate serifs; lachrymal terminals; moderate aperture; italic fully subjugated to roman.

adnate: flowing into the stem; *lachrymal*: tear-drop shaped

ROMANTIC (18th & 19th centuries): high contrast; intensified rationalist axis; abrupt, thin serifs; round terminals; small aperture; fully subjugated italic. In Neoclassical and Romantic letters alike, the *primary* axis is usually vertical and the *secondary* axis oblique.

Historical
Synopsis

abpfoe

abpfoe

REALIST (19th & early 20th centuries): unmodulated stroke; implied vertical axis; small aperture; serifs absent or abrupt and of equal weight with main strokes; italic absent or replaced by sloped roman.

abpfoe

abpfoe

GEOMETRIC MODERNIST (20th century): unmodulated stroke; bowls often circular (no axis); moderate aperture; serifs absent or of equal weight with main strokes; italic absent or replaced by sloped roman. The modelling, however, is often much more subtle than it first appears.

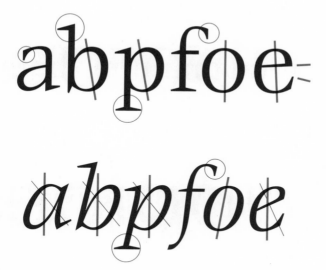

LYRICAL MODERNIST (20th century): rediscovery of Renaissance form: modulated stroke; humanist axis; pen-formed serifs and terminals; large aperture; italic partially liberated from roman.

POSTMODERNIST (late 20th century): frequent parody of Neoclassical and Romantic form: rationalist axis; sharply modelled serifs and terminals; moderate aperture; italic subjugated to roman. (There are many kinds of Postmodernist letter. This is one example.)

rigo Habraam numerā
ı a moſaica lege(ſeptim
r)ſed naturalı fuit ratio
idit enim Habraam deᴄ
m quoqꝛ gentium patr
ıs oés gentes hoc uıdelıᴄ
m eſt:cuius ille iuſtıtiæ
us eſt:qui poſt multas ᴄ
ᴉmum omnium diuinᴄ
ɔ naſcerétur tradidit:uᴇ
gnum:uel ut hoc quaſ
ſuos imitari conaret':au
um nobis modo eſt.Po

Roman type cut in 1469 by Nicolas Jenson, a French typographer working in Venice. The original is approximately 16 pt. The type is shown here
as Jenson printed it, but at twice actual size. This is the ancestor of the
type (Bruce Rogers's Centaur) shown at the top of page 12.

THE GRAND DESIGN

1.1.1 *Typography exists to honor content.*

1

Like oratory, music, dance, calligraphy – like anything that lends its grace to language – typography is an art that can be deliberately misused. It is a craft by which the meanings of a text (or its absence of meaning) can be clarified, honored and shared, or knowingly disguised.

In a world rife with unsolicited messages, typography must often draw attention to itself before it will be read. Yet in order to be read, it must relinquish the attention it has drawn. Typography with anything to say therefore aspires to a kind of statuesque transparency. Its other traditional goal is durability: not immunity to change, but a clear superiority to fashion. Typography at its best is a visual form of language linking timelessness and time.

One of the principles of durable typography is always legibility; another is something more than legibility: some earned or unearned interest that gives its living energy to the page. It takes various forms and goes by various names, including serenity, liveliness, laughter, grace and joy.

These principles apply, in different ways, to the typography of business cards, instruction sheets and postage stamps, as well as to editions of religious scriptures, literary classics and other books that aspire to join their ranks. Within limits, the same principles apply even to stock market reports, airline schedules, milk cartons, classified ads. But laughter, grace and joy, like legibility itself, all feed on meaning, which the writer, the words and the subject, not the typographer, must generally provide.

In 1770, a bill was introduced in the English Parliament with the following provisions:

... all women of whatever age, rank, profession, or degree, whether virgins, maids, or widows, that shall ... impose upon, seduce, and betray into matrimony, any of His Majesty's subjects, by the scents, paints, cosmetic washes, artificial teeth, false hair, Spanish wool, iron stays, hoops, high heeled shoes [or] bolstered hips shall incur

the penalty of the law in force against witchcraft ... and ... the marriage, upon conviction, shall stand null and void.

The function of typography, as I understand it, is neither to further the power of witches nor to bolster the defences of those, like this unfortunate parliamentarian, who live in terror of being tempted and deceived. The satisfactions of the craft come from elucidating, and perhaps even ennobling, the text, not from deluding the unwary reader by applying scents, paints and iron stays to empty prose. But humble texts, such as classified ads or the telephone directory, may profit as much as anything else from a good typographical bath and a change of clothes. And many a book, like many a warrior or dancer or priest of either sex, may look well with some paint on its face, or indeed with a bone in its nose.

1.1.2 *Letters have a life and dignity of their own.*

Letterforms that honor and elucidate what humans see and say deserve to be honored in their turn. Well-chosen words deserve well-chosen letters; these in their turn deserve to be set with affection, intelligence, knowledge and skill. Typography is a link, and it ought, as a matter of honor, courtesy and pure delight, to be as strong as the others in the chain.

Writing begins with the making of footprints, the leaving of signs. Like speaking, it is a perfectly natural act which humans have carried to complex extremes. The typographer's task has always been to add a somewhat unnatural edge, a protective shell of artificial order, to the power of the writing hand. The tools have altered over the centuries, and the exact degree of unnaturalness desired has varied from place to place and time to time, but the character of the essential transformation between manuscript and type has scarcely changed.

The original purpose of type was simply copying. The job of the typographer was to imitate the scribal hand in a form that permitted exact and fast replication. Dozens, then hundreds, then thousands of copies were printed in less time than a scribe would need to finish one. This excuse for setting texts in type has disappeared. In the age of photolithography, digital scanning and offset printing, it is as easy to print directly from handwritten copy as from text that is typographically composed. Yet the typographer's task is little changed. It is still to give the illusion of superhuman speed and stamina – and of superhuman patience and precision – to the writing hand.

Typography is just that: idealized writing. Writers themselves now rarely have the calligraphic skill of earlier scribes, but they evoke countless versions of ideal script by their varying voices and literary styles. To these blind and often invisible visions, the typographer must respond in visible terms.

In a badly designed book, the letters mill and stand like starving horses in a field. In a book designed by rote, they sit like stale bread and mutton on the page. In a well-made book, where designer, compositor and printer have all done their jobs, no matter how many thousands of lines and pages, the letters are alive. They dance in their seats. Sometimes they rise and dance in the margins and aisles.

Simple as it may sound, the task of creative non-interference with letters is a rewarding and difficult calling. In ideal conditions, it is all that typographers are really asked to do – and it is enough.

1.1.3 *There is a style beyond style.*

Literary style, says Walter Benjamin, "is the power to move freely in the length and breadth of linguistic thinking without slipping into banality." Typographic style, in this large and intelligent sense of the word, does not mean any particular style – my style or your style, or Neoclassical or Baroque style – but the power to move freely through the whole domain of typography, and to function at every step in a way that is graceful and vital instead of banal. It means typography that can walk familiar ground without sliding into platitudes, typography that responds to new conditions with innovative solutions, and typography that does not vex the reader with its own originality in a self-conscious search for praise.

Typography is to literature as musical performance is to composition: an essential act of interpretation, full of endless opportunities for insight or obtuseness. Much typography is far removed from literature, for language has many uses, including packaging and propaganda. Like music, it can be used to manipulate behavior and emotions. But this is not where typographers, musicians or other human beings show us their finest side. Typography at its best is a slow performing art, worthy of the same informed appreciation that we sometimes give to mu-

From part 2 of Benjamin's essay on Karl Kraus, in *Illuminationen* (Frankfurt, 1955). There is an English translation in Walter Benjamin, *Reflections*, ed. Peter Demetz (New York, 1978).

sical performances, and capable of giving similar nourishment and pleasure in return.

The same alphabets and page designs can be used for a biography of Mohandas Gandhi and for a manual on the use and deployment of biological weapons. Writing can be used both for love letters and for hate mail, and love letters themselves can be used for manipulation and extortion as well as to bring delight to body and soul. Evidently there is nothing inherently noble and trustworthy in the written or printed word. Yet generations of men and women have turned to writing and printing to house and share their deepest hopes, perceptions, dreams and fears. It is to them, not to the extortionist – nor to the opportunist or the profiteer – that the typographer must answer.

1.2 TACTICS

1.2.1 *Read the text before designing it.*

The typographer's one essential task is to interpret and communicate the text. Its tone, its tempo, its logical structure, its physical size, all determine the possibilities of its typographic form. The typographer is to the text as the theatrical director to the script, or the musician to the score.

1.2.2 *Discover the outer logic of the typography in the inner logic of the text.*

A novel often purports to be a seamless river of words from beginning to end, or a series of unnamed scenes. Research papers, textbooks, cookbooks and other works of nonfiction rarely look so smooth. They are often layered with chapter heads, section heads, subheads, block quotations, footnotes, endnotes, lists and illustrative examples. Such features may be obscure in the manuscript, even if they are clear in the author's mind. For the sake of the reader, each requires its own typographic identity and form. Every layer and level of the text must be consistent, distinct, yet (usually) harmonious in form.

The first task of the typographer is therefore to read and understand the text; the second task is to analyze and map it. Only then can typographic interpretation begin.

If the text has many layers or sections, it may need not only heads and subheads but running heads as well, reappearing on every page or two-page spread, to remind readers which intellectual neighborhood they happen to be visiting.

Novels seldom need such signposts, but they often require typographic markers of other kinds. Peter Matthiessen's novel *Far Tortuga* (New York, 1975; designed by Kenneth Miyamoto) uses two sizes of type, three different margins, free-floating block paragraphs and other typographic devices to separate thought, speech and action. Ken Kesey's novel *Sometimes a Great Notion* (New York, 1964) seems to flow like conventional prose, yet it shifts repeatedly in mid-sentence between roman and italic to distinguish what characters say to each other from what they say in silence to themselves.

In poetry and drama, a larger typographic palette is sometimes required. Some of Douglass Parker's translations from classical Greek and Dennis Tedlock's translations from Zuni use roman, italic, bold, small caps and full caps in various sizes to emulate the dynamic markings of music. Robert Massin's typographic performances of Eugène Ionesco's plays use intersecting lines of type, stretched and melted letters, inkblots, pictograms, and a separate typeface for each person in the play. In the works of other artists such as Guillaume Apollinaire and Guy Davenport, boundaries between author and designer sometimes vanish. Writing merges with typography, and the text becomes its own illustration.

See for example
Aristophanes,
Four Comedies
(Ann Arbor,
Michigan, 1969);
Dennis Tedlock,
*Finding the
Center* (New
York, 1972);
Eugène Ionesco,
*La Cantatrice
chauve* (Paris,
1964), and
Délire à deux
(Paris, 1966).
There are samples of Massin's
work in *Typographia* n.s. 11
(1965).

The typographer must analyze and reveal the inner order of the text, as a musician must reveal the inner order of the music he performs. But the reader, like the listener, should in retrospect be able to close her eyes and see what lies inside the words she has been reading. The typographic performance must reveal, not replace, the inner composition. Typographers, like other artists and craftsmen – musicians, composers and authors as well – must as a rule do their work and disappear.

1.2.3 *Make the visible relationship between the text and other
elements (photographs, captions, tables, diagrams, notes)
a reflection of their real relationship.*

If the text is tied to other elements, where do they belong? If there are notes, do they go at the side of the page, the foot of the page, the end of the chapter, the end of the book? If there are photographs or other illustrations, should they be embedded in the text or should they form a special section of their own? And if the photographs have captions or credits or labels, should these sit close beside the photographs or should they be separately housed?

If there is more than one text – as in countless publications issued in Canada, Switzerland, Belgium and other multilingual countries – how will the separate but equal texts be arrayed? Will they run side by side to emphasize their equality (and perhaps to share in a single set of illustrations), or will they be printed back-to-back, to emphasize their distinctness?

No matter what their relation to the text, photos or maps must sometimes be grouped apart from it because they require a separate paper or different inks. If this is the case, what typographic cross-references will be required?

These and similar questions, which confront the working typographer on a daily basis, must be answered case by case. The typographic page is a map of the mind; it is frequently also a map of the social order from which it comes. And for better or for worse, minds and social orders change.

1.2.4 *Choose a typeface or a group of faces that will honor and elucidate the character of the text.*

This is the beginning, middle and end of the practice of typography: choose and use the type with sensitivity and intelligence. Aspects of this principle are explored throughout this book and considered in detail in chapters 6, 7 and 10.

Letterforms have tone, timbre, character, just as words and sentences do. The moment a text and a typeface are chosen, two streams of thought, two rhythmical systems, two sets of habits, or if you like, two personalities, intersect. They need not live together contentedly forever, but they must not as a rule collide.

The root metaphor of typesetting is that the alphabet (or in Chinese, the entire lexicon) is a system of interchangeable parts. The word *form* can be surgically revised, instead of rewritten, to become the word *farm* or *firm* or *fort* or *fork* or *from*, or with a little more trouble, to become the word *pineapple*. The old compositor's typecase is a partitioned wooden tray holding hundreds of such interchangeable bits of information. These sub-semantic particles, these bits – called *sorts* by letterpress printers – are letters cast on standardized bodies of metal, waiting to be assembled into meaningful combinations, then dispersed and reassembled in a different form. The compositor's typecase is one of the primary ancestors of the computer – and it is no surprise that while typesetting was one of the last crafts to be mechanized, it was one of the first to be computerized.

But the bits of information handled by typographers differ in one essential respect from the computer programmer's bits. Whether the type is set in hard metal by hand, or in softer metal by machine, or in digital form on paper or film, every comma, every parenthesis, every *e*, and in context, even every empty space, has style as well as bald symbolic value. Letters are microscopic works of art as well as useful symbols. They mean what they are as well as what they say.

Typography is the art and craft of handling these doubly meaningful bits of information. A good typographer handles them in intelligent, coherent, sensitive ways. When the type is poorly chosen, what the words say linguistically and what the letters imply visually are disharmonious, dishonest, out of tune.

1.2.5 *Shape the page and frame the textblock so that it honors and reveals every element, every relationship between elements, and every logical nuance of the text.*

Selecting the shape of the page and placing the type upon it is much like framing and hanging a painting. A cubist painting in an eighteenth-century gilded frame, or a seventeenth-century still-life in a slim chrome box, will look no sillier than a nineteenth-century text from England set in types that come from seventeenth-century France, asymmetrically positioned on a German Modernist page.

If the text is long or the space is short, or if the elements are many, multiple columns may be required. If illustrations and text march side by side, does one take precedence over the other? And does the order or degree of prominence change? Does the text suggest perpetual symmetry, perpetual asymmetry, or something in between?

Again, does the text suggest the continuous unruffled flow of justified prose, or the continued flirtation with order and chaos evoked by flush-left ragged-right composition? (The running heads and sidenotes on the odd-numbered pages of this book are set flush left, ragged right. On the even numbered pages, they are ragged left. Leftward-reading alphabets, like Arabic and Hebrew, are perfectly at home in ragged-left text, but with rightward-reading alphabets like Latin, Greek or Thai, ragged-left setting emphasizes the end, not the beginning, of the line. This makes it a poor choice for extended composition.)

Shaping the page goes hand in hand with choosing the type, and both are permanent typographical preoccupations. The subject of page shapes and proportions is addressed in greater detail in chapter 8.

Tactics

1.2.6 *Give full typographic attention even to incidental details.*

Some of what a typographer must set, like some of what any musician must play, is simply passage work. Even an edition of Plato or Shakespeare will contain a certain amount of routine text: page numbers, scene numbers, textual notes, the copyright claim, the publisher's name and address, and the hyperbole on the jacket, not to mention the passage work or background writing that is implicit in the text itself. But just as a good musician can make a heart-wrenching ballad from a few banal words and a trivial tune, so the typographer can make poignant and lovely typography from bibliographical paraphernalia and textual chaff. The ability to do so rests on respect for the text as a whole, and on respect for the letters themselves.

Perhaps the principle should read: Give full typographic attention *especially* to incidental details.

1.3 SUMMARY

There are always exceptions, always excuses for stunts and surprises. But perhaps we can agree that, as a rule, typography should perform these services for the reader:

- invite the reader into the text;
- reveal the tenor and meaning of the text;
- clarify the structure and the order of the text;
- link the text with other existing elements;
- induce a state of energetic repose, which is the ideal condition for reading.

While serving the reader in this way, typography, like a musical performance or a theatrical production, should serve two other ends. It should honor the text for its own sake – always assuming that the text is worth a typographer's trouble – and it should honor and contribute to its own tradition: that of typography itself.

24

2.1 HORIZONTAL MOTION

2

An ancient metaphor: thought is a thread, and the raconteur is a spinner of yarns – but the true storyteller, the poet, is a weaver. The scribes made this old and audible abstraction into a new and visible fact. After long practice, their work took on such an even, flexible texture that they called the written page a *textus,* which means cloth.

The typesetting device, whether it happens to be a computer or a composing stick, functions like a loom. And the typographer, like the scribe, normally aims to weave the text as evenly as possible. Good letterforms are designed to give a lively, even texture, but careless spacing of letters, lines and words can tear this fabric apart.

Another ancient metaphor: the density of texture in a written or typeset page is called its *color.* This has nothing to do with red or green ink; it refers only to the darkness or blackness of the letterforms in mass. Once the demands of legibility and logical order are satisfied, *evenness of color* is the typographer's normal aim. And color depends on four things: the design of the type, the spacing between the letters, the spacing between the words, and the spacing between the lines. None is independent of the others.

2.1.1 *Define the word space to suit the size and natural letterfit of the font.*

Type is normally measured in picas and points (explained in detail on pages 294–295), but horizontal spacing is measured in *ems,* and the em is a sliding measure. One em is a distance equal to the type size. In 6 point type, an em is 6 points; in 12 pt type it is 12 points, and in 60 pt type it is 60 points. Thus a one-em space is *proportionately* the same in any size.

12 pt em	18 pt em	24 pt em	36 pt em

Typesetting machines generally divide the em into units. Ems of 18, 36 or 54 units, for example, are commonly found in the older machines. In newer devices, the em may be a thousand units. Typographers are more likely to divide the em into simple fractions: half an em, a third of an em, and so on, knowing that the unit value of these fractions will vary from one machine to the next. Half an em is called an *en*.

If text is set ragged right, the *word space* (the space between words) can be fixed and unchanging. If the text is *justified* (set flush left and right, like the text in this book), the word space must be elastic. In either case, the size of the ideal word space varies from one circumstance to another, depending on factors such as letterfit, type color, and size. A loosely fitted or bold face will need a larger interval between the words. At larger sizes, when letterfit is tightened, the spacing of words can be tightened as well. For a normal text face in a normal text size, a typical value for the word space is a quarter of an em, which can be written M/4. (A quarter of an em is typically about the same as, or slightly more than, the set-width of the letter t.)

Language has some effect on the word space as well. In highly inflected languages, such as Latin, most word boundaries are marked by grammatical tags, and a smaller space is therefore sufficient. In English and other uninflected languages, good word spacing makes the difference between a line that has to be deciphered and a line that can be efficiently read.

If the text is justified, a reasonable *minimum* word space is a fifth of an em (M/5), and M/4 is a good average to aim for. A reasonable maximum in justified text is M/2. If it can be held to M/3, so much the better. But for loosely fitted faces, or text set in a small size, M/3 is often a better average to aim for, and a better minimum is M/4. In a line of widely letterspaced capitals, a word space of M/2 or more may be required.

2.1.2 *Choose a comfortable measure.*

Anything from 45 to 75 characters is widely regarded as a satisfactory length of line for a single-column page set in a serifed text face in a text size. The 66-character line (counting both letters and spaces) is widely regarded as ideal. For multiple-column work, a better average is 40 to 50 characters.

If the type is well set and printed, lines of 85 or 90 characters will pose no problem in discontinuous texts, such as bibliographies, or, with generous leading, in footnotes. But even with generous leading, a line that averages more than 75 or 80 characters is likely to be too long for continuous reading.

A reasonable working minimum for justified text in English is the 40-character line. Shorter lines may compose perfectly well with sufficient luck and patience, but in the long run, justified lines averaging less than 38 or 40 characters will lead to white acne or pig bristles: a rash of erratic and splotchy word spaces or an epidemic of hyphenation. When the line is short, the text should be set ragged right. In large doses, even ragged-right composition may look anorexic if the line falls below 30 characters, but in small and isolated patches – ragged marginal notes, for example – the minimum line (if the language is English) can be as little as 12 or 15 characters.

When the counters of the letterforms themselves, not just the spaces between words, are elastic, justification can be carried to greater extremes. See pages 189–191 for details.

These line lengths are in every case averages, and they include empty spaces and punctuation as well as letters. The simplest way of computing them is with a copyfitting table like the one on page 29. Measure the length of the basic lowercase alphabet – abcdefghijklmnopqrstuvwxyz – in any face and size you are considering, and the table will tell you the average number of characters to expect on a given line. In most text faces, the 10 pt roman alphabet will run between 120 and 140 points in length, but a 10 pt *italic* alphabet might be 100 points long or even less, while a 10 pt bold might run to 160. The 12 pt alphabet is, of course, about 1.2 times the length of the 10 pt alphabet – but not exactly so unless it is generated from the same master design and the letterfit is unchanged.

On a conventional book page, the measure, or length of line, is usually around 30 times the size of the type, but lines as little as 20 or as much as 40 times the type size fall within the expectable range. If, for example, the type size is 10 pt, the measure might be around $30 \times 10 = 300$ pt, which is $300/12 = 25$ picas. A typical lowercase alphabet length for a 10 pt text font is 128 pt, and the copyfitting table tells us that such a font set to a 25-pica measure will yield roughly 65 characters per line.

2.1.3 *Set ragged if ragged setting suits the text and the page.*

In justified text, there is always a trade-off between evenness of word spacing and frequency of hyphenation. The best available compromise will depend on the nature of the text as well as on the specifics of the design. Good compositors like to avoid consecutive hyphenated line-ends, but frequent hyphens are better than sloppy spacing, and ragged setting is better yet.

Narrow measures – which prevent good justification – are commonly used when the text is set in multiple columns. Setting ragged right under these conditions will lighten the page and decrease its stiffness, as well as preventing an outbreak of hyphenation.

Many unserifed faces look best when set ragged no matter what the length of the measure. And monospaced fonts, which are common on typewriters, always look better set ragged, in standard typewriter style. A typewriter (or a computer-driven printer of similar quality) that justifies its lines in imitation of typesetting is a presumptuous machine, mimicking the outer form instead of the inner truth of typography.

When setting ragged text with a computer, take a moment to refine your software's understanding of what constitutes an honest rag. Many programs are predisposed to invoke a minimum as well as a maximum line. If permitted to do so, they will hyphenate words and adjust spaces regardless of whether they are ragging or justifying the text. Ragged setting under these conditions produces an orderly ripple down the righthand side, making the text look like a neatly pinched piecrust. This approach combines the worst features of justification with the worst features of ragged setting, while eliminating the principal virtues of both. Unless the measure is excruciatingly narrow, it is usually better to set a hard rag. This means a fixed word space, no minimum line, and no hyphenation beyond what is inherent in the text. In a hard rag, hyphenated linebreaks may occur in words like *self-consciousness*, which are hyphenated anyway, but they can only occur with manual intervention in words like *hyphenation* or *pseudosophisticated*, which are not.

2.1.4 *Use a single word space between sentences.*

In the nineteenth century, which was a dark and inflationary age in typography and type design, many compositors were encouraged to stuff extra space between sentences. Generations of twentieth-century typists were then taught to do the same, by hitting the spacebar twice after every period. Your typing as well as your typesetting will benefit from unlearning this quaint

AVERAGE CHARACTER COUNT PER LINE

	10	12	14	16	18	20	22	24	26	28	30	32	34	36	38	40
80	40	48	56	64	72	80	88	96	104	112	120	128	136	144	152	160
85	38	45	53	60	68	76	83	91	98	106	113	121	129	136	144	151
90	36	43	50	57	64	72	79	86	93	100	107	115	122	129	136	143
95	34	41	48	55	62	69	75	82	89	96	103	110	117	123	130	137
100	33	40	46	53	59	66	73	79	86	92	99	106	112	119	125	132
105	32	38	44	51	57	63	70	76	82	89	95	101	108	114	120	127
110	30	37	43	49	55	61	67	73	79	85	92	98	104	110	116	122
115	29	35	41	47	53	59	64	70	76	82	88	94	100	105	111	117
120	28	34	39	45	50	56	62	67	73	78	84	90	95	101	106	112
125	27	32	38	43	48	54	59	65	70	75	81	86	91	97	102	108
130	26	31	36	41	47	52	57	62	67	73	78	83	88	93	98	104
135	25	30	35	40	45	50	55	60	65	70	75	80	85	90	95	100
140	24	29	34	39	44	48	53	58	63	68	73	77	82	87	92	97
145	23	28	33	37	42	47	51	56	61	66	70	75	80	84	89	94
150	23	28	32	37	41	46	51	55	60	64	69	74	78	83	87	92
155	22	27	31	36	40	45	49	54	58	63	67	72	76	81	85	90
160	22	26	30	35	39	43	48	52	56	61	65	69	74	78	82	87
165	21	25	30	34	38	42	46	51	55	59	63	68	72	76	80	84
170	21	25	29	33	37	41	45	49	53	57	62	66	70	74	78	82
175	20	24	28	32	36	40	44	48	52	56	60	64	68	72	76	80
180	20	23	27	31	35	39	43	47	51	55	59	62	66	70	74	78
185	19	23	27	30	34	38	42	46	49	53	57	61	65	68	72	76
190	19	22	26	30	33	37	41	44	48	52	56	59	63	67	70	74
195	18	22	25	29	32	36	40	43	47	50	54	58	61	65	68	72
200	18	21	25	28	32	35	39	42	46	49	53	56	60	63	67	70
210	17	20	23	27	30	33	37	40	43	47	50	53	57	60	63	67
220	16	19	22	25	29	32	35	38	41	45	48	51	54	57	60	64
230	15	18	21	24	27	30	33	36	40	43	46	49	52	55	58	61
240	15	17	20	23	26	29	32	35	38	41	44	46	49	52	55	58
250	14	17	20	22	25	28	31	34	36	39	42	45	48	50	53	56
260	14	16	19	22	24	27	30	32	35	38	41	43	46	49	51	54
270	13	16	18	21	23	26	29	31	34	36	39	42	44	47	49	52
280	13	15	18	20	23	25	28	30	33	35	38	40	43	45	48	50
290	12	15	17	20	22	24	27	29	32	34	37	39	41	44	46	49
300	12	14	17	19	21	24	26	28	31	33	35	38	40	42	45	47
320	11	13	16	18	20	22	25	27	29	31	34	36	38	40	43	45
340	10	13	15	17	19	21	23	25	27	29	32	34	36	38	40	42
360	10	12	14	16	18	20	22	24	26	28	30	32	34	36	38	40

Read down, in the left column: lowercase alphabet length in points. *Read across,* in the top row: line length in picas.

Victorian habit. As a general rule, no more than a single space is required after a period, a colon or any other mark of punctuation. Larger spaces (e.g., en spaces) are *themselves* punctuation.

The rule is usually altered, however, when setting classical Latin and Greek, romanized Sanskrit, phonetics or other kinds of texts in which sentences begin with lowercase letters. In the absence of a capital, a full *en space* (M/2) between sentences will generally be welcome.

2.1.5 *Add little or no space within strings of initials.*

Names such as W. B. Yeats and J.C.L. Prillwitz need hair spaces, thin spaces or no spaces at all after the intermediary periods. A normal word space follows the *last* period in the string.

2.1.6 *Letterspace all strings of capitals and small caps, and all long strings of digits.*

Acronyms such as CIA and PLO are frequent in some texts. So are abbreviations such as CE and BCE or AD and BC. The normal value for letterspacing these sequences of small or full caps is 5% to 10% of the type size.

With digital fonts, it is a simple matter to assign extra width to all small capitals, so that letterspacing occurs automatically. The width values of full caps are normally based on the assumption that they will be used in conjunction with the lower case, but letterspacing can still be automated through the use of kerning tables (see pages 33–34).

In titles and headings, extra letterspacing is often desirable. Justified lines of letterspaced capitals are generally set by inserting a normal word space (M/5 to M/4) between letters. This corresponds to letterspacing of 20% to 25% of the type size. But the extra space between letters will also require more space between lines. A Renaissance typographer setting a multi-line head in letterspaced text-size capitals would normally set blanks between the lines: the hand compositor's equivalent of the keyboard operator's extra hard return, or double spacing.

There is no generalized optimum value for letterspacing capitals in titles or display lines. The effective letterspacing of caps in good classical inscriptions and later manuscripts ranges from 5% to 100% of the nominal type size. The quantity of space is far less important than its balance. Sequences like LA or

30

AVA may need no extra space at all, while sequences like N N and
H I H beg to be pried open.

W A V A D O P A T T I M M I L T L

WAVADOPATTIMMILTL

Letterspaced caps, above; kerned but unletterspaced, below.

   Many typographers like to letterspace all strings of numbers
as well. Spacing is essential for rapid reading of long, fundamentally meaningless strings, such as serial numbers, and it is
helpful even for shorter strings such as phone numbers and
dates. Numbers set in very short strings – triplets or pairs –
need not be letterspaced. This is the rationale behind the long-
standing European habit of setting phone numbers in the form
oo oo oo instead of o o o - o o o o.

2.1.7 *Don't letterspace the lower case without a reason.*

A man who would letterspace lower case would steal sheep,
Frederic Goudy liked to say. If this wisdom needs updating, it is
chiefly to add that a woman who would letterspace lower case
would steal sheep as well.

   Nevertheless, like every rule, this one extends only as far as
its rationale. The reason for not letterspacing lower case is that
it hampers legibility. But there are some lowercase alphabets to
which this principle doesn't apply.

   Headings set in exaggeratedly letterspaced, condensed, unserifed capitals are now a hallmark, if not a cliché, of postmodern
typography. In this context, secondary display can be set perfectly well in more modestly letterspaced, condensed, unserifed
lower case. Moderate letterspacing can make a face such as lowercase Univers bold condensed *more* legible rather than less. Ines-
sential ligatures are, of course, omitted from letterspaced text.

wharves and wharfingers

Lowercase Univers bold condensed, letterspaced 10%.

   It would be possible, in fact, to make a detailed chart of
lowercase letterforms, plotting their inherent resistance to let-

31

terspacing. Near the top of the list (most unsuitable for letterspacing) would be Renaissance italics, such as Arrighi, whose structure strongly implies an actual linkage between one letter and the next. A little farther along would be Renaissance romans. Still farther along, we would find faces like Syntax, which echo the forms of Renaissance roman but lack the serifs. Around the middle of the list, we would find other unserifed faces, such as Helvetica, in which nothing more than wishful thinking bonds the letters to each other. Bold condensed sanserifs would appear at the bottom of the list. Letterspacing will always sabotage a Renaissance roman or italic. But when we come to the other extreme, the faces with no calligraphic flow, letterspacing of lowercase letters can sometimes be of genuine benefit.

Because it isolates the individual elements, letterspacing has a role to play wherever words have ceased to matter and letters are what count. Where letters function one by one, like numbers – as in acronyms, web-site and e-mail addresses – letterspacing is likely to help, no matter whether the letters are caps, small caps or lower case.

Outside the domain of roman and italic type, the letterspacing of text has other traditional functions. Blackletter faces have, as a rule, no companion italic or bold, and no small caps. The simplest methods of emphasis available are underlining and letterspacing. The former was the usual method of the scribes, but letterspacing is easier for letterpress printers. In digitial typography, however, underlining is just as easy as letterspacing and sometimes does less damage to the page.

In Cyrillic, the normal lower case is full of forms resembling small caps, and a separate small cap font is therefore out of the question. A Russian typographer calls for разрядка (letterspacing) in Cyrillic where small caps would be used in the Latin alphabet. But a true cursive (*курсивный*) Cyrillic, like a true italic, should rarely or never be letterspaced.

2.1.8 *Kern consistently and modestly or not at all.*

Inconsistencies in letterfit are inescapable, given the forms of the Latin alphabet, and small irregularities are after all essential to the legibility of roman type. *Kerning* – altering the space between selected pairs of letters – can increase consistency of spacing in a word like Washington or Toronto, where the combinations *Wa* and *To* are kerned. But names like Wisconsin,

32

Tübingen, Tbilisi and Los Alamos, as well as common words like The and This, remain more or less immune to alteration.

Hand compositors rarely kern text sizes, because their kerning pairs must be manually fitted, one at a time. Computerized typesetting makes extensive kerning easy, but judgment is still required, and the computer does not make good judgment any easier to come by. Too little kerning is preferable to too much, and inconsistent kerning is worse than none.

In digital type, as in foundry type, each letter has a standard width of its own. But computerized typesetting systems can modify these widths in many ways. Digital fonts are generally kerned through the use of *kerning tables*, which can specify a reduction or increase in spacing for every possible pair of letters, numbers or symbols. By this means, space can be automatically added to combinations like HH and removed from combinations like Ty. Prefabricated kerning tables are now routine components of well-made digital fonts, but they still sometimes require extensive editing to suit individual styles and requirements. If you use an automatic kerning program, test it thoroughly before trusting its decisions, and take the time to repair its inevitable shortcomings.

Kerning tables generally subtract space from combinations such as Av, Aw, Ay, 'A, 'A, L', and all combinations in which the first element is T, V, W or Y and the second element is a, c, d, e, g, m, n, o, p, q, r, s, u, v, w, x, y or z. Not all of these combinations occur in English, but any kerning system should accommodate names like Tchaikovsky, Tmolos, Tsimshian and Ysaÿe.

The table also normally adds space to sequences like f', f), f], f?, f!, (f, [f, (J and [J. In some italics, space must also be added to gg and gy. If your text includes them, other sequences – gf, gj, qf, qj, for instance – may need attention as well.

Especially at larger sizes, it is common to kern combinations involving commas and periods, such as r, / r. / v, / v. / w, / w. / y, / y. But use care in kerning combinations such as F. / P. / T. / V. Capitals need their space, and some combinations are easy to misread. P. F. Didot may be misread as R E Didot if too enthusiastically kerned.

Numbers are often omitted from kerning tables, but numbers frequently need kerning more than anything else. The digit *one* is usually thinner in form than the other numbers, but it is often assigned the same set-width, so columns of typeset figures will align. Many fonts include an alternative version of the digit

To

(f"

w,

one (the so-called 'fitted one') with a narrower set-width, intended for use in text. Other combinations of digits often need more subtle adjustment, and all digits need careful kerning in relation to the en dash.

Horizontal Motion

1640–1842   **1640–1842**

Unkerned numerals, left, and kerned numerals, right

Whatever kerning you do, make sure it does not result in collisions with floating accents. Wolf can be kerned more than Wölfflin in many faces, and Tennyson more than Tête-à-tête. Also beware the composite effect of sequential kerns. The apostrophes in L'Hôtel and D'Artagnan can be brought up fairly close, but in L'Anse aux Meadows, two close kerns in a row will produce a collision.

A kerning table written for one language will need subtle alteration before it can do justice to another. In English, for example, it is normal to kern the combinations 'd 'm 'r 's 't, which appear in common contractions. In French, 'a 'â 'e 'é 'è 'ê 'o 'ô are kerned instead, because these appear in elisions. In Czech, it is best to kern the combinations d' and t', which are used as separate letters distinct from d and t. For Spanish, one kerns the combinations '¿ and "¿. For German, a fastidious typographer will take space out of the combinations ‚T „T ‚V „V ‚W „W and frequently add it to ‚J and „J.

The letter *c* is not a full-fledged member of the German alphabet, and in former times it was always restricted, in German, to the ligatures *ch* and *ck*. English-speaking readers often find these combinations kerned too close for comfort in German-made fonts – or they find the right side-bearing of the *c* too close-cut to begin with. In fonts from the Netherlands, unusually tight kerning is common in the sequence *ij* instead.

Binomial kerning tables are powerful and useful typographic tools, but they eliminate neither the need nor the pleasure of making final adjustments by hand. Names like T.V.R. Murti and T.R.V. Murti, for example, pose microscopic typographic problems that no binomial kerning table can solve. Fonts with polynomial kerning capabilities – the ability to kern a given pair of letters in different ways according to context – now exist, and these are discussed in §9.2.3.

's

d'

"¿

ck

ij

34

2.1.9 *Don't alter the widths or shapes of letters without cause.*

Type design is an art practiced by few and mastered by fewer –
but font-editing software makes it possible for anyone to alter
in a moment the widths and shapes of letters to which an artist
may have devoted decades of study, years of inspiration and a
rare concentration of skill. The power to destroy such a type designer's work should be used with caution. And arbitrarily condensing or expanding letterforms is the poorest of all methods
for fitting uneditable copy into unalterable space.

In many fonts, the exclamation mark, question mark, semicolon and colon need a wider left sidebearing than manufacturers have given them, but the width of any character should be
altered for one purpose only: to improve the set of the type.

Typographic letters are made legible not only by their forms
and by the color of the ink that prints them but also by the
sculpted empty space between and around them. When type is
cast and set by hand, that space is physically defined by blocks
of metal. When the type is reduced to a *face*, photographically
or digitally stored, the letter still has a room of its own, defined
by its stated body height and width. But in the world of digital
type, it is very easy for a designer or compositor with no regard
for letters to squish them into cattle trains and ship them to the
slaughter.

letterfit   letterfit

When letters are maltreated in this way, their reserve of legibility is sapped. They can do little in their turn except short-
change and brutalize the reader.

2.1.10 *Don't stretch the space until it breaks.*

Lists, such as contents pages and recipes, are opportunities to
build architectural structures in which the space between the
elements both separates and binds. The two favorite ways of destroying such an opportunity are setting great chasms of space
that the eye cannot leap without help from the hand, and setting unenlightening rows of dots (*dot leaders*, they are called)
that force the eye to walk the width of the page like a prisoner
being escorted back to its cell.

The following examples show two among many ways of

handling a list. Splitting titles and numbers apart, setting one flush left and the other flush right, with or without dot leaders, would only muffle the information:

2.2 VERTICAL MOTION

2.2.1 *Choose a basic leading that suits the typeface, text and measure.*

Time is divisible into any number of increments. So is space. But for working purposes, time in music is divided into a few proportional intervals: halves, quarters, eighths, sixteenths and so on. And time in most music is measured. Add a quarter note to a bar whose time is already accounted for and, somewhere nearby, the equivalent of that quarter note must come out. Phrasing and rhythm can move in and out of phase – as they do in the singing of Billie Holiday and the trumpet solos of Miles Davis – but the force of blues phrasing and syncopation vanishes if the beat is actually lost.

Space in typography is like time in music. It is infinitely divisible, but a few proportional intervals can be much more useful than a limitless choice of arbitrary quantities.

The metering of horizontal space is accomplished almost unconsciously in typography. You choose and prepare a font, and you choose a measure (the width of the column). When you set the type, the measure fills with the varied rhythm of repeating letter shapes, which are music to the eye.

Vertical space is metered in a different way. You must choose not only the overall measure – the depth of the column or page – but also a basic rhythmical unit. This unit is the leading, which is the distance from one baseline to the next.

Eleven-point type *set solid* is described as 11/11. The theoretical face of the type is 11 points high (from the top of *d* to the bottom of *p*, if the type is full on the body), and the distance from the baseline of line one to the baseline of line two is also 11 points. Add two points of lead (interlinear space), and the type is set 11/13. The type size has not changed, but the distance from baseline to baseline has increased to 13 points, and the type has more room to breathe.

The text of the book you are reading, to take an example, is set 10/12 × 21. This means that the type size is 10 pt, the added lead is 2 pt, giving a total leading of 12 pt, and the line length is 21 picas.

A short burst of advertising copy or a title might be set with negative leading (18/15, for example), so long as the ascenders and descenders don't collide:

this is an example
of negative leading

Continuous text is very rarely set with negative leading, and only a few text faces read well when set solid. Most text requires positive leading. Settings such as 9/11, 10/12, 11/13 and 12/15 are routine. Longer measures need more lead than short ones. Dark faces need more lead than light ones. Large-bodied faces need more lead than smaller-bodied ones. Faces like Bauer Bodoni, with substantial color and a rigid vertical axis, need much more lead than faces like Bembo, whose color is light and whose axis is based on the writing hand. And unserifed faces often need more lead (or a shorter line) than their serifed counterparts.

Extra leading is also generally welcome where the text is thickened by superscripts, subscripts, mathematical expressions, or the frequent use of full capitals. A text in German would ideally have a little more lead than the same text in Latin or French, purely because of the increased frequency of capitals.

2.2.2 *Add and delete vertical space in measured intervals.*

For the same reason that the tempo must not change arbitrarily in music, leading must not change arbitrarily in type.

Pages and columns are set most often to uniform depth, but ragged depths are better in some situations. A collection of short texts, such as catalog entries, set in multiple-column pages, is likely to look better and read more easily if the text is not sawed into columns of uniform depth. A collection of short poems is bound to generate pages of varying depth as well – and so much the better.

Continuous prose offers no such excuse for variation. It is therefore usually set in pages of uniform depth, designed in symmetrical pairs. The lines and blocks of text on facing pages in this format should align, and the lines on the front and back of the leaf (the recto and verso pages) should align as well. Typographers check their reproduction proofs by holding them up to the light in pairs, to see that the text and crop marks match from page to page. Press proofs are checked in the same way, by holding them up to the light to see that textblocks *back each other up* when the sheet is printed on both sides.

Headings, subheads, block quotations, footnotes, illustrations, captions and other intrusions into the text create syncopations and variations against the base rhythm of regularly leaded lines. These variations can and should add life to the page, but the main text should also return after each variation precisely on beat and in phase. This means that the total amount of vertical space consumed by each departure from the main text should be an even multiple of the basic leading. If the main text runs 11/13, intrusions to the text should equal some multiple of 13 points: 26, 39, 52, 65, 78, 91, 104 and so on.

Subheads in this book are leaded in the simplest possible way, with a *white line* (that is, in keyboard terms, a hard return) before and after. They could just as well be leaded asymmetrically, with more space above than below, so long as the total additional lead is equivalent to an even number of text lines.

If you happen to be setting a text 11/13, subhead possibilities include the following:

- subheads in 11/13 small caps, with 13 pt above the head and 13 pt below;
- subheads in 11/13 bold *u&lc* (upper and lower case), with 8 pt above the head and 5 pt below, since 8 + 5 = 13;
- subheads in 11/13 caps with 26 pt above and 13 pt below;
- one-line subheads in 14/13 italic u&lc, with 16 pt above the head and 10 pt below. (The negative leading is merely to minimize coding in this case. If the heads are one line long, no cramping will occur.)

2.2.3 *Don't suffocate the page.*

Most books now printed in the Latin alphabet carry from 30 to 45 lines per page. The average length of line in most of those books is 60 to 66 characters. In English and the Romance languages, a word is typically assumed to average five letters plus a space. Ten or eleven such words fit on a line of 60 to 66 characters, and the page, if it is full, holds from 300 to 500 words.

Outside these conventional boundaries lie many interesting typographic problems. If the text deserves the honor, a handsome page can be made with very few words. A page with 17 lines of 36 characters each, as an example, will carry only 100 words. At the other extreme, a page with 45 lines of 70 characters each will carry 525 words. If you want more than 500 words to the page, it is time to consider multiple columns. A two-column book page will comfortably carry 750 words. If it must, it can carry a thousand.

However empty or full it may be, the page must breathe, and in a book – that is, in a long text fit for the reader to live in – the page must breathe in both directions. The longer the line, the more space necessary between lines. Two columns of short lines are therefore more compact than a single column of long lines.

2.3 BLOCKS & PARAGRAPHS

2.3.1 *Set opening paragraphs flush left.*

The function of a paragraph indent is to mark a pause, setting the paragraph apart from what precedes it. If a paragraph is preceded by a title or subhead, the indent is superfluous and can therefore be omitted, as it is here.

2.3.2 *In continuous text, mark all paragraphs after the first with an indent of at least one en.*

Typography like other arts, from cooking to choreography, involves a balance between the familiar and the unfamiliar, the dependably consistent and the unforeseen. Typographers generally take pleasure in the unpredictable length of the paragraph while accepting the simple and reassuring consistency of the paragraph indent. The prose paragraph and its verse counterpart, the stanza, are basic units of linguistic thought and literary style. The typographer must articulate them enough to make them clear, yet not so strongly that the form instead of the content steals the show. If the units of thought, or the boundaries between thoughts, look more important than the thoughts themselves, the typographer has failed.

Blocks and Paragraphs

❧ Ornaments can be placed in the paragraph indents, but few texts actually profit from ornamentation.

Paragraphs can also be marked, as this one is, by drop lines, but dropline paragraphs grow tiresome in long texts. They also increase the labor of revisions and corrections. ¶ Pilcrows, boxes and bullets can be used to mark the breaks in a stream of continuous text, sometimes with excellent results. This format is more economical of space than conventional indented paragraphs, but again, extra labor and expense may arise with emendations and corrections.

Outdented paragraphs and indented paragraphs are the two most obvious possibilities that remain. And outdented paragraphs bring with them other possibilities, such as the use of enlarged marginal letters.

All these variants, and others, have their uses, but the plainest, most unmistakable yet unobtrusive way of marking paragraphs is the simple indent: a white square.

How much indent is enough? The most common paragraph indent is one em. Another standard value is *one lead*. If your text is set 11/13, the indent would then be either 11 pt (one em) or 13 pt (one lead). One en (half an em) is the practical minimum.

Where the line is long and margins are ample, an indent of 1½ or 2 ems may look more luxurious than one em, but paragraph indents larger than three ems are generally counterproductive. Short last lines followed by new lines with large indents produce a tattered page.

Block paragraphs open flush left and are separated vertically from their neighbors by extra lead, usually a white line. Block paragraphs are common in business letters and memos, and because they suggest precision, crispness and speed, they can be useful in short documents of other kinds. In longer sequences, they may seem soulless and uninviting.

2.3.3 *Add extra lead before and after block quotations.*

Block quotations can be distinguished from the main text in many ways. For instance: by a change of face (usually from roman to italic), by a change in size (as from 11 pt down to 10 pt or 9 pt), or by indention.

Combinations of these methods are often used, but one device is enough. If your paragraph indent is modest, you may for consistency's sake want to use the same indent for quotations. And even if your block quotations are set in a size smaller than normal text, you may want to leave the leading unchanged. If the main text runs 10/12, the block quotations might run 10/12 italic or 9/12 roman. If you prefer greater density or are eager to save space, you might set them 9/11 or 9/10½.

However the block quotations are set, there must be a visible distinction between main text and quotation, and again between the quotation and subsequent text. This usually means a white line or half-line at the beginning and end of the block. But if the leading within the block quotation differs from the leading of the main text, these blanks before and after the quotation must be elastic. They afford the only opportunity for bringing the text back into phase.

Suppose your main text is 11/13 and a five-line block quotation set 10/12 intervenes. The depth of the quotation is $5 \times 12 = 60$. This must be bulked up to a multiple of 13 to bring the text back into phase. The nearest multiple of 13 is $5 \times 13 = 65$. The remaining space is $65 - 60 = 5$, and $5/2 = 2.5$, which is not enough. Adding 2.5 points before and after the quotation will not give adequate separation. The next multiple of 13 is $6 \times 13 = 78$, which is better: $78 - 60 = 18$, and $18/2 = 9$. Add 9 pt lead before and after the quotation, and the text will realign.

2.3.4 *Indent or center verse quotations.*

Verse is usually set flush left and ragged right, and verse quotations within prose should not be deprived of their chosen form. But to distinguish verse quotations from surrounding prose, they should be indented or centered on the longest line. Centering is preferable when the prose measure is substantially longer than the verse line. The following passage, for example, is centered on the first and longest line.

> *God guard me from those thoughts men think*
> *In the mind alone;*
> *He that sings a lasting song*
> *Thinks in a marrow bone.*

William Butler
Yeats, "A Prayer
for Old Age."

Suppose your main text is set on a 24-pica measure and you have decided to set verse quotations in italic at the text size. Suppose that the longest line in your quotation measures 269 points. The indent for this quotation might be computed as follows: $24 \times 12 = 288$ pt, which is the full prose measure, and $288 - 269 = 19$ pt, which is the difference between the measure and the longest verse line. The theoretically perfect left indent for the verse quotation is $19/2 = 9.5$ pt. But if another indent close to 9.5 pt is already in use, either for block quotations in prose, or as a paragraph indent, then the verse quotation might just as well be indented to match.

Suppose however that the longest line in the verse is 128 points. The measure, again, is 288 points, and $288 - 128 = 160$. Half of 160 is 80 points. No other indent in the vicinity of 80 points is likely to be in use. The verse quotation would then be indented by precisely that amount.

2.4 ETIQUETTE OF HYPHENATION & PAGINATION

The rules listed below are traditional craft practice for the setting of justified text. Except for the last rule, they are all programmable, but the operation of these rules necessarily affects the spacing of words and thus the texture and color of the page. If decisions are left to the software, they should be checked by a trained eye – and no typesetting software should be permitted to compress, expand or letterspace the text automatically and arbitrarily as a means of fitting the copy. Copyfitting problems should be solved by creative design, not fobbed off on the reader and the text nor cast like pearls before machines.

2.4.1 *At hyphenated line-ends, leave at least two characters behind and take at least three forward.*

Fi-nally is conventionally acceptable line-end hyphenation, but final-ly is not, because it takes too little of the word ahead to the next line.

2.4.2 *Avoid leaving the stub-end of a hyphenated word, or any word shorter than four letters, as the last line of a paragraph.*

2.4.3 *Avoid more than three consecutive hyphenated lines.*

2.4.4 *Hyphenate proper names only as a last resort unless they occur with the frequency of common nouns.*

2.4.5 *Hyphenate according to the conventions of the language.*

In English we hyphenate *cab-ri-o-let* but in French *ca-brio-let*. The old German rule which hyphenated *Glockenspiel* as *Glok-kenspiel* was changed by law in 1998, but when *össze* is broken in Hungarian, it still turns into *ösz-sze*. In Spanish the double consonants *ll* and *rr* are never divided. (The only permissible hyphenation in the phrase *arroz con pollo* is thus *arroz con po-llo*.) The conventions of each language are a part of its typographic heritage and should normally be followed, even when setting single foreign words or brief quotations.

Hart's Rules for Compositors (39th ed, Oxford, 1983) includes a good, brief guide to hyphenation and punctuation rules for several European languages. But it is always worthwhile to consult a style manual written in and for the language at issue – e.g., for French, the *Lexique des règles typographiques en usage à l'imprimerie nationale* (Paris, 1990).

2.4.6 *Link short numerical and mathematical expressions with hard spaces.*

All you may see on the keyboard is a space bar, but typographers use several invisible characters: the word space, fixed spaces of various sizes (em space, en space, thin space, figure space, etc) and a *hard space* or *no-break space*. The hard space will stretch, like a normal word space, when the line is justified, but it will not convert to a linebreak. Hard spaces are useful for preventing linebreaks within phrases such as *6.2 mm, 3 in., 4 × 4,* or in phrases like *page 3* and *chapter 5*.

When it is necessary to break longer algebraic or numerical expressions, such as $a + b = c$, the break should come at the equal sign or another clear logical pause.

2.4.7 *Avoid beginning more than two consecutive lines with the same word.*

2.4.8 *Never begin a page with the last line of a multi-line paragraph.*

The typographic terminology is telling. Isolated lines created when paragraphs *begin* on the *last* line of a page are known as *orphans*. They have no past, but they do have a future, and they need not trouble the typographer. The stub-ends left when paragraphs *end* on the *first* line of a page are called *widows*. They have a past but not a future, and they look foreshortened and forlorn. It is the custom – in most, if not in all, the world's typographic cultures – to give them one additional line for company. This rule is applied in close conjunction with the next.

2.4.9 *Balance facing pages by moving single lines.*

Pages with more than two columns often look best with the columns set to varying depths. This is the vertical equivalent of ragged-right composition. Where there are only one or two main text columns per page, paired columns and facing pages (except at the end of a chapter or section) are usually set to a uniform depth.

Balance facing pages not by adding extra lead or puffing up the word space, but by exporting or importing single lines to and from the preceding or following spreads. The same technique is used to avoid widows, and to extend or shorten any chapters that would otherwise end with a meager few lines on the final page. But this balancing should be performed with a gentle hand. In the end, no spread of continuous text should have to run more than a single line short or a single line long.

2.4.10 *Avoid hyphenated breaks where the text is interrupted.*

Style books sometimes insist that both parts of a hyphenated word must occur on the same page: in other words, that the last line on a page must never end with a hyphen. But turning the page is not, in itself, an interruption of the reading process. It is far more important to avoid breaking words in those locations where the reader is likely to be distracted by other information. That is, whenever a map, a chart, a photograph, a pull-quote, a sidebar or other interruption intervenes.

2.4.11 *Abandon any and all rules of hyphenation and pagination that fail to serve the needs of the text.*

3.1 SIZE

3.1.1 *Don't compose without a scale.*

The simplest scale is a single note, and sticking with a single note draws more attention to other parameters, such as rhythm and inflection. The early Renaissance typographers set each book in a single font – one face in one size – supplemented by hand-drawn or specially engraved large initial letters for the openings of chapters. Their pages show what sensuous evenness of texture and variety of rhythm can be attained with a single font of type: very much greater than on a typewriter, where letters have, more often than not, a single width and a single stroke weight as well as a single size.

In the sixteenth century, a series of common sizes developed among European typographers, and the series survived with little change and few additions for 400 years. In the early days, the sizes had names rather than numbers, but measured in points, the traditional series is this:

a a a a a a a a a a a a a a a a a
6 7 8 9 10 11 12 14 16 18 21 24 36 48 60 72

This is the typographic equivalent of the diatonic scale. But modern equipment makes it possible to set, in addition to these sizes, all the sharps and flats and microtonal intervals between. Twenty-point, 22-point, 23-point, and 10½-point type are all available for the asking. The designer can now choose a new scale or tone-row for every piece of work.

These new resources are useful, but rarely all at once. Use the old familiar scale, or use new scales of your own devising, but limit yourself, at first, to a modest set of distinct and related intervals. Start with one size and work slowly from there. In time, the scales you choose, like the faces you choose, will become recognizable features of personal style.

A few examples of the many older names for type sizes:

6 pt: *nonpareil*
7 pt: *minion*
8 pt: *brevier* or *small text*
9 pt: *bourgeois* or *galliard*
10 pt: *long primer* or *garamond*
11 pt: *small pica* or *philosophy*
12 pt: *pica*
14 pt: *english* or *augustin*
18 pt: *great primer*

3.2.1 *Use titling figures with full caps, and text figures in all other circumstances.*

Numerals,
Capitals
and
Small Caps

The date is 23 August 1832, and it is 3:00 AM in Apartment 6-B, 213-A Beacon Street; it is 27° C or 81° F; the price is $47,000 US or £28,200. The postal codes are NL 1034 WR Amsterdam; SF 00170 Helsinki 17; Honolulu 96814; London WC1 2NN; New Delhi 110 003; Toronto M5S 2G5, and Dublin 2.

BUT IT IS 1832 AND 81° IN FULL CAPITALS.

Arabic numerals – known in Arabic as Indian numerals, *arqām hindiyya*, because the Arabs obtained them from India – entered the scribal tradition of Europe in the thirteenth century. Before that (and for many purposes afterward) European scribes used roman numerals, written in capitals when they occurred in the midst of other capitals, and in lowercase in the midst of lowercase letters. Typographers have naturally inherited this custom of setting roman numerals so that they harmonize with the words:

Number xiii lowercase AND XIII UPPERCASE
AND THE NUMBER XIII IN SMALL CAPITALS
and the roman numeral xiii in italic

When arabic numerals joined the roman alphabet, they too were given both lowercase and uppercase forms. Typographers call the former *text figures, hanging figures, lowercase figures,* or *old-style figures,* and make a point of using them whenever the surrounding text is set in lowercase letters or small caps. The alternative forms are called *titling figures, ranging figures* or *lining figures,* because they range or align with one another and with the upper case.

Text 1234567890 figures
TITLING 1234567890 FIGURES
FIGURES 1234567890 WITH SMALL CAPS
Italic text 1234567890 figures

Text figures were the common form in European typography between 1540 and 1800. But in the mid-eighteenth century, when European shopkeepers and merchants were apt to write more numbers than letters, handwritten numerals developed proportions of their own. These quite literally middleclass figures entered the realm of typography in 1788, when a British punchcutter named Richard Austin cut a font of three-quarter-height lining figures for the founder John Bell.

Bell letters and 1234567890 figures in roman *and 1234567890 italic*

In the nineteenth century, which was not a great age for typography, founders stretched these figures up to cap height, and titling figures became the norm in commercial typography. Renaissance letterforms were revived in the early twentieth century, and text figures found their way back into books. But in news and advertising work, titling figures remained routine. In the 1960s, phototypesetting machines with their truncated fonts once again made text figures difficult to find. The better digital foundries now offer a wide selection of fonts with text figures and small caps. These are often sold separately and involve extra expense, but they are essential to good typography. It is better to have one good face with all its parts, including text figures and small caps, than fifty faces without.

It is true that text figures are rarely useful in classified ads, but they are useful for setting almost everything else, including good magazine and newspaper copy. They are basic parts of typographic speech, and they are a sign of civilization: a sign that dollars are not really twice as important as ideas, and numbers are not afraid to consort on an equal footing with words.

It is also true that a number of excellent text faces, both serifed and unserifed, have been issued without text figures. Examples include Adrian Frutiger's Méridien, Eric Gill's Gill Sans, Paul Renner's Futura, Hans Eduard Meier's Syntax, Hermann Zapf's Comenius and Optima, Gudrun Zapf-von Hesse's Carmina, and Ron Carpenter's Amasis and Calisto. In several of these cases, there is evidence to prove that, even though they were never issued, text figures were part of the original conception or even the finished design. With any text face that is missing text figures, it is reasonable to enquire whether commercial intimidation or, in effect, commercial censorship may not have played a role.

During most of the nineteenth and twentieth centuries, lining figures were widely known as 'modern' and text figures as 'old-style.' Modernism was preached as a sacred duty, and numbers, in a sense, were actually deified. Modernism is nothing if not complex, but its gospel was radical simplicity. Many efforts were made to reduce the Latin alphabet back to a single case. (The telegraph, the teletype, and theater marquees, with their announcements all in capitals, are also products of that time.) These efforts failed, on the larger front, where letters were concerned. With numbers, their success rate was much greater. Typewriters came to have upper- and lowercase letters but uppercase numbers alone. And from typewriters have come computer keyboards.

Numerals, Capitals and Small Caps

Typographic civilization seems, nonetheless, determined to proceed. Text figures are again a normal part of type design – and can, after all, be retroactively supplied to faces that were earlier denied them.

3.2.2 *For abbreviations and acronyms in the midst of normal text, use spaced small caps.*

This is a good rule for just about everything except two-letter geographical acronyms and acronyms that stand for personal names. Thus: 3:00 AM, 3:00 PM, the ninth century AD, 450 BC to AD 450, the OAS and NATO; World War II or WWII; but JFK and Fr J.A.S. O'Brien, OMI; HMS *Hypothesis* and USS *Ticonderoga*; Washington, DC, and Mexico, DF; J.S. Bach's Prelude and Fugue in B♭ minor, BWV 867.

Some typographers prefer to use small caps for postal abbreviations (San Francisco, CA 94119), and for geographical acronyms longer than two letters. Thus, the USA, or in Spanish, *los EEUU*, and Sydney, NSW. But the need for consistency intervenes when long and short abbreviations fall together. From the viewpoint of the typographer, small caps are preferable in faces with fine features and small x-height, full caps in faces with large x-height and robust form.

Genuine small caps are not simply shrunken versions of the full caps. They differ from large caps in stroke weight, letterfit, and internal proportions as well as in height. Any good set of small caps is designed as such from the ground up. Thickening, shrinking and squashing the full caps with digital modification routines will only produce a parody.

48

Sloped small capitals – A B C D E F G – have been designed and cut for relatively few faces in the history of type design. They can be faked with digital machinery, by sloping the roman small caps, but it is better to choose a face (such as this one, Robert Slimbach's Minion) which includes them, or to live without. Sloped (italic) text figures, on the other hand, are part of the basic requirement and are included in most good text fonts.

3.2.3 *Refer typographic disputes to the higher courts of speech and thinking.*

Type is idealized writing, and its normal function is to record idealized speech. Acronyms such as CD and TV or USA and UFO are set in caps because that is the way we pronounce them. Acronyms like UNESCO, ASCII and FORTRAN, which are pronounced not as letters but as words, are in the process of becoming precisely that. When a writer accepts them fully into her speech and urges readers to do likewise, it is time for the typographer to accept them into the common speech of typography by setting them in lower case: Unesco, Ascii (or ascii) and Fortran. Other acronymic words, like *laser* and *radar,* have long since travelled the same road.

Logograms pose a more difficult question. An increasing number of persons and institutions, from e.e. cummings to WordPerfect, now come to the typographer in search of special treatment. In earlier days it was kings and deities whose agents demanded that their names be written in a larger size or set in a specially ornate typeface; now it is business firms and mass-market products demanding an extra helping of capitals, or a proprietary face, and poets pleading, by contrast, to be left entirely in the vernacular lower case. But type is visible speech, in which gods and men, saints and sinners, poets and business executives are treated fundamentally alike. And the typographer, by virtue of his trade, honors the stewardship of *texts* and implicitly opposes private ownership of *words.*

Logotypes and logograms push typography in the direction of hieroglyphics, which tend to be looked at rather than read. They also push it toward the realm of candy and drugs, which tend to provoke dependent responses, and away from the realm of food, which tends to promote autonomous being. Good typography is like bread: ready to be admired, appraised and dissected before it is consumed.

3.3.1 *Use the ligatures required by the font, and the characters required by the language, in which you are setting type.*

Ligatures

In most roman faces the letter f reaches into the space beyond it. In most italics, the *f* reaches into the space on both sides. Typographers call these overlaps *kerns*. Only a few kerns, like those in the arm of the *f* and the tail of the *j*, are implicit in a normal typefont, while others, like the overlap in the combination *To,* are optional refinements, independent of the letterforms.

Reaching into the space in front of it, the arm of the f will collide with certain letters – b, f, h, i, j, k, l – and with question marks, quotation marks or parentheses, if these are in its way.

Most of the early European fonts were designed primarily for setting Latin, in which the sequences fb, fh, fj and fk do not occur, but the sequences ff, fi, fl, ffi and ffl are frequent. The same set of ligatures was once sufficient for English, and these five ligatures are standard in traditional roman and italic fonts. As the craft of typography spread through Europe, new regional ligatures were added. An fj and æ were needed in Norway and Denmark for words like *fjeld* and *fjord* and *nær*. In France an œ, and in Germany an ß (*eszett* or double-s) were required, along with accented and umlauted vowels. Double letters which are read as one – *ll* in Spanish, *ij* in Dutch, and *ch* in German, for example – were cast as single sorts for regional markets. New individual letters were added, like the Polish ł, the Spanish ñ, and the Danish and Norwegian ø. Purely decorative ligatures were added to many fonts as well.

English continues to absorb and create new words – *fjord, gaffhook, halfback, hors d'œuvre* – that call for ligatures beyond the Latin list. As an international language, English must also accommodate names like *Youngfox, al-Hajji* and *Asdzą́ą́ Yołgai.* These sometimes make demands on the roman alphabet which earlier designers didn't foresee. In the digital world, many of these compound characters and ligatures can, in effect, take care of themselves. There is no burning need for a specially crafted fb ligature or even a prefabricated ą when the digital forms can be cleanly superimposed. Recent type designers, alive to these polylingual demands on the alphabet, have often simplified the problem further by designing faces in which no sequence of letters involves a collision.

æœ as ch ct ff ffi ffl fi fl fr
ij is ll q̃ st ʃch ʃh ʃi ʃl ʃp ʃʃ ß ʃʃi ʃʃl ʃt ʃz us
Æ Œ æ œ æ œ ß ß ff fi fl ffi ffl ffi ffl
ct st ct st fh fi fl ff ft ʃh ʃi ʃl ʃʃ ʃt

Top two lines: Ligatures from an italic font cut in the 1650s by Christoffel van Dijck. *Second two lines*: Ligatures from Adobe Caslon roman and italic, by Carol Twombly, after William Caslon, about 1750. These are Baroque typefaces. As such, they include a set of ligatures with *f* and a second set formed with the long s. Long s and its ligatures were normal in European typography until late in the eighteenth century, though fonts designed to do without them were cut as early as the 1640s.

   Separation of the letters *f* and *i* is sometimes crucial. In Turkish, *i* with a dot and *ı* without – or in capitals, *İ* and *I* – are two different letters. A typeface whose lowercase *f* disguises the difference between the two forms of *i* is therefore, for Turkish, an unacceptable design.
   This does not do away with the question of the five Latin ligatures. Older typefaces – Bembo, Garamond, Caslon, Baskerville and other distinguished creations – are, thankfully, still with us, in metal and in digital revivals. Many new faces also perpetuate the spirit of these earlier designs. These faces are routinely supplied with the five basic ligatures because they require them. And for digital typographers, software is available that will automatically insert them.

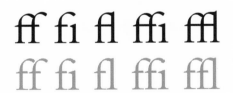

Bembo, set with ligatures (above) and without (below)

   The double-f ligatures are admittedly of greater importance when setting in metal than when setting in digital form, where letters are free to overlap. In a number of faces, only two of the

51

old ligatures, fi and fl, are crucial for digital setting. In some
faces, only the fi ligature is actually required. Others need no ligatures at all. But true fi and fl ligatures, like true small caps, are
designed instead of concocted. A fake ligature assembled from f
and the dotless i will rarely have the desired form.

Ligatures

Any face that needs an fi ligature will need an fj too, for setting words like *fjord*. When the fj is missing from the font, the
typographer must generally make do. In metal, it is simple
enough to pare the dot off a *j* and kern it under the *f*. Digital
font editing programs make the same trick nearly as easy. Font
editors also bring fully customized ligatures within range. A
novelist who wants an orchestra conductor to say "Defffini-
tively!" can be accommodated without grievous expense, and
without any serious lapse in typographic quality or speed.

fi fi fi *fi fi fi*

Above: Adobe Caslon, set with an *fi* ligature (left), *f* + *dotless i* (center)
and colliding letters (right). In faces such as this, ligatures are essential.
Below: Ligatured and unligatured combinations in Sabon, Trump Mediäval, Mendoza and Aldus. In faces such as these, *f*-ligatures are optional
– and in most such faces, only a partial set of ligatures exists.

fi fi *fi fi* fi fi *fi fi*
fi fi *fi fi* fi fi *fi fi*

3.3.2 *If you wish to avoid ligatures altogether, restrict yourself to
faces that don't require them.*

It is quite possible to avoid the use of ligatures completely and
still set beautiful type. All that is required is a face with non-
kerning roman and italic *f* – and some of the finest twentieth-
century faces have been deliberately equipped with just this feature. Aldus, Melior, Mendoza, Palatino, Sabon, Trajanus and
Trump Mediäval, for example, all set handsomely without ligatures. Full or partial ligatures do exist for these faces, and the

52

ligatures may add a touch of refinement – but when ligatures are omitted from these faces, no unsightly collisions occur.

The choice is wider still among sanserifs. Ligatures are important to the design of Eric Gill's Gill Sans, Ronald Arnholm's Legacy Sans, and Martin Majoor's Scala Sans, but they are irrelevant to many unserifed faces. (Dummy ligatures, consisting of separate letters, are nevertheless often present on the fonts for convenience in running standardized typesetting routines.)

3.4 TRIBAL ALLIANCES & FAMILIES

3.4.1 *To the marriage of type and text, both parties bring their cultural presumptions, dreams and family obligations. Accept them.*

Each text, each manuscript (and naturally, each language) has its own requirements and expectations. Some types are more adaptable than others in meeting these demands. But typefaces too have their individual habits and presumptions. Many of them, for instance, are rich with historical and regional connections – a subject pursued at greater length in chapter 7. For the moment, consider just the sociology of typefaces. What kinds of families and alliances do they form?

The union of uppercase and lowercase roman letters – in which the upper case has seniority but the lower case has the power – has held firm for twelve centuries. This constitutional monarchy of the alphabet is one of the most durable of European cultural institutions.

Ornamental initials, small caps and arabic figures were early additions to the roman union. Italics were a separate tribe at first, refusing to associate with roman lower case, but forming an alliance of their own with roman (not italic) capitals and small caps. Sloped caps developed only in the sixteenth century. Roman, italic and small caps formed an enlarged tribal alliance at that time, and most text families continue to include them.

Bold and condensed faces became a fashion in the nineteenth century, partially displacing italics and small caps. Bold weights and sets of titling figures have been added retroactively to many earlier faces, though they lack any historical justification. Older text faces, converted from metal to digital form, are usually available in two fundamentally different versions. The better digital foundries supply authentic reconstructions; oth-

	Primary:	roman lower case	1.1
	Secondary:	Roman Upper Case	2.1
		ROMAN SMALL CAPS	2.2
		roman text figures: 123	2.3
		italic lower case	2.4
Tribal	Tertiary:	*True Italic (Cursive) Upper Case*	3.1
Alliances		*italic text figures: 123*	3.2
and		*SLOPED SMALL CAPS*	3.3
Families		Roman Titling Figures: 123	3.4
		bold lower case	3.5
	Quaternary:	*False Italic (Sloped Roman) Upper Case*	4.1
		Bold Upper Case	4.2
		BOLD SMALL CAPS	4.3
		bold text figures: 123	4.4
		bold italic lower case	4.5
	Quintary:	*Italic Titling Figures: 123*	5.1
		Bold Italic (Sloped Roman) Upper Case	5.2
		bold italic text figures: 123	5.3
		Bold Titling Figures: 123	5.4
	Sextary:	***Bold Italic Titling Figures: 123***	6.1

ers supply the fonts without small caps, text figures and other essential components, and usually burden them instead with an inauthentic bold.

Among recent text faces, two basic family structures are now common. The simplified model consists only of roman, italic and titling figures, in a range of weights – light, medium, bold and black, for example. The more elaborate family structure includes small caps and text figures, though these are sometimes present only in the lighter weights.

A family with all these elements forms a hierarchical series, based not on historical seniority but on general adaptability and frequency of use. And the series works the way it does not so much from force of custom as from the force of physiology. The monumentality of the capitals, the loudness of the bold face, the calligraphic flow and slope of italic, stand out effectively against a peaceful roman ground. Reverse the order and the text not only looks peculiar, it causes the reader physical strain.

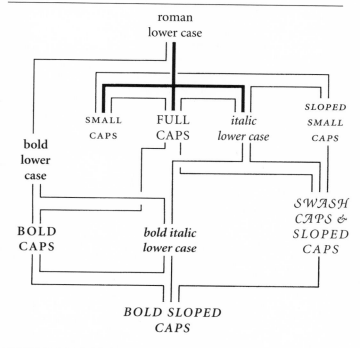

roman
lower case

SMALL CAPS

FULL CAPS

italic lower case

SLOPED SMALL CAPS

bold lower case

BOLD CAPS

bold italic lower case

SWASH CAPS & SLOPED CAPS

BOLD SLOPED CAPS

The chart at left is a grammatical road map of a conventional large family of type. (The heavy rules show the extent of the basic nuclear family.) The typographer can move directly along any of the lines – e.g., from roman lower case to bold lower case or to small or full caps. A sudden shift from roman lower case to bold caps or sloped caps, however, is elliptical. That is, it short-circuits the conventions of typographic grammar.

Fonts in each of these categories are called into use, through a surprisingly complex grammar of editorial and typographic rules, by fonts in the category above. The typographer can intervene in this process at will, and alter it to any degree. But good type is good because it has natural strength and beauty. The best results come, as a rule, from finding the best type for the work and then guiding it with the gentlest possible hand.

The standard North American reference on the editorial tradition is *The Chicago Manual of Style*.

3.4.2 *Don't use a font you don't need.*

The marriage of type and text requires courtesy to the in-laws, but it does not mean that all of them ought to move in, nor even that all must come to visit.

Boldface roman type did not exist until the nineteenth century, and bold italic is even more recent. Generations of good typographers were quite content without such variations. Font manufacturers nevertheless now often sell these extra weights as part of a basic package, thereby encouraging typographers –

beginners especially – to use bold roman and italic whether they need them or not.

Bold and semibold faces do have their value. They can be used, for instance, to flag items in a list, to set titles and subheads u&lc in small sizes, to mark the opening of the text on a complex page, or to thicken the texture of lines that will be printed in pale ink or as dropouts (negative images) in a colored field. Sparingly used, they can effectively emphasize numbers or words, such as the headwords, keywords and definition numbers in a dictionary. They can also be used (as they often are) to shout at readers, putting them on edge and driving them away; or to destroy the historical integrity of a typeface designed before boldface roman was born; or to create unintentional anachronisms, something like adding a steam engine or a fax machine to the stage set for *King Lear*.

3.4.3 *Use sloped romans sparingly and artificially sloped romans more sparingly still.*

It is true that most romans are upright and most italics slope to the right – but flow, not slope, is what really differentiates the two. Italics have a more cursive structure than romans, which is to say that italic is closer to longhand or continuous script. Italic serifs are usually *transitive*; they are direct entry and exit strokes, depicting the pen's arrival from the previous letter and its departure for the next. Roman serifs, by contrast, are generally *reflexive*. They show the pen doubling back onto itself, emphasizing the end of the stroke. Italic serifs therefore tend to slope at a natural writing angle, tracing the path from one letter to another. Roman serifs, especially at the baseline, tend to be level, tying the letters not to each other but to an invisible common line.

Some italics are more cursive than others; so are some romans. But any given italic is routinely more cursive than the roman with which it is paired.

e   e   l   l   m   m   u   u

Baskerville roman and italic. Baskerville has less calligraphic flow than most earlier typefaces, but the italic serifs are, like their predecessors, transitive and oblique, showing the path of the pen from letter to letter. The roman serifs are reflexive and level, tying letters to a common line.

56

Early italic fonts had only modest slope and were designed to be used with upright roman capitals. There are some beautiful fifteenth-century manuscript italics with no slope whatsoever, and some excellent typographic versions, old and new, that slope as little as 2° or 3°. Yet others slope as much as 25°.

Italic and roman lived quite separate lives until the middle of the sixteenth century. Before that date, books were set in either roman *or* italic, but not in both. In the late Renaissance, typographers began to use the two for different features in the same book. Typically, roman was used for the main text and italic for the preface, headnotes, sidenotes and for verse or block quotations. The custom of combining italic and roman *in the same line*, using italic to emphasize individual words and mark specific classes of information, developed in the sixteenth century and flowered in the seventeenth. Baroque typographers liked the extra activity this mixing of fonts gave to the page, and the convention proved so useful to editors and authors that no subsequent change of typographic taste has ever driven it entirely away. Modulation between roman and italic is now a basic and routine typographic technique, much the same as modulation in music between major and minor keys. (The system of linked major and minor keys in music is, of course, another Baroque invention.)

Since the seventeenth century, many attempts have been made to curb the cursive, fluid nature of italic and to refashion it on the roman model. Many so-called italics designed in the last two hundred years are actually not italics at all, but sloped romans – otherwise known as obliques. And many are hybrids between the two.

As lowercase italic letterforms mutated toward sloped roman, their proportions changed as well. Most italics (though not all) are 5% to 10% narrower than their roman counterparts. But most sloped romans (unless designed by Eric Gill) are as wide or wider than their upright roman companions.

Renaissance italics were designed for continuous reading, and modern italics based on similar principles tend to have similar virtues. Baroque and Neoclassical italics were designed to serve as secondary faces only, and are best left in that role. Sloped romans, as a general rule, are even more devotedly subsidiary faces. They have been with us for ten centuries or more, but have rarely succeeded in rising above the status of calligraphic stunts or short-term perturbations of the upright roman.

Harmony and Counterpoint

In addition to families consisting of upright and sloped roman, there are now several families consisting of upright (or nearly upright) and sloped *italic*. Hermann Zapf's Zapf Chancery (ITC, 1979) is an example. The 'roman' is an italic with a slope of 4°; the 'italic' is also an italic, but with swash caps and a slope of 14°. Another example is Jean-Renaud Cuaz's Cerigo (ITC, 1993), in which the 'roman' is an italic with a slope of 0° and the 'italic' is in essence the same alphabet with a slope of 10°.

1 adefmpru *adefmpru*

2 adefmpru *adefmpru*

3 adefmpru *adefmpru*

4 adefmpru *adefmpru*

5 adefmpru *adefmpru*

1 Adrian Frutiger's Méridien roman and italic; **2** Lucida Sans roman and italic, by Kris Holmes & Charles Bigelow; **3** Perpetua roman and its italic, which is a hybridized sloped roman, by Eric Gill; **4** Univers roman and oblique (a pure sloped roman), by Adrian Frutiger; **5** Romulus roman and oblique (again a pure sloped roman), designed by Jan van Krimpen.

Typesetting software is capable of distorting letters in many different ways: condensing, expanding, outlining, shadowing, sloping, and so on. If the only difference between a roman and its companion font were slope, the roman font alone would be enough for the computer. Sloped versions could be generated at will. But italic is not sloped roman, and even a good sloped roman is more than simply roman with a slope.

Direct electronic sloping of letterforms changes the weight of vertical and sloped strokes, while the weight of the horizontal strokes remains the same. Strokes that run northwest-southeast in the parent form – like the right leg of the A or the upper right and lower left corners of the O – are rotated toward the vertical when the letter is given a slope. Rotation toward the vertical causes these strokes to thicken. But strokes running northeast-southwest, like the left leg of the A, and the other corners of the O, are rotated farther away from the vertical. Rotation away from the vertical thins them down. Stroke curvature is altered in this translation process as well. The natural inclinations of a calligrapher drawing a sloped roman differ from what is convenient for the machine. Even 'italic' capitals – which nowadays are rarely anything except sloped roman – require individual shaping and editing to reach a durable form.

Through the collaborative efforts of calligraphers, typographers and engineers, software for the design and editing of typographic letterforms continues to improve. As it does, it continues to mimic more and more closely those subtle and primitive tools that lie at the root of all typography: the stick, the brush, the chisel and the broadnib pen. Rules for transforming roman into good sloped roman forms, instead of into parodies, can surely be derived through close analysis of what the best scribes do. When parts of the procedure can be stated with mechanical precision, they can also be entrusted to machines. But rules for translating roman into *italic* cannot be stated clearly because no such rules exist. The two kinds of letterform have different genealogies, like apples and bananas. They form a common heritage and share an evolutionary source, yet neither one is a modification of the other.

$$A \quad A \quad A \quad O \quad O \quad O$$

Adobe Caslon roman, the same roman sloped electronically, and the true 'italic' capitals as drawn. Caslon italics have an average slope of 20°.

$$a \quad a \quad a \quad o \quad o \quad o$$

Palatino roman, the same roman sloped electronically, and the genuine italic, whose average slope is 9°.

$$\mathcal{A} \quad \mathcal{E} \quad \mathcal{M} \quad \mathcal{R} \quad \mathcal{S} \quad \mathcal{T} \quad \mathcal{Y}$$

True italic capitals: the swash forms from Robert Slimbach's Minion italic. It is the structure, not the slope, of the letters that marks them as italic.

Once in a while, nevertheless, a typographer will pine for a sloped version of a font such as Haas Clarendon or André Gürtler's Egyptian 505, for which no italic, nor even a sloped roman, has been drawn. On such occasions, a sloped roman generated by computer may suffice as a temporary solution. But the slope should be modest (perhaps 10° maximum), because less slope yields less distortion.

3.5.1 *Change one parameter at a time.*

When your text is set in a 12 pt medium roman, it should not be necessary to set the heads or titles in 24 pt bold italic capitals. If boldface appeals to you, begin by trying the bold weight of the text face, u&lc, *in the text size.* As alternatives, try u&lc italic, or letterspaced small caps, or letterspaced full caps in the text weight and size. If you want a larger size, experiment first with a larger size of the text face, u&lc in the text weight. For a balanced page, the weight should *decrease* slightly, not increase, as the size increases.

Contrast

3.5.2 *Don't clutter the foreground.*

When boldface is used to emphasize words, it is usually best to leave the punctuation in the background, which is to say, in the basic text font. It is the words, not the punctuation, that merit emphasis in a sequence such as the following:

> … on the islands of **Lombok, Bali, Flores, Timor** and **Sulawesi,** the same textiles …

But if the same names are emphasized by setting them in italic rather than bold, there is no advantage in leaving the punctuation in roman. With italic text, italic punctuation normally gives better letterfit and thus looks less obtrusive:

> … on the islands of *Lombok, Bali, Flores, Timor* and *Sulawesi,* the same textiles …

If spaced small caps are used for emphasis – changing the stature and form of the letters instead of their weight or slope, and thereby minimizing the surface disturbance on the page – the question of punctuation does not arise. The punctuation used with small caps is (except for question and exclamation marks) the same as roman punctuation; it is only necessary to check it for accurate spacing:

> … on the islands of LOMBOK, BALI, FLORES, TIMOR and SULAWESI, the same textiles …

STRUCTURAL FORMS & DEVICES

4

4.1.1 *Make the title page a symbol of the dignity and presence of the text.*

If the text has immense reserve and dignity, the title page should have these properties as well – and if the text is devoid of dignity, the title page should in honesty be the same.

Think of the blank page as alpine meadow, or as the purity of undifferentiated being. The typographer enters this space and must change it. The reader will enter it later, to see what the typographer has done. The underlying truth of the blank page must be infringed, but it must never altogether disappear – and whatever displaces it might well aim to be as lively and peaceful as it is. It is not enough, when building a title page, merely to unload some big, prefabricated letters into the center of the space, nor to dig a few holes in the silence with typographic heavy machinery and then move on. Big type, even huge type, can be beautiful and useful. But poise is usually far more important than size – and poise consists primarily of emptiness. Typographically, poise is made of white space. Many fine title pages consist of a modest line or two near the top, and a line or two near the bottom, with little or nothing more than taut, balanced white space in between.

4.1.2 *Don't permit the titles to oppress the text.*

In books, spaced capitals of the text size and weight are often perfectly adequate for titles. At the other extreme, there is a fine magazine design by Bradbury Thompson, in which the title, the single word *boom*, is set in gigantic bold condensed caps that fill the entire two-page spread. The text is set in a tall narrow column *inside the stem* of the big B. The title has swallowed the text – yet the text has been reborn, alive and talkative, like Jonah from the whale.

Most unsuccessful attempts at titling fall between these two extremes, and their problem is often that the title throws its weight around, unbalancing and discoloring the page. If the

For examples of Thompson's work, see Bradbury Thompson, *The Art of Graphic Design* (New Haven, Conn., 1988).

title is set in a larger size than the text, it is often best to set it u&lc in a light titling font or a lightened version of the text font. Inline capitals (like the Castellar initials on pages 64 and 160) are another device that typographers have used since the fifteenth century to get large size without excessive weight.

Openings

There are other ways of creating large letters of light weight, but some only arise at the film-making and printing stage. The typographer can, for instance, *screen* the type (that is, break up the solid image with an optical or electronic filter) or, if the budget permits, instruct the printer to print it in a second ink of a paler color.

10 20 30 40 50
60 70 80 90 100

Screened text. The numbers indicate the percentage of ink coverage permitted by the screen.

4.1.3 *Set titles and openings in a form that contributes to the overall design.*

Renaissance books, with their long titles and ample margins, generally left no extra space at the heads of chapters. In modern books, where the titles are shorter and the margins have been eaten by inflationary pressure, a third of a page sometimes lies vacant just to celebrate the fact that the chapter begins. But space alone is not enough to achieve the sense of richness and celebration, nor is absence of space necessarily a sign of typographic poverty.

Narrow row houses flush with the street are found not only in urban slums but in the loveliest of the old Italian hill towns and Mediterranean villages. A page full of letters presents the same possibilities. It can lapse into a typographic slum, or grow into a model of architectural grace, skilled engineering and simple economy. Broad suburban lawns and wide typographical front yards can also be uninspiringly empty or welcoming and graceful. They can display real treasure, including the treasure of empty space, or they can be filled with souvenirs of wishful thinking. Neoclassical birdbaths and effigies of liveried slaves, stable boys and faded pink flamingoes all have counterparts in the typographic world.

4.1.4 *Mark each beginning and resumption of the text.*

The simplest way of beginning any block of prose is to start from the margin, flush left, as this paragraph does. On a peaceful page, where the text is announced by a head or subhead, this is enough. But if the text, or a new section of text, begins at the top of a page with no heading to mark it, a little fanfare will probably be required. The same is true if the opening page is busy. If there is a chapter title, an epigraph, a sidenote, and a photograph and caption, the opening of the text will need a banner, a ten-gallon hat or a bright red dress to draw the eye.

Fleurons (typographic ornaments) are often used to flag text openings, and are often printed in red, the typographer's habitual second color. The opening phrase, or entire first line, can also be set in small caps or in bold u&lc. Another excellent method of marking the start of the text, inherited from ancient scribal practice, is a large initial capital: a *versal* or *lettrine*. Versals can be treated in many ways. Indented or centered, they can stick up from the text. Flush left, they can be nested into the text (typographers call these *drop caps*, as opposed to *elevated* or *stick-up caps*). If there is room, they can hang in the left margin. They can be set in the same face as the text or in something outlandishly different. In scribal and typographic tradition alike, where the budget permits, versals too are generally red or another color in preference to black.

Elevated caps are easier to set well from a keyboard, but drop caps have closer links with the scribal and letterpress tradition. And the tooling and fitting of drop caps is something typographers do for fun, to test their skill and visual intuition. It is common practice to set the first word or phrase after the versal in caps, small caps or boldface, as a bridge between versal and normal text. Examples are shown on the following page.

In English, if the initial letter is A, I or O, a question can arise: is the initial letter itself a word? The answer to this question must come in the spacing of the text in relation to the versal. If the first word of the text is *Ahead,* for example, excessive space betwen the initial A and the rest of the word is bound to cause confusion.

O SCULETUR me osculo oris sui; quia meliora sunt ubera tua vino, ¶ fragantia unguentis optimis. Oleum effusum nomen tuum; ideo adolescentulae dilexerunt te.

T RAHE ME, post te curremus in odorem unguentorum tuorum. Introduxit me rex in cellaria sua; exsultabimus et laetabimur in te, memores uberum tuorum super vinum. Recti diligunt te.

« N IGRA SUM, sed formosa, filiae Ierusalem, sicut tabernacula Cedar, sicut pelles Salomonis. Nolite me considerare quod fusca sim, quia decoloravit me sol. Filii matris meae pugnaverunt contra me.... »

" A DIURO VOS, filiae Ierusalem, per capreas cervosque camporum, ne suscitetis, neque evigilare faciatis

dilectam, quoadusque ipsa velit."

V OX DILECTI MEI; ecce iste venit, saliens in montibus, transiliens colles. ¶ Similis est dilectus meus capreae, hinnuloque cervorum. En ipse stat post parietem nostrum, respiciens per fenestras, prospiciens per cancellos. En dilectus meus loquitur mihi.

S URGE, propera, amica mea, columba mea, formosa mea, et veni. ¶ Iam enim hiems transiit; imber abiit, et recessit. ¶ Flores apparuerunt in terra nostra....

L AVI PEDES MEOS, quomodo inquinabo illos? ¶ Dilectus meus misit manum suam per foramen, et venter meus intremuit ad tactum eius. ¶ Surrexit ut aperirem dilecto meo; manus meae stillaverunt myrrham, et digiti mei pleni myrrha probatissima. Pessulum ostii mei....

4.1.5 *If the text begins with a quotation, include the initial quotation mark.*

Quotation marks have a long scribal history as editorial signs added after the fact to other people's texts, but they did not come into routine typographic use until late in the sixteenth century. Then, because they interfered with established habits for positioning large initials, they were commonly omitted from the openings of texts. Some style books still prescribe this concession to convenience as a fixed procedural rule. But digital typography makes it simple to control the size and placement of the opening quotation mark, whether or not the text begins with a versal. For the reader's sake, it should be there.

4.2 HEADINGS & SUBHEADS

4.2.1 *Set headings in a form that contributes to the style of the whole.*

Headings can take many forms, but one of the first choices to make is whether they will be symmetrical or asymmetrical. Symmetrical heads, which are centered on the measure, are known to typographers as *crossheads*. Asymmetrical heads usually take the form of *left sideheads*, which is to say they are set flush left, or modestly indented or outdented from the left. *Right sideheads* work well in certain contexts, but more often as main heads than as subheads. A short, one-line head set flush right needs substantial size or weight to prevent the reader from missing it altogether.

One way to make heads prominent without making them large is to set them entirely in the margin, like the running heads (in typographic terms, they are running shoulders) used throughout this book.

4.2.2 *Use as many levels of headings as you need: no more and no fewer.*

As a rule it is best to choose a predominantly symmetrical or asymmetrical form for subheads. Mixing the two haphazardly leads to stylistic as well as logical confusion. But the number of levels available can be slightly increased, if necessary, by judicious combinations. If symmetrical heads are added to a basically asymmetrical series, or vice versa, it is usually better to put the visiting foreigners at the top or bottom of the hierarchical pile. Two six-level series of subheads are shown, by way of example, on the following pages.

In marking copy for typesetting, the various levels of subheads are generally given letters rather than names: A-heads, B-heads, C-heads, and so on. Using this terminology, the heads on the following pages run from A through F.

These principles are reversed, of course, when setting leftward-reading alphabets such as Arabic and Hebrew.

∾ Main Section Title ∾

Headings and Subheads

I F A MAN walk in the woods for love of them half of each day, he is in danger of being regarded as a loafer; but if he spends his whole day as a speculator, shearing off those woods and making earth bald before her time, he is esteemed an industrious and enterprising citizen.

MAIN CROSSHEAD

The ways by which you may get money almost without exception lead downward. To have done anything by which you earned money *merely* is to have been truly idle or worse.... If you would get money as a writer or lecturer, you must be popular, which is to go down perpendicularly....

Heavy Crosshead

In proportion as our inward life fails, we go more constantly and desperately to the post office. You may depend on it, that the poor fellow who walks away with the greatest number of letters ... has not heard from himself this long while.

MEDIUM CROSSHEAD

I do not know but it is too much to read one newspaper a week. I have tried it recently, and for so long it seems to me that I have not dwelt in my native region. The sun, the clouds, the snow, the trees say not so much to me....

Light Crosshead

You cannot serve two masters. It requires more than a day's devotion to know and to possess the wealth of a day.... Really to see the sun rise or go down every day, so to relate ourselves to a universal fact, would preserve us sane forever.

hypethral:
from Greek
ἐν ὑπαίθρῳ:
'in the open air'

RUN-IN SIDEHEAD Shall the mind be a public arena...? Or shall it be a quarter of heaven itself, an hypethral temple, consecrated to the service of the gods?

Main Section Title

❊ IF I AM TO BE a thoroughfare, I prefer that it be of the mountain brooks, the Parnassian streams, and not the town sewers.... I believe that the mind can be permanently profaned by attending to trivial things, so that all our thoughts shall be tinged with triviality.

MAIN CROSSHEAD

Our very intellect shall be macadamized, as it were: its foundation broken into fragments for the wheels of travel to roll over; and if you would know what will make the most durable pavement, surpassing rolled stones, spruce blocks, and asphaltum, you have only to look into some of our minds....

❦ ORNAMENTED CROSSHEAD ❦

Read not the Times. Read the Eternities.... Even the facts of science may dust the mind by their dryness, unless they are in a sense effaced each morning, or rather rendered fertile by the dews of fresh and living truth.

MEDIUM SIDEHEAD

Knowledge does not come to us by details, but in flashes of light from heaven. Yes, every thought that passes through the mind helps to wear and tear it, and to deepen the ruts, which, as in the streets of Pompeii, evince how much it has been used.

Light Sidehead

When we want culture more than potatoes, and illumination more than sugar-plums, then the great resources of a world are taxed and drawn out, and the result, or staple production, is not slaves, nor operatives, but ... saints, poets, philosophers....

Run-in Sidehead In short, as a snowdrift is formed where there is a lull in the wind, so, one would say, where there is a lull of truth, an *institution* springs up....

Structural Forms and Devices

The texts on this and the facing page are excerpts from HENRY DAVID THOREAU'S "Life Without Principle," *c.* 1854, first published in 1863. The type on the facing page is Adobe Caslon 10/12 × 21, and on this page, Monotype Centaur & *Arrighi* 11/12 × 21.

4.3.1 *If the text includes notes, choose the optimum form.*

If notes are used for subordinate details, it is right that they be set in a smaller size than the main text. But the academic habit of relegating notes to the foot of the page or the end of the book is a mirror of Victorian social and domestic practice, in which the kitchen was kept out of sight and the servants were kept below stairs. If the notes are permitted to move around in the margins – as they were in Renaissance books – they can be present where needed and at the same time enrich the life of the page.

Notes

Footnotes are the very emblem of fussiness, but they have their uses. If they are short and infrequent, they can be made economical of space, easy to find when wanted and, when not wanted, easy to ignore. Long footnotes are inevitably a distraction: tedious to read and wearying to look at. Footnotes that extend to a second page (as some long footnotes are bound to do) are an abject failure of design.

Endnotes can be just as economical of space, less trouble to design and less expensive to set, and they can comfortably run to any length. They also leave the text page clean except for a peppering of superscripts. They do, however, require the serious reader to use two bookmarks and to read with both hands as well as both eyes, swapping back and forth between the popular and the persnickety parts of the text.

Sidenotes give more life and variety to the page and are the easiest of all to find and read. If carefully designed, they need not enlarge either the page or the cost of printing it.

Footnotes rarely need to be larger than 8 or 9 pt. Endnotes are typically set in small text sizes: 9 or 10 pt. Sidenotes can be set in anything up to the same size as the main text, depending on their frequency and importance, and on the overall format of the page.

4.3.2 *Check the weight and spacing of superscripts.*

If they are not too frequent, sidenotes can be set with no superscripts at all (as in this book), or with the same symbol (normally an asterisk) constantly reused, even when several notes appear on a single page. For endnotes, superscript numbers are standard. For footnotes, symbols can be used if the notes are few. (The traditional order is * † ‡ § ‖ ¶. But beyond the asterisk, dagger and double dagger, this order is not familiar to most readers, and never was.) Numbers are more transparent, and their order is much less easy to confuse.

Many fonts include sets of superscript numbers, but these are not always of satisfactory size and design. Text numerals set at a reduced size and elevated baseline are sometimes the best or only choice. Establishing the best size, weight and spacing for superscripts will, however, require some care. In many faces, smaller numbers in semibold look better than larger numbers of regular weight. And the smaller the superscripts are, the more likely they are to need increased character space.

Superscripts frequently come at the ends of phrases or sentences. If they are high above the line, they can be kerned over a comma or period, but this may endanger readability, especially if the text is set in a modest size.

4.3.3 *Use superscripts in the text but full-size numbers in the notes themselves.*

In the main text, superscript numbers are used to indicate notes because superscript numbers minimize interruption. They are typographic asides: small because that is an expression of their relative importance, and raised for two reasons: to keep them out of the flow of the main text, and to make them easier to find. In the note itself, the number is not an aside but a target. Therefore the number in the note should be full size.[1]

To make them easy to find, the numbers of footnotes or endnotes can be hung to the left (like the marginal numbers on the following two pages and the footnote number below). Punctuation, apart from empty space, is not normally needed between the number and text of the note.

4.3.4 *Avoid ambiguity in the numbering and placement of endnotes.*

Readers should never be forced to hunt for the endnotes. As a rule, this means the endnotes should not appear in small

---

1 This footnote is flagged by a superscript in the text, but the note itself is introduced by an outdented figure of the same size used for the text of the note. The main text on this page is set 10/12 × 21, and the note is 8/11.

clumps at the end of each chapter. It is better to place them together at the end of the book. Wherever possible, they should also be numbered sequentially from the beginning to end of the book, and the notes themselves should be designed so the numbers are readily visible. If the notes are numbered anew for each section or chapter or essay, running heads will be needed along with the notes to point the way. If the running heads accompanying the notes say, for instance, "Notes to Pages 44–62," readers will know their way. But if the running heads say something like "Notes to Chapter 5," then chapter 5 must be identified as such by running heads of its own.

Notes

4.4 TABLES & LISTS

4.4.1 *Edit tables with the same attention given to text, and set them as text to be read.*

For graphic alternatives to typographic tables, see Edward R. Tufte, The Visual Display of Quantitative Information and Envisioning Information.

Tables are notoriously time-consuming to typeset, but the problems posed are often editorial as much as typographic. If the table is not planned in a readable form to begin with, the typographer can render it readable only by rewriting or redesigning it from scratch.

Tables, like text, go awry when approached on a purely technical basis. Good typographic answers are not elicited by asking questions such as "How can I cram this number of characters into that amount of space?"

If the table is approached as merely one more form of text, which must be made both good to read and good to look at, several principles will be clear:

1 All text should be horizontal, or in rare cases oblique. Setting column heads vertically as a space-saving measure is quite feasible if the text is in Japanese or Chinese, but not if it is written in the Latin alphabet.

2 Letterforms too small or too condensed for comfortable reading are not part of the solution.

3 There should be a minimum amount of furniture (rules, boxes, dots and other guiderails for travelling through typographic space) and a maximum amount of information.

4 Rules, tint blocks or other guides and dividers, where they are necessary at all, should run in the predominant reading direction: vertically in the case of lists, indices and some numerical tables, and horizontally otherwise.

5 A rule located at the edge of a table, separating the first or final column from the adjacent empty space, ordinarily serves no function.

6 A table, like any other text in multiple columns, must contain within itself an adequate amount of white space.

4.4.2 *Avoid overpunctuating lists.*

A list is an inherently spatial and numerical arrangement. Speakers reciting lists often enumerate on their fingers, and lists set in type often call for equivalent typographic gestures. This means that the list should be clarified as much as possible through spatial *positioning* and *pointing*, usually done with bullets, dashes or numerals. (Examples occur on these two pages and throughout this book.) If the numbers are made visible either through position (e.g., by hanging them in the margin) or through prominence (e.g., by setting them in a contrasting face), additional punctuation – extra periods, parentheses or the like – should rarely be required.

Dot leaders (lines of dots leading the eye from one word or number to another) are rarely beneficial in tables.

4.4.3 *Set lists and columns of figures to align flush right or on the decimal.*

The numerals in most fonts are all of equal width, though there is often an alternative, narrower form of the numeral one. This *fitted one* is generally used when setting figures in the midst of text, while the *unfitted one* (of standard numeral width) is often used when setting figures in columns. The font itself or the composition software will also include a *figure space* – a fixed blank space corresponding to the width of a standard, unkerned numeral. This makes it a simple matter to compose lists and columns of figures in rigorous mechanical alignment.

If you alter the set-widths of numerals, kern numeral combinations, or use the fitted one when setting columns or lists, the individual digits will not align, but *columns* of figures can still be aligned. For much tabular matter (as for the first table overleaf) this is sufficient. If notes are required in a table with flush-right columns, the superscripts should be hung to the right (as in column 3, line 2 of the first example overleaf) so they will not disrupt the alignment.

8	98	998	9.75
9	99	999*	10
10	100	1000	10.25
11	101	1001	10.5

Above: aligning columns of nonaligning figures, with a hanging asterisk.

Below: columns in mixed alignment.

Aster	$2:3$	24×36	0.667	$a = 2b$
Valerian	$271:20$	813×60	13.550	$6a = c$

4.4.4 *For text and numerals alike, choose harmonious and legible tabular alignments.*

Simple tables and lists of paired items, like the sample tables of contents on page 36, are often best aligned against each other, the left column flush right and the right column flush left. Financial statements and other numerical tables usually follow the opposite pattern: a column of words, on the left, aligns flush left, while the subsequent columns of numbers all align flush right or on the decimal. Any repeating character – a dimension sign or equal sign, for instance – is potentially of use in tabular alignment. But many columns with many different alignments can generate overall visual chaos. Occasionally it is better, in such cases, to set all columns or most columns either flush right or flush left, for the sake of general clarity.

4.5 FRONT & BACK MATTER

4.5.1 *Leave adequate space at the beginning and end of every publication.*

A brief research paper may look its best with no more space at beginning and end than is provided by the standard page margins. The same is rarely true of a book, whose text should generally be, and should seem to be, a living and breathing entity, not aged and shrink-wrapped meat. A chapbook or saddle-stitched booklet can begin directly with the title page. Otherwise, a half-title is customary, preceding the title page. It is equally customary to leave a blank leaf, or at least a blank page, at the end of a book. These blanks provide a place for inscriptions and notes and allow the text to relax in its binding.

4.5.2 *Give adequate space to the prelims.*

A text preceded by an interminable chain of forewords, prefaces, introductions and prologues is unlikely to be read. But a dedication that is stuffed, like a typographic afterthought, onto an already overfilled copyright page is no dedication at all. And a list of contents which is incomplete (or missing altogether), and which does not have the page to itself, is usually a sign of typographic desperation or of disregard for the reader.

4.5.3 *Balance the front and back matter.*

Books are normally built up from *gatherings* or signatures – printed and folded sheets – with each signature forming a unit of 8, 12, 16, 24 or 32 pages. The 16-page signature is by far the most common. Typographers therefore work to make most of their books seem divinely ordained and conceived to be some multiple of 16 pages in length. Seasoned book typographers recite in their meditations not only the mantra of points and picas – 12, 24, 36, 48, 60, 72 … – but also the mantra of octavo signatures: 16, 32, 48, 64, 80, 96, 112, 128, 144, 160, 176, 192, 208, 224, 240, 256, 272, 288, 304, 320, 336, 352, 368, 384, 400…. These are the lengths of the books that we read.

In a work of continuous prose, the illusion of divine love for the number sixteen is obtained by straightforward copyfitting. If the length of the text is accurately measured, the page can be designed to yield a book of appropriate length. More complicated books are often surrounded by paraphernalia – not only the standard half-title, title page, copyright page, dedication page and some blanks, but also perhaps a detailed table of contents, a list of charts, illustrations and maps, a table of abbreviations, a page or two of acknowledgements, and a preface, counterbalanced by appendices, endnotes, bibliography, index and a colophon. Copyfitting the main text for a volume of this kind may be highly complex, and room may be taken up or conserved in the large aura of front and back matter. But for complex books and simple books alike, it is up to the typographer to balance the front matter, back matter and text. A wad of blank leaves at the end of a book is a sign of carelessness, not of kindliness toward readers who like to take notes.

ABCDEFGHIKL
MNOPQ RSTV
XYZabcdefghil
mnopqrsʃtuvxyz
1234567890,.ʼ!?;:-⁹‿
Æ æ ɕ ff fi fl œ ſſ ſi ſt ſl ℞
&ãáàâçẽéèêëẹĩíìîïſ

Iuris præcepta ſunt hæc , Honeſté viuere , alterum
non lædere , ſuum cuíq̃; tribuere . Huius ſtudij duæ
ſunt poſitiones, Publicum & priuatum. Publicum
ius eſt , quod ad ſtatum rei Romanæ ſpectat. Priua
tum , quod ad ſingulorum vtilitatem pertinet .
Dicendum eſt igitur de iure priuato, quòd triperti-
tum eſt : collectum eſt enim ex naturalibus præcep-
tis, aut gẽtium aut ciuilibus . Ius naturale eſt quòd

A 42 pt roman titling font (cut *c.*1530, revised *c.*1550) and a 16 pt italic
text font (*c.*1539). Both were cut by Claude Garamond, Paris. The italic
is shown actual size and the roman reduced by about one fifth. Matrices
for the roman font survive at the Plantin-Moretus Museum, Antwerp.

ANALPHABETIC SYMBOLS

5

5.1 ANALPHABETIC STYLE

It falls to the typographer to deal with an increasing herd of
flicks, squiggles, dashes, dots and ideographs that travel with
the alphabet yet never quite belong. The most essential of these
marks – period, comma, parenthesis, and the like – are signs of
logical pause and intonation, much like the rests and slurs in a
musical score. Some, like the dollar and per cent signs, are stylized abbreviations. Others, like the asterisk and the dagger, are
silent typographical cross-references. And a few that are normally unspoken have tried to sneak their way into the oral tradition. Speakers who say *quote unquote* or *who slash what* or
That's it, period! are, of course, proving their debt to these para-
literary signs.

Approached through the scribal and typographic tradition,
the palette of analphabetic symbols is much more supple and
expressive than it appears through the narrow grill of the typewriter keyboard. A typographer will not necessarily use more
analphabetic symbols per page than a typist. In fact, many good
typographers use fewer. But even the most laconic typographer
learns to speak this sign language with an eloquence that conventional word processors and typewriters preclude.

5.1.1 *To invoke the inscriptional tradition, use the midpoint.*

The earliest alphabetic inscriptions have no analphabetic furniture at all, not even spaces between the words. As writing spread
through Greece and Italy, spaces appeared between the words,
and a further sign was added: the centered dot, for marking
phrases or abbreviations. That dot, the *midpoint* or small bullet,
remains one of the simplest, most effective forms of typographic punctuation – useful today in lists and letterheads and
signage just as it was on engraved marble twenty centuries ago.

Suite 6 · 325 Central Park South

Roman calligraphers lettered their inscriptions with a flat
brush held in the right hand. The flat brush – thick in one di-

rection, thin in the other, like a broadnib pen – produces a *modulated* stroke. That is to say, the weight of the stroke varies predictably with direction. The letter O is an example. Because the brush is held in the scribe's right hand, the strokes are thickest in the northwest/southeast direction, at the natural inclination of the forearm and the hand. Using the same brush, Roman calligraphers also developed the subtle choreography of twists and turns at the stroke-ends that produces the imperial Roman serif. Roman capital letters have retained these forms for two thousand years.

O · I · M

When the centered dot or midpoint is made in the same way with the same tool, it becomes a small, curved wedge: a clockwise twist of the brush, with a short tail. Falling to the baseline, this tailed dot became our comma. The same inscriptional and calligraphic traditions have left us other useful marks, such as the double dot or colon (:), the virgule (/), the hyphen (-), and the long dash (—).

5.1.2 *Use analphabetic symbols and diacritics that are in tune with the basic font.*

A normal font of type now includes about two dozen mutant forms of the few ancient signs of punctuation (period, comma, colon, quotation marks, brackets, parentheses, dashes, and so on). It also includes about a dozen diacritics (acute and grave accents, the circumflex, tilde, ogonek, umlaut, and others), some legal and commercial logograms (@ # $ % ‰ etc) and a few arithmetical symbols. In the iso Latin character sets (font tables defined by the International Organization for Standardization and now used as a standard by most digital foundries in Europe and North America), analphabetic symbols outnumber the basic Latin alphabet three to one.

On some fonts, these analphabetic characters are beautifully designed; on others they are not designed at all. Often they are simply borrowed from another font, which may have been drawn in a different weight and style.

Several analphabetic characters are notorious for poor design and should always be inspected when assessing a new font. These problem characters include *square brackets* [ ], which are

愛さ

In Asian and European scripts alike, modulated strokes are usually serifed and unmodulated strokes are usually not. Transitive brush serifs are evident in the *mincho* typeface above, designed by Takaichi Hori. The same *kanji* and *kana* are shown below in an unserifed face designed by Yasubumi Miyake. *Mincho katsuji* or 'Ming Dynasty script' is, roughly, the Japanese counterpart of serifed roman – but its serif structure is more cursive, like that of italic.

76

often too dark; *parentheses* ( ), which are often too symmetrical and skinny; the *asterisk* *, the *pilcrow* ¶ and the *section sign* §, which are often stiff and bland; and the *octothorp* or numeral sign #, which is frequently too large for anything more interesting than chain-store propaganda. Fonts equipped with good versions of these characters must often lend them to those without. But not just any good version will do.

a * & § & ';!?
1 2 3 4 5 6 † z

Neoclassical analphabetics, after John Baskerville, above, and the neohumanist analphabetics of Hermann Zapf's Palatino, below. The analphabetics differ from one face to another, and from one historical period to another, just as much as the letterforms do – and they differ in essentially the same ways.

a * & § & ';!?
1 2 3 4 5 6 † z

Baskerville, which is an eighteenth-century Neoclassical typeface, requires a Neoclassical asterisk: one with an even number of lobes, each in symmetrical teardrop form. But a twentieth-century neohumanist face like Palatino requires an asterisk with more calligraphic character – sharper, slightly asymmetrical lobes, more likely five than six in number, showing the trace of the broadnib pen. Well-made fonts are distinguished by similar differences in the question and exclamation marks, quotation marks and commas. Not even simple periods are freely interchangeable. Some are elliptical, diamond-shaped or square instead of round. Their weight and fitting varies as well. The *visible invisibility* of the marks of punctuation, which is essential to their function, depends on these details. So, therefore, does the visible invisibility of the typeface as a whole.

5.1.3 *In heads and titles, use the best available ampersand.*

Earlier typographers made liberal use of ampersands, especially when setting italic – and relished their variety of form. The 16th-century French printer Christophe Plantin sometimes uses four quite different ampersands in the course of a single paragraph, even when setting something as unwhimsical as the eight-volume polylingual Bible on which he risked his fortune and to which he devoted more than six years of his life.

The ampersand is a symbol evolved from the Latin *et,* meaning and. It is one of the oldest alphabetic abbreviations, and it has assumed over the centuries a wonderful variety of forms. Contemporary offerings are for the most part uninspired, stolid pretzels: unmusical imitations of the treble clef. Often the italic font is equipped with an ampersand less repressed than its roman counterpart. Since the ampersand is more often used in display work than in ordinary text, the more creative versions are often the more useful. There is rarely any reason not to borrow the italic ampersand for use with roman text.

Shakespeare & Co.
Brown & Son
Smith & Daughter

Trump Mediäval italic (above), designed by Georg Trump; Pontifex roman (center), by Friedrich Poppl; Pontifex roman with italic ampersand (below).

5.1.4 *Consider even the lowly hyphen.*

It is worth taking a close look at hyphens, which were once more subtle and various than they tend to be today. The hyphen was originally a simple pen stroke, often the thinnest stroke the broadnib pen could make, at an angle of 20° to 45° above horizontal. To distinguish the hyphen from the comma (which could also be written as a simple, canted stroke), the hyphen was often doubled, like an equal sign heading uphill.

Many Renaissance typographers preferred the canted hyphen with italic and the level hyphen with roman. Others mixed the two at random – one of several techniques once used to give a touch of scribal variety to the typeset page. But after the death of the master printer Robert Estienne in 1559 and of Claude Garamond in 1561, the level hyphen was the norm.

Most hyphens currently offered are short, blunt, thick, and perfectly level, like refugees from a font of Helvetica. This has sometimes been the choice of the designer, sometimes not. The double hyphen designed by Hermann Zapf in 1953 for his typeface Aldus, as an example, was omitted when the face was commercially issued in 1954. Foundry Centaur, designed by Bruce Rogers, had a hyphen inclined at 48°, but Monotype replaced it with a level bar when the face was adapted for machine composition in 1929. And the original Linotype issue of W.A. Dwiggins's Electra had a subtly tapered hyphen inclined at 7° from the horizontal; later copies of the face have substituted a bland, anonymous form.

If you are tempted to redesign an existing font, using a digital font editor, the hyphen is a good character to start on. It is a comparatively simple character, and you may be able to restore instead of subvert the designer's original intentions.

A few alternatives to the blunt and level hyphen are also still in circulation, and these are worth stealing on occasion for use with another face. The hyphen in Monotype Poliphilus is canted (as in the original design) at 42°. The hyphen in Monotype Blado (the companion italic to Poliphilus) is canted at 35° and tapered as well. The hyphens in most of Frederic Goudy's text faces are canted at angles ranging from 15° to 50°. Some digital versions preserve this feature; others are more homogenized. Canted and tapered hyphens are also to be found in many of the faces of Oldřich Menhart. (In the original version of Menhart's Figural, for example, the roman hyphen is tapered one way and the italic hyphen the other.) Frederic Warde's Arrighi, José Mendoza's Photina italic, and Warren Chappell's Trajanus all have hyphens that are level but asymmetrically serifed, which gives them a slight angular movement. The hyphen in Bram de Does's Trinité, a model of subtlety, is essentially level and unserifed but has a slight calligraphic lift at one end.

g-h

g-h

Poliphilus & *Blado*, above; Kennerley below.

g-h

g-h

fine-tuned / **eagle-eye**

Arrighi, left, and Trajanus, right

Hyphens also once varied considerably in width, but most now are standardized to a quarter of an em. Sometimes a shorter hyphen is better. Some of Gerard Unger's and Martin Majoor's economical Dutch hyphens (in faces such as Swift, Flora and Scala) measure no more than a fifth of an em.

Line-end hyphens are often best hung in the right margin, like the line-end hyphens on this and the facing page. This was easy to do for the scribes, who made it a common practice, but

79

it is tedious to emulate in metal. Digital typography makes it potentially easy once again – though not all typesetting software is equally eager to oblige.

5.2 DASHES, SLASHES & DOTS

5.2.1 *Use spaced en dashes – rather than em dashes or hyphens – to set off phrases.*

Standard computer keyboards and typewriters include only one dash, but a normal font of roman or italic type includes at least three. These are the hyphen and two sizes of long dash: the *en* dash – which is one en (half an em, M/2) in width – and the *em* dash—which is one em (two ens) wide. Many fonts also include a subtraction sign, which may or may not be the same length and weight as the en dash. And some include a figure dash (equal to the width of a standard numeral), a *three-quarter em* dash, and a *three-to-em* dash, which is one third of an em (M/3) in length.

In typescript, a double hyphen (--) is often used for a long dash. Double hyphens in a typeset document are a sure sign that the type was set by a typist, not a typographer. A typographer will use an em dash, three-quarter em, or en dash, depending on context or personal style. The em dash is the nineteenth-century standard, still prescribed in many editorial style books, but the em dash is too long for use with the best text faces. Like the oversized space between sentences, it belongs to the padded and corseted aesthetic of Victorian typography.

Used as a phrase marker – thus – the en dash is set with a normal word space either side.

5.2.2 *Use close-set en dashes or three-to-em dashes between digits to indicate a range.*

Thus: 3–6 November; 4:30–5:00 PM; 25–30 mm. Set close in this way (and with careful attention to character spacing), the dash stands for the word *to*. The hyphen is too short to serve this function, and in some faces the en dash (which is traditionally prescribed) appears too long. A *three-to-em* (M/3) dash is often the best choice. Three-to-em dashes are missing from many type fonts, but they are easily made on digital equipment, by condensing or shortening an en dash.

When compound terms are linked with a dash in the midst of running prose, subtle clues of size and spacing can be crucial, and confusion can easily arise. A sentence such as *The office will be closed 25 December – 3 January* is a linguistic and typographic trap. When it stands all alone in a schedule or list, the phrase *25 December – 3 January* will be clear, but in running prose it is better both editorially and typographically to omit the dash and insert an honest preposition: *25 December to 3 January.*

5.2.3 *Use the em dash to introduce speakers in narrative dialogue.*

The em dash, followed by a thin space (M/5) or word space, is the normal European method of marking dialogue, and it is much less fussy than quotation marks:

— So this is a French novel? she said.
— No, he said, it's Manitoban.

5.2.4 *In lists and bibliographies, use a three-em rule when required as a sign of repetition.*

Set without spaces, a line of true em dashes forms a continuous midline rule. A three-em rule (three consecutive em dashes) is the old standard bibliographical sign for the repetition of a name. For example:

Boas, Franz. *Primitive Art.* Oslo: Aschehoug, 1927. Reissued Cambridge, MA: Harvard University Press, 1928; New York: Dover, 1955.
———. *Tsimshian Mythology.* BAE Ann. Rep. 31. Washington, DC: Bureau of American Ethnology, 1916.

In recent years, most professional scholars have abandoned this style of bibliography, but the three-em rule still has many nonacademic uses.

5.2.5 *Use the virgule with words and dates, the solidus with split-level fractions.*

The slash, like the dash, is more various in real life than it is on the typewriter keyboard. A normal font of type includes a vertical bar and two slashes of differing inclinations. The steeper slash is the virgule (/), an alternative form of the comma. It is useful in dates (6/6/99 = 6.VI.99 = 6 June 99) and in text where a comma or parenthesis might otherwise have been used.

Wednesday / August 3 / 1977
Tibetan Guest House / Thamel / Kathmandu
Victoria University, Toronto / Ontario
he/she hit him/her

The other slash mark on the font is a solidus or fraction bar, used to construct fractions such as ³⁄₃₂. The solidus generally slopes at close to 45° and kerns on both sides. The virgule, not the solidus, is used to construct *level* fractions, such as 2π/3. (Notice, for instance, the difference in slope and kerning between the two slash marks in the type specification 8/9½.)

5.2.6 *Use a dimension sign instead of a serifed* x *when dimensions are given.*

A picture is 26 × 42 cm; studs are 2 × 4 and shelving is 2 × 10 inches; North American letter paper is 8½ × 11.

5.2.7 *Use ellipses that fit the font.*

Most digital fonts now include, among other things, a prefabricated *ellipsis* (a row of three baseline dots). Many typographers nevertheless prefer to make their own. Some prefer to set the three dots flush ... with a normal word space before and after. Others prefer ... to add *thin* spaces between the dots. Thick spaces (M/3) are prescribed by the Chicago Style Manual, but these are another Victorian eccentricity. In most contexts, the Chicago ellipsis is much too wide.

Flush-set ellipses work well with some fonts and faces but not with all. At small text sizes – in 8 pt footnotes, for example – it is generally better to add space (as much as M/5) between the dots. Extra space may also look best in the midst of light, open letterforms, such as Baskerville, and less space in the company of a dark font, such as Trajanus, or when setting in bold face. (The ellipsis generally used in this book is part of the font and sets as a single character.)

In English (but usually not in French), when the ellipsis occurs at the end of a sentence, a fourth dot, the period, is added and the space at the beginning of the ellipsis disappears....

i ... j

k....

l..., l

l, ... l

m...?

n...!

When the ellipsis combines with a comma, exclamation mark or question mark, the same typographic principle applies. Otherwise, a word space is required fore and aft.

5.2.8 *Treat the punctuation as notation, not expression, most of the time.*

Now and again the typographer finds on his desk a manuscript in which the exclamation marks and question marks stand six or nine together. Certain words may be written in bold capitals and others may be underlined five times. If the page has been written by hand, the dashes may get longer, and the screamers (exclamations) may get taller as they go. With sufficient equipment and time, the typographer can actually come close to reproducing what he sees; he can even increase its dramatic intensity in any of several ways. Theatrical typography is a genre that flourished throughout most of the twentieth century, yet whose limits are still largely unexplored.

Most writing and typography nevertheless remain contentedly abstract, like a theater script or a musical score. The script of *Macbeth* does not need to be bloodstained and spattered with tears; it needs to be legible. And the score of Beethoven's *Hammerklavier Sonata* does not need bolder notes to mark fortissimos nor fractured notes to mark the broken chords. The score is abstract code and not raw gesture. The typeset script or musical score is also a performance in its way – but only of the text. The score is silent so the pianist can play. The script can whisper while the actors roar.

William Faulkner, like most American novelists of his generation, typed his final drafts. Noel Polk, a literary scholar and a specialist on Faulkner, has prepared new editions of these novels in recent years. He found that Faulkner usually typed three hyphens for a long dash and four or five dots for an ellipsis, but that once in a while he hammered away at the key, typing hyphens or dots a dozen or more in a row. Polk decided not to try to replicate Faulkner's keyboard jigs exactly, but he did not want to edit them entirely away. He evolved the rule of converting two, three or four hyphens to an em dash, and five or more hyphens to a two-em dash. Anything up to six dots, he replaced with a standard ellipsis, and he called for seven dots wherever Faulkner had typed seven dots or more.

These are typographic decisions that other editors or ty-

See Joseph Blotner & Noel Polk, "Note on the Texts," in William Faulkner, *Novels 1930–1945* (New York: Library of America, 1985), p 1021, and *Novels 1936– 1940* (1990), p 1108. Photoreproductions of Faulkner's holographs and typescripts have also been published in 25 volumes as *The Faulkner Manuscripts* (New York: Garland, 1986–7).

pographers might have made in other ways. But the principle underlying them is sound. That principle is: punctuation is cold notation; it is not frustrated speech; it is typographic code.

Faulkner, we can presume, did not resort to bouts of extravagant punctuation because he was unable to express himself in words. He may, however, have been looking for some of the keys that the typewriter just doesn't have. The typographer's task is to know the vocabulary and grammar of typography, and to put them to meaningful use on Faulkner's behalf.

Dashes,
Slashes
and Dots

5.3 PARENTHESES

5.3.1 *Use the best available brackets and parentheses, and set them with adequate space.*

Typographic parentheses are traditionally pure line, like the virgule (/), the en dash (–) and the em dash (—). They are curved rules – usually portions of perfect circles, with no variation in weight – and in many older fonts they were loosely fitted, or set with plenty of space between them and the text they enclose. Parentheses in the form of swelled rules – thick in the middle and pointed at the ends – first appeared in the early Baroque, faded from view again in the Neoclassic age, and became the fashion, along with lining figures, in the nineteenth century. Many of the best twentieth-century text faces (Bruce Rogers's Centaur and the Monotype Corporation's Bembo, for example) were historical revivals that reasserted the older form.

In older German typeface classifications, *Antiqua* means roman and *mediäval* actually means Renaissance – because Italian Renaissance architects and scribes revived and updated romanesque and Carolingian forms from the medieval period. *Trump Mediäval Antiqua,* or Trump Medieval roman, despite its name, stems from late Renaissance forms.

$(abc) \quad (abc)$

Monotype Centaur and Monotype Baskerville, above. Georg Trump's Trump Mediäval Antiqua and Karl-Erik Forsberg's Berling, below.

$(abc) \quad (abc)$

The parentheses of some recent faces, such as Georg Trump's Trump Mediäval Antiqua and Hermann Zapf's Comenius, are modulated, asymmetrical strokes, based on the natural forms of the broadnib pen. In other recent designs (Zapf's Melior and Zapf International, and Karl-Erik Forsberg's Berling, for example), the parentheses are symmetrically thick in the middle and thin at the ends, like the nineteenth-century standard, but they are stretched into the form of a partial superellipse, which gives them greater tension and poise.

Parentheses in the form of nineteenth-century swelled rules are found by default on many digital fonts and have frequently been added, by mistake or by design, to alphabets with which they don't belong – historical revivals of the printing types of Garamond and Baskerville for example.

If you are forced to work with a font whose parentheses fall below standard, borrow a better pair from elsewhere. And whatever parentheses you use, check that they are not too tightly fitted (as in recent fonts they very often are).

5.3.2 *Use upright (i.e., "roman") rather than sloped parentheses, square brackets and braces, even if the context is italic.*

Parentheses and brackets are not letters, and it makes little sense to speak of them as roman or italic. There are vertical parentheses and sloped ones, and the parentheses on italic fonts are almost always sloped, but vertical parentheses are generally to be preferred. That means they must come from the roman font, and may need extra spacing when used with italic letterforms.

$$(efg) \; (efg)$$

The sloped square brackets usually found on italic fonts are, if anything, even less useful than sloped parentheses. If, perish the thought, there were a book or film entitled *The View from My [sic] Bed*, sloped brackets might be useful as a way of indicating that the brackets and their contents are actually part of the title. Otherwise, vertical brackets should be used, no matter whether the text is roman or italic: "The View from My [sic] Bed" and *"the view from my* [sic] *bed."*

This rule has been broken more often than followed since the end of the 16th century. It was followed more often than broken by the best of the early typographers who set books in italic: Aldus Manutius, Gershom Soncino, Johann Froben, Simon de Colines, Robert Estienne, Ludovico degli Arrighi and Henri Estienne II.

5.4.1 *Minimize the use of quotation marks, especially with Renaissance faces.*

Quotation Marks and Other Intrusions

Typographers got by quite well for centuries without quotation marks. In the earliest printed books, quotation was marked merely by naming the speaker – as it still is in most editions of the Vulgate and King James Bibles. In the High Renaissance, quotation was generally marked by a change of font: from roman to italic or the other way around. Quotation marks were first cut in the middle of the sixteenth century, and by the seventeenth, some printers liked to use them profusely. In books from the Baroque and Romantic periods, quotation marks are sometimes repeated at the beginning of every line of a long quotation. When these distractions were finally omitted, the space they had occupied was frequently retained. This is the origin of the indented block quotation. Renaissance block quotations were set in a contrasting face at full size and full measure.

Three forms of quotation mark are still in common use. Inverted and raised commas – "quote" and 'quote' – are generally favored in Britain and North America. But baseline and inverted commas – „quote" – are more widely used in Germany, and many typographers prefer them to take the shape of sloped primes („–") instead of tailed commas („–"). *Guillemets,* otherwise known as *duck foot quotation marks, chevrons,* or *angle quotes* – «quote» and ‹quote› – are the normal form in France and Italy, and are widely used in the rest of Europe. French and Italian typographers set their guillemets with the points out, «thus», while German-speaking typographers usually set them »the opposite way«. In either case, thin spaces are customary between the guillemets and the text they enclose.

An informative history of punctuation is M.B. Parkes, *Pause and Effect* (Berkeley, 1993).

Quotation marks are sufficiently ingrained in modern editorial sign language that it is difficult, in many kinds of texts, to do entirely without them. But many nonprofessional writers overuse quotation marks. Good editors and typographers will reduce their appearance to a minimum, retaining only those that contribute real information.

When quotation marks (including guillemets) are used, the question remains, how many should there be? The usual British practice is to use single quotes first, and doubles within singles. 'So does "analphabetic" mean what I think it means?' she said

86

suspiciously. When this convention is followed, most quotation marks will be singles and therefore less obtrusive.

Common American practice is the reverse. "So," she said, "does 'analphabetic' mean…?" This convention, using singles within doubles instead of doubles within singles, ensures that quotation flags will stand out. But some faces – Matthew Carter's Galliard, for example – have prominent quotation marks, while others have forms that are more discreet. Consider the face as well as the text when deciding which convention to follow in marking quotations.

Analphabetic Symbols

5.4.2 *Position quotation marks consistently in relation to the rest of the punctuation.*

Punctuation is normally placed inside a closing single or double guillemet if it belongs to the quotation, and outside otherwise. With other quotation marks, usage is less consistent. Most North American editors like their commas and periods inside the raised commas, "like this," but their colons and semicolons outside. Many British editors prefer to put all punctuation outside, with the milk and the cat. The kerning capabilities of digital typesetters, especially in the hands of advertising typographers, have evolved an intermediate third style, in which closing quotation marks are kerned over the top of commas and periods. Typographically, this is a good idea with some faces in large sizes, but a bad idea with many faces at text sizes, where a kerned quotation mark or apostrophe may look much like a question or exclamation mark.

"kern, 'kerning,' kerned."

When quotation marks are not kerned, it makes no *typographic* difference whether they follow commas and periods or precede them. The difference is one of editorial rather than visual discretion. But typographers, like editors, should be consistent, whichever route they choose.

5.4.3 *Omit the apostrophe from numerical plurals.*

Houses are built with 2 × 4s; children and parents live through the terrible twos; Europeans killed as many Europeans in the 1930s as they did Native Americans and Africans in the 1800s.

5.4.4 *Eliminate other unnecessary punctuation.*

Omit the period after metric units and other self-evident abbreviations. Set 5.2 m and 520 cm but 36 in. or 36", and in bibliographical references, p 36f, or pp 306–314.

   North American editors and typesetters tend to put periods after all abbreviations or (more rarely) after none. The former practice produces a text full of birdshot and wormholes; the latter can cause confusion. As a form of compromise, the Oxford house style, which is widely followed in Britain, has much to commend it. This rule is: use a period only when the word stops prematurely. The period is omitted if the abbreviation begins with the first letter of the word and ends with the last. Thus: Mrs Bodoni, Mr John Adams Jr and Ms Lucy Chong-Adams, Dr McBain, St Thomas Aquinas, Msgr Kuruwezi and Fr O'Malley; but Prof. Czesław Miłosz and Capt. James Cook.

   Periods are equally unnecessary in acronyms and other abbreviations commonly written with small or large capitals. Thus: 3:00 AM and 450 BC; Washington, DC, and Mexico, DF; Vancouver, BC, and Darwin, NT.

   In the interests of typographic hygiene, unnecessary hyphens should likewise be omitted. Thus: avant garde, bleeding heart, halfhearted, postmodern, prewar, silkscreen and typeface, in preference to the hyphenated alternatives. (It is good editorial practice, however, to hyphenate compound adjectives unless they can be fused into single words or will stand out as proper nouns. Thus, one finds twentieth-century typefaces in limited-edition books but publishes a limited edition at the end of the twentieth century and rides the New York Subway in New York. But one finds lowercase letters in the lower case.)

   Apostrophes are needed for some plurals, but not for others, and inconsistency is better than a profusion of unnecessary marks. Thus: do's and don'ts; the ayes have it but the I's don't; the ewes are coming but the you's are staying home.

5.4.5 *Add punctuation, or preserve it, where it is necessary to meaning.*

The phrase *twenty one night stands* is ambiguous when written, but if the speaker knows what he means, it will be perfectly clear when spoken. Typography answers to vocal inflection in distinguishing *twenty one-night stands* from *twenty-one nightstands.*

In the careful language of science and poetry, hyphens can be more important still. Consider the following list of names: Douglas-fir, balsam fir, Oregon ash, mountain-ash, redcedar, yellowcedar, Atlas cedar, white pine, yellow pine, blue spruce. All these names are correct as they stand. They would be less so if an eager but ignorant editor, or a typographer obsessed with graphic hygiene, tried to standardize the hyphens. The terms are written differently because some are made from nouns that are only borrowed, others from nouns that are generic. The balsam fir is what it claims to be: a fir; the Douglas-fir is not; it is a separate genus waiting for a proper English name. The Oregon ash, likewise, is an ash, but the mountain-ash is not, and the Atlas cedar is a cedar, but redcedar and yellowcedar (or yellow-cedar) are not. The differences, though subtle, are perfectly audible in the speech of knowledgeable speakers (who say **bal**sam *fir* and **Doug**las-**fir** and **moun**tain-**ash** and **Or**egon *ash*). A good typographer will make the same distinctions subtly visible as well. In the present state of typographic art and editorial convention, this is done not by spattering the page with boldface syllables but by the judicious and subtle placement of hyphens.

5.5 DIACRITICS

5.5.1 *Use the accents and alternate sorts that proper names and imported words and phrases require.*

Simplicity is good, but so is plurality. Typography's principal function (not its only function) is communication, and the greatest threat to communication is not difference but sameness. Communication ceases when one being is no different from another: when there is nothing strange to wonder at and no new information to exchange. For that reason among others, typography and typographers must honor the variety and complexity of human language, thought and identity, instead of homogenizing or hiding it.

Typography was once a fluently multilingual and multicultural calling. The great typographers of the fifteenth and sixteenth centuries worked willingly with North Italian whiteletter, German blackletter, French script, Ashkenazi and Sephardic Hebrew, orthotic and cursive and chancery Greek. The best typographers of the twentieth century have followed their lead. But typographic ethnocentricity and racism also have thrived in the last hundred years, and much of that narrow-mindedness is institutionalized in the workings of machines. Unregenerate, uneducated fonts and keyboards, defiantly incapable of setting anything beyond the most rudimentary Anglo-American alphabet, are still not difficult to find.

Diacritics Recent digital technology has made it possible for any typographer to create special characters on demand – a luxury most have been without since the seventeenth century. Prepackaged fonts of impeccable design, with character sets sufficient to set any word in all European and many Asian languages, and the software to compose and kern these characters, are also now available even to the smallest home and desktop operations. Yet there are large-circulation newspapers in North America still deliberately incapable of typesetting even the names of major cities, composers and statesmen, or the annual list of winners of the Nobel Prize, for want of letters like ñ and é.

Neither typographers nor their tools should labor under the sad misapprehension that no one will ever mention crêpes flambées or aïoli, no one will have a name like Antonín Dvořák, Søren Kierkegaard, Stéphane Mallarmé or Chloë Jones, and no one will live in Óbidos or Århus, in Kroměříž or Øster Vrå, Průhonice or Nagykőrös, Dalasýsla, Kırkağaç or Köln.

5.5.2 *Remap the font driver and keyboard to suit your own requirements.*

The conventional computer keyboard includes a number of characters – @ # ^ + = { } | \ ~ < > – rarely required by most typesetters, while frequently needed characters, such as the en dash, em dash, acute accent, midpoint and ellipsis, are nowhere to be seen. Unless your keyboard fits your needs as is, remap it. It should give you ready access to whatever accented and analphabetic characters you regularly use.

You may also want to edit your roman and italic fonts so that text figures, upright parentheses and upright brackets set automatically, in place of the more rarely needed lining and sloping forms.

Unless your composition software places ligatures automatically, you may find it easiest to insert them through a substitution routine after the text is fully set. Open and close quotes can be inserted at the same time in the same way, but many typesetters like to assign them specific keys.

Compositors who seldom use accented characters often prefer to set them through mnemonic codes, using a function key that momentarily redefines the keyboard. Software that operates in this way may produce ó from the combination o + /, ř from r + v, Ů from U + o, and so on. But if you use accented characters with any frequency, you may find it worth your while to map them directly to the keyboard.

A typical customized keyboard for the roman font is shown on the following page. The purpose of this particular layout is general multilingual text work. This could mean something as complex as polylingual manuals and packaging for technical products sold on the global market, or something as simple as addressing an envelope to Poland, or spelling the names correctly in the program for a symphony performance in Detroit.

The keyboard layout shown is missing two characters (the tailed N and the barred T) required for Lapp and one (the barred H) required for Maltese. With those exceptions, it will accommodate all European and North Asian languages that use the Latin alphabet: Albanian, Basque, Breton, Catalan, Croatian, Czech, Danish, Dutch, English, Estonian, Faroese, Finnish, Flemish, French, Frisian, Gaelic, German, Greenlandic, Hungarian, Icelandic, Italian, Kurdish, Latvian, Lithuanian, Moldavian, Norwegian, Polish, Portuguese, Romansch, Romany, Rumanian, Slovak, Slovene, Sorbian, Spanish, Swedish, Turkish and Welsh. It will also accommodate most Pacific languages written in Latin script (including Bahasa Indonesia, Bikol, Cebuano, Fijian, Hiligaynon, Ilocano, Malay, Maori, Tagalog and Tahitian); dozens of Native American languages; upwards of twenty common African languages; the standard romanized forms of Arabic, Chinese, Greek, Hebrew, Hindi, Japanese, Pali, Persian and Sanskrit, and romanized forms of all the languages commonly written in Cyrillic.

This particular layout assumes the primary languages to be English, Spanish and French, but it is equally fast for German, Italian, Portuguese and the Scandinavian languages. If the primary languages were, for instance, English and Turkish, or English, Polish and Czech, several minor rearrangements might be made.

The individual characters are identified and discussed in appendix A, page 271.

Analphabetic Symbols

Tagalog is the primary language of the Philippines. Bikol, Cebuano, Hiligaynon and Ilocano are other Philippine languages with several million speakers each.

Sample Layout for an Expanded Keyboard

Cntrl	¡	ő	ű	£	Ő	Ű	ª	º	†	‡		×
SHIFT	!	´	`	$	%	°	&	*	(	)	–	+
Plain	1	2	3	4	5	6	7	8	9	0	-	=
Alt	1	2	3	4	5	6	7	8	9	0	–	—

Cntrl	Ø	Ů	é	Å	Þ	Ÿ	ú	í	ó	¶	ŵ	ŷ
SHIFT	Q	W	E	R	T	Y	U	I	O	P	â	ê
Plain	q	w	e	r	t	y	u	i	o	p	[	]
Alt	ø	ů	è	å	þ	ÿ	ù	ì	ò	î	ô	û

Cntrl	á	§	Đ	Ä	Ë	Ï	Ö	Ü	Ł	ı	"
SHIFT	A	S	D	F	G	H	J	K	L	:	"
Plain	a	s	d	f	g	h	j	k	l	;	'
Alt	à	ß	ð	ä	ë	ï	ö	ü	ł	đ	'

Cntrl	Ã	Õ	Ç	^	~	Ñ	µ	«	»	¿	…	Æ
SHIFT	Z	X	C	V	B	N	M	‹	›	?	˙	Œ
Plain	z	x	c	v	b	n	m	,	.	/	•	œ
Alt	ã	õ	ç	ˇ	˘	ñ	¯	,	·	˛	.	æ

Ambiguous characters are as follows. **Row 1**: *Shift-2* is the floating acute. *Shift-3* is the floating grave. *Shift-6* is the degree sign. *Cntrl-7* is the ordinal A. *Cntrl-8* is the ordinal O. *Shift-hyphen* is a subtraction sign. *Alt-hyphen* is an en dash, and *Alt-equal* is an em dash. **Row 3**: *Cntrl-colon* is a dotless i. The double-quote key is a double close-quote. *Cntrl-double-quote* is the double open-quote. *Alt-apostrophe* is the single open-quote (inverted comma). **Row 4**: *Cntrl-V* is the floating circumflex. *Alt-v* is the floating caron. *Cntrl-B* is the floating tilde. *Alt-b* is the floating breve. *Alt-m* is the floating macron. *Shift-comma* and *Shift-period* are single guillemets rather than angle brackets. *Alt-comma* is a cedilla. *Alt-period* is a midpoint. The *slash* key is a virgule, not a fraction bar or solidus. *Alt-slash* is an ogonek (nasal hook). The two extra keys shown to the right in the bottom row are placed in different positions by different keyboard manufacturers. On an ordinary keyboard, one of these keys carries the backslash and pipe; the other carries the swung dash and open quote or floating grave. Here, the backslash key carries the bullet, underdot, overdot and ellipsis. The swung dash key is converted to carry the four typographic diphthongs or ligatured vowels.

"Alt" and "Cntrl" are keyboard codes of the IBM persuasion. The Macintosh equivalents are "Option" and "Shift-Option."

6.1 TECHNICAL CONSIDERATIONS

6

6.1.1 *Consider the medium for which the typeface was originally designed.*

Typographic purists like to see every typeface used with the technology for which it was designed. Taken literally, this means that virtually all faces designed before 1950 must be set in metal and printed letterpress, and the majority must be set by hand. Most typographers apply this principle in a more relaxed and complex way, and settle for preserving something rather than everything of a type's original character.

On the technical side, several things can be done to increase the chance that a letterpress typeface will survive translation to digital composition and offset printing.

6.1.2 *When using digital adaptations of letterpress faces, choose fonts that are faithful to the spirit as well as the letter of the old designs.*

Letterpress printing places the letterform *into* the paper, while offset printing lays it on the surface. Many subtle differences result from these two approaches to printing. The letterpress adds a little bulk and definition to the letter, especially in the thin strokes, and increases the prominence of the ends of thin serifs. Metal typefaces are designed to take advantage of these features of letterpress printing.

On the offset press – and in the photographic procedures by which camera-ready art and offset printing plates are prepared – thin strokes tend to get thinner and the ends of delicate serifs are eaten away. In a face like Bembo, for instance, offset printing tends to make features like the feet of i and l, and the heads and feet of H and I, slightly convex, while letterpress printing tends to make them slightly concave.

Ili

Faces designed for photographic manipulation and offset printing are therefore weighted and finished differently from letterpress designs. And adapting a letterpress face for digital composition is a far from simple task.

Digital fonts poorly translated from metal originals are sometimes too dark or light or blunt throughout, or uneven in stroke weight, or faithless in their proportions. They sometimes lack text figures or other essential components of the original design. But digital translations can also be *too faithful* to the original. They sometimes neglect the subtle adjustments that the shift from three-dimensional letterpress to two-dimensional offset printing requires.

6.1.3 *Choose faces that will survive, and if possible prosper, under the final printing conditions.*

Bembo and Centaur, Spectrum and Palatino, are subtle and beautiful alphabets, but if you are setting 8 pt text with a laser printer on plain paper at 300 dpi, the refined forms of these faces will be rubbed into the coarse digital mud of the imaging process. If the final output will be 14 pt text set directly to film at 3000 dpi, then printed by good offset lithography on the best coated paper, every nuance may be crystal clear, but the result will still lack the character and texture of the letterpress medium for which these faces were designed.

Some of the most innocent looking faces are actually the most difficult to render by digital means. Optima, for example – an unserifed and apparently uncomplicated face – is constructed entirely of subtle tapers and curves that can be adequately rendered only at the highest resolutions.

Faces with blunt and substantial serifs, open counters, gentle modelling and minimal pretensions to aristocratic grace stand the best chance of surviving the indignities of low resolution. Amasis, Caecilia, Lucida, Stone and Utopia, for example, while they prosper at high resolutions, are faces that will also survive under cruder conditions lethal to Centaur, Spectrum, Linotype Didot or almost any version of Bodoni.

6.1.4 *Choose faces that suit the paper you intend to print on, or paper that suits the faces you wish to use.*

Most Renaissance and Baroque types were made to be pressed into robust, lively papers by fairly robust means. They wilt when placed on the glossy, hard-surfaced sheets that came into vogue toward the end of the eighteenth century. Most Neoclassical and Romantic types, on the other hand, were designed to require smooth papers. Rough, three-dimensional papers break their fragile lines. Geometric Modernist types such as Futura, and overhauled Realist types such as Helvetica, can be printed on rough and smooth papers alike, because they are fundamentally *monochrome*. (That is to say, the stroke is nearly uniform in width.) But the aura of machine precision that emanates from a type like Futura is reinforced by a smooth paper and contradicted (*or* counterbalanced) by a paper that feels homespun.

These historical categories are summarized on pp 12–15 and explored in greater detail in chapter 7.

6.2 PRACTICAL TYPOGRAPHY

6.2.1 *Choose faces that suit the task as well as the subject.*

You are designing, let us say, a book about bicycle racing. You have found in the specimen books a typeface called Bicycle, which has spokes in the O, an A in the shape of a racing seat, a T that resembles a set of racing handlebars, and tiny cleated shoes perched on the long, one-sided serifs of ascenders and descenders, like pumping feet on the pedals. Surely this is the perfect face for your book?

Actually, typefaces and racing bikes are very much alike. Both are ideas as well as machines, and neither should be burdened with excess drag or baggage. Pictures of pumping feet will not make the type go faster, any more than smoke trails, pictures of rocket ships or imitation lightning bolts tied to the frame will improve the speed of the bike.

The best type for a book about bicycle racing will be, first of all, an inherently good type. Second, it will be a good type for books, which means a good type for comfortable long-distance reading. Third, it will be a type sympathetic to the theme. It will probably be lean, strong and swift; perhaps it will also be Italian. But it is unlikely to be carrying excess ornament or freight, and unlikely to be indulging in a masquerade.

6.2.2 *Choose faces that can furnish whatever special effects you require.*

If your text includes an abundance of numerals, you may want a face whose numerals are especially well designed. Palatino, Pontifex, Trump Mediäval and Zapf International, for example, all recommend themselves. But if you prefer three-quarter-height lining numerals, your options include Bell, Trajanus and Weiss.

If you need small caps, faces that lack them (such as Frutiger, Méridien and Syntax) are out of the running. But if you need a range of weights, faces such as Centaur and Spectrum are disqualified instead. If you need a matching phonetic face, your choices include Lucida Sans, Stone and Times Roman. If you need a matching Cyrillic, you might choose Minion, Lazurski, Lucida, Officina or Futura. And for the sake of a matching sanserif, you might choose Charlotte, Legacy, Lucida, Officina, Scala or Stone. These matters are explored in more detail in chapter 10, which discusses individual typefaces.

Practical
Typography

Special effects can also be obtained through more unorthodox combinations, which are the subject of §6.5.

6.2.3 *Use what there is to the best advantage.*

If there is nothing for dinner but beans, one may hunt for an onion, some pepper, salt, cilantro and sour cream to enliven the dish, but it is generally no help to pretend that the beans are really prawns or chanterelles.

When the only font available is Cheltenham or Times Roman, the typographer must make the most of its virtues, limited though they may be. An italic, small caps and text figures will help immensely if they can be added, but there is nothing to be gained by pretending that Times Roman is Bembo or Cheltenham is Aldus in disguise.

As a rule, a face of modest merits should be handled with great discretion, formality and care. It should be set in modest sizes (better yet, in one size only) with the caps well spaced, the lines well leaded, and the lower case well fitted and modestly kerned. The line length should be optimal and the page impeccably proportioned. In short, the typography should be richly and superbly *ordinary*, so that attention is drawn to the quality of the composition, not to the individual letterforms. Only a face that warrants close scrutiny should be set in a form that invites it.

Using what there is to best advantage almost always means using less than what is available. Baskerville, Helvetica, Palatino and Times Roman, for example – which are four of the most widely available typefaces – are four faces with nothing to offer

Baskerville roman
and its italic

Helvetica roman
and its oblique

Palatino roman
and its italic

Times New Roman
and its italic

Baskerville is an English Neoclassical face designed in Birmingham in the 1750s by John Baskerville. It has a rationalist axis, thoroughgoing symmetry and delicate finish.

Helvetica is a twentieth-century Swiss revision of a late nineteenth-century German Realist face. The first weights were drawn in 1956 by Max Miedinger, based on the Berthold Foundry's old Odd-job Sanserif, or Akzidenz Grotesk, as it is called in German. The heavy, unmodulated line and tiny aperture evoke an image of uncultivated strength, force and persistence. The very light weights issued in recent years have done much to reduce Helvetica's coarseness but little to increase its readability.

Palatino is a lyrical modernist face with a neohumanist architecture, which is to say that it is *written*, not drawn, and that it is based on Renaissance forms. It was created in 1948 by Hermann Zapf.

Times Roman – properly Times *New* Roman – is an historical pastiche drawn by Victor Lardent for Stanley Morison in London in 1931. It has a humanist axis but Mannerist proportions, Baroque weight, and a sharp, Neoclassical finish.

The traditional account of the origin of Times Roman is given here, but it is currently a subject of hot dispute. Mike Parker has argued in detail that the roman was designed in the usa by Starling Burgess as early as 1904. See Parker, "Starling Burgess, Type Designer," *Printing History* 31/32 (1994): 52–108.

one another except public disagreement. None makes a good companion face for any of the others, because each of them is rooted in a different concept of what constitutes a letterform. If the available palette is limited to these faces, the first thing to do is choose *one* for the task at hand and ignore the other three.

6.3 HISTORICAL CONSIDERATIONS

Typography, like other arts, preys on its own past. It can do so with the callousness of a grave robber, or with the piety of unquestioning ancestor worship. It can also do so in thoughtful, enlightened and deeply creative ways.

Roman type has been with us for more than five centuries. Its root components – the roman upper and lower case, basic analphabetic symbols, and the arabic numerals – have been with us for much longer yet. There are typographers who resolutely avoid using any typeface designed in an earlier era, but even they must learn something of how the older letterforms functioned, because the ancient forms are living in the new. Typographers who willingly use the old faces, and who wish to use them intelligently, need to know all they can learn about the heritage they enjoy.

6.3.1 *Choose a face whose historical echoes and associations are in harmony with the text.*

Any contemporary North American library will furnish examples of typographic anachronism. There are books on contemporary Italy and on seventeenth-century France set in typefaces such as Baskerville and Caslon, cut in eighteenth-century England. There are books about the Renaissance set in faces that belong to the Baroque, and books about the Baroque set in faces from the Renaissance. To a good typographer it is not enough merely to avoid these kinds of laughable contradictions. The typographer seeks to *shed light* on the text, to generate insight and energy, by setting every text in a face and form in which it actually belongs.

It is not that good typographers object to mixing centuries and cultures. Many take delight in doing so – especially when they have no other choice. A text from ancient Athens, for example, cannot be set in an ancient Athenian version of roman type. A face designed in North America in the 1990s may well be used instead. Texts from seventeenth-century France or eighteenth-century England also might be set perfectly well in faces of recent design. But a face that truly suits an historical text is likely to have some fairly clear historical content of its own. There is no typeface *equally suited* to texts from Greek antiquity, the French Baroque and the English Neoclassical period – though faces equally *unsuited* to each of them abound.

The historical affiliations of individual typefaces are discussed in chapters 7 and 10.

6.3.2 *Allow the face to speak in its natural idiom.*

Books that leap historical boundaries and mix historical subjects can pose complex and exciting typographic problems. But often, if a text calls for a Renaissance type, it calls for Renaissance typography as well. This usually means Renaissance page proportions and margins, and an absence of bold face. It may also mean large Renaissance versals, Renaissance style in the handling of quotations, and the segregation of roman and italic. If the text calls for a Neoclassical type, it likewise often calls for Neoclassical page design. When you undertake to use an historical typeface, take the trouble to learn the typographic idiom for which it was intended. (Works of reference that may be useful in solving particular problems are listed in appendix F, page 327.)

6.4 CULTURAL & PERSONAL CONSIDERATIONS

6.4.1 *Choose faces whose individual spirit and character is in keeping with the text.*

Accidental associations are rarely a good basis for choosing a typeface. Books of poems by the twentieth-century Jewish American poet Marvin Bell, for example, have sometimes been set in Bell type – which is eighteenth-century, English and Presbyterian – solely because of the name. Puns of this kind are a private amusement for typographers. But a typographic page so well designed that it attains a life of its own must be based on something more than an inside joke.

Letterforms have character, spirit and personality. Typographers learn to discern these features through years of working first-hand with the forms, and through studying and comparing the work of other designers, present and past. On close inspection, typefaces reveal many hints of their designers' times and temperaments, and even their nationalities and religious faiths. Faces chosen on these grounds are likely to give more interesting results than faces chosen through mere convenience of availability or coincidence of name.

If, for example, you are setting a text by a woman, you might prefer a face designed by a woman. Such faces were rare or nonexistent in earlier centuries, but there are now many to choose from. They include Gudrun Zapf-von Hesse's Alcuin, Carmina, Diotima and Nofret; Elizabeth Friedländer's Elizabeth; Kris Holmes's Sierra, Lucida and Kolibri; Kris Holmes's and Janice Prescott Fishman's Shannon; Carol Twombly's Charlemagne, Lithos, Nueva and Trajan; Zuzana Ličko's Journal; Cynthia Hollandsworth's Hiroshige and Tiepolo, and Ilse Schüle's Rhapsodie. For some purposes, one might also go back to the work of Elizabeth Colwell, whose Colwell Handletter, issued by ATF in 1916, was the first American typeface designed by a woman.

But perhaps a text by a French author, or a text dealing with France, might best be set in a French typeface, without regard to the gender of author or designer. The choices include Garamond, Jannon, Mendoza, Méridien, Vendôme and many others, but even this abbreviated list covers considerable range. Garamond – of which there are many recent revivals – was designed in sixteenth-century Paris. It owes much to Italian forms and belongs to the world of Renaissance Catholicism. Jannon is equally elegant but nonconformist. It belongs to the Reformation rather than the Renaissance, and its designer, Jean Jannon, was a French Protestant who suffered all his life from religious persecution. Vendôme, designed by François Ganeau, is a witty twentieth-century face much indebted to Jannon. Mendoza, designed in Paris in 1990, goes back to the tough humanist roots from which Garamond sprang. Méridien, from the 1950s, is more in touch with the secular spirit of twentieth-century Swiss industrial design, yet it includes a regal, even imperious, upper case and a very crisp and graceful italic. These five different faces invite additional differences in page design, paper, and binding as well as different texts, just as different musical instruments invite different phrasings, different tempi, different musical modes or keys.

Even nations such as Greece and Thailand, which have alphabets of their own, share in a multinational tradition of type

Garamond roman
and its italic

Jannon roman
and its italic

Mendoza roman
and its italic

Méridien roman
and its italic

Vendôme roman
and its oblique

Stempel Garamond is the Stempel Foundry's replica of a text roman and italic designed by Claude Garamond (*c.* 1490–1561). (Compare the reproductions of some of Garamond's actual type on page 74.)

Monotype 'Garamond' 156 is a revival of a type designed by Jean Jannon (1580–1658), the greatest typecutter of the French Baroque. Jannon's type was once misidentified as Garamond's and is still often sold under his name.

Mendoza is a recent design by José Mendoza y Almeida. Méridien, by Adrian Frutiger, and Vendôme, by François Ganeau, are both products of the 1950s. Ganeau – who worked as a painter, sculptor and set designer more than as a typographer – based Vendôme on Jannon's letters, but moved them playfully in the direction of French Neoclassicism.

design. Nevertheless, some typefaces seem more redolent of national character than others. Frederic Goudy, for example, is widely regarded as the most ebulliently American of all American type designers. The sensitive typographer would not choose one of Goudy's faces to set, let us say, the text of the Canadian or Mexican constitution.

This subject is a lifelong study, and for serious typographers it is a lifelong source of discovery and delight. Here it is pursued at greater length in chapter 10. Appendix C (page 299) is a cross-indexed list of type designers.

6.5 THE MULTICULTURAL PAGE

Consistency is one of the forms of beauty. Contrast is another. A fine page, even a fine book, can be set from beginning to end in one type in one size. It can also teem with variety, like an equatorial forest or a modern city.

6.5.1 *Start with a single typographic family.*

Most pages, and most entire documents, can be set perfectly well with only one family of type. But perhaps the page confronting you requires a chapter title, two or three levels of subheads, an epigraph, a text in two languages, block quotations within the text, a couple of mathematical equations, a bar graph, several explanatory sidenotes, and captions for photographs and a map. An extended type family, such as Legacy, Lucida or Stone, may provide sufficient resources even for this task. Another possibility is Gerard Unger's comprehensive series known as Demos, Praxis and Flora – which is a family with no surname to unite it. Each of these series includes both roman and italic in a range of weights, matching serifed and unserifed forms, and other variations. If you restrict yourself to faces within the family, you can have variety and homogeneity at the same time: many shapes and sizes but a single typographic culture. Such an approach is well suited to some texts, poorly suited to others.

You can also, of course, mix faces at random, by drawing them out of a hat.

Between these two extremes is the wide arena of thoughtful mixing and matching, in which the typographic intelligence often does its most creative work and play.

6.5.2 *Respect the integrity of roman, italic & small caps.*

It has been the normal practice of type designers since the middle of the sixteenth century to offer text faces in the form of a matched triad, consisting of roman, italic and small caps. Because some of these marriages are more successful than others, it is wise to examine the roman and the italic both separately and together when choosing a text face.

There are several celebrated instances in which an italic designed by one artist has been happily and permanently married to another designer's roman. These matches always involve some redrawing (and the face that is most heavily redrawn is almost always the italic, which is the subsidiary and 'feminine' font in post-Renaissance typography). There are also instances in which a roman and its italic have been designed by the same artist many years apart. But casual liaisons, in which the roman of one family is paired momentarily with the italic of another, have little hope of success. Mixing small caps from one face with full caps from another is even less likely to succeed.

If you use type strictly in the Renaissance manner, treating the roman and italic as separate but equal, not mixing them on the line, you may find that greater latitude is possible. Jan van Krimpen's Lutetia italic mixes well with his later Romanée roman, for example, if the two are not too intimately combined. One is visibly more mature than the other, but they are close in color and structure, and they are patently the work of the same designer.

6.5.3 *Consider bold faces on their own merits.*

The original boldface printing types are the blackletters used by Gutenberg in the 1440s. For the next two centuries, blackletter fonts were widely used not only in Germany but in France, Spain, the Netherlands and England. (That is why blackletter fonts are occasionally sold in the USA as 'Olde English.')

Boldface romans, however, are a nineteenth-century invention. Bold italic is even more recent, and it is hard to find a successful version designed before 1950. Bold romans and italics have been added retroactively to many earlier faces, but they are often simply parodies of the original designs.

Before using a bold weight, especially a bold italic, ask yourself whether you really need it at all. If the answer is yes, you may want to avoid type families such as Bembo, Garamond or Baskerville, to which bold weights have been retroactively added but do not in fact belong. You might, instead, choose a twentieth-century family such as Méridien, Nofret or Utopia, in which a range of weights is part of the original design.

If your text face lacks a bold weight, you may also find an appropriate bold close by. Hermann Zapf's Aldus, for example, is a twentieth-century family on the Renaissance model, limited to roman, italic and small caps. But Aldus is a close cousin of the same designer's Palatino family, which does include a bold, and Palatino bold sits reasonably well with Aldus text.

a aardvark; **b** balloon; **3** thruppence

Aldus roman with Palatino bold

Equally interesting results can often be obtained by reaching much farther afield. The normal function of boldface type is, after all, to contrast with the roman text. If the bold is used in small amounts, and bold and roman are not too intimately combined, a difference in structure as well as weight may be an asset. Under these conditions, a typographer is free to choose both roman and bold on their own merits, seeking basic compatibility rather than close genetic connection.

c coelacanth; **d** daffodil; **4** Franciscan

Sabon roman with Zapf International bold

A text might be set in Sabon, for example, with Zapf International as a titling face and Zapf International bold for subheads and flags. Structurally, these are very different faces, with very different pedigrees. But Sabon has the calm and steady flow required for setting text, while Zapf International's vitality makes it a good face for titling – and this vitality persists even in the boldest weights. Most of the bold fonts structurally closer to Sabon, on the other hand, look splayed and deformed.

Fifteenth-century typographers – Nicolas Jenson for example – rarely mixed fonts except when mixing languages. They loved an even page. Bold roman is therefore an appendage they did happily without. If, nevertheless, you were using one of the fine text faces based on Jenson's single roman font and wanted to embellish it with bold, you might consider using Jenson's kind of bold. The only dark faces he cut were blackletters.

Elève elephant; **fool** filibuster; **lvi** phytogenic

Bruce Rogers's Centaur (here 16 pt) with Karlgeorg Hoefer's San Marco (12 pt). Centaur is based on the roman that Nicolas Jenson cut at Venice in 1469. San Marco is based on the rotundas he cut there in the 1470s.

6.5.4 *Choose titling and display faces that reinforce the structure of the text face.*

Titling faces, display faces and scripts can be chosen on much the same principles as bold faces. Incestuous similarity is rarely a necessity, but empathy and compatibility usually are. A geometrically constructed, high-contrast face such as Bauer Bodoni, beautiful though it may be, has marginal promise as a titling face for a text set in Garamond or Bembo, whose contrast is low and whose structure is fundamentally calligraphic. (Bodoni mixes far more happily with Baskerville – of which it is not a contradiction but rather an exaggeration.)

6.5.5 *Pair serifed and unserifed faces on the basis of their inner structure.*

When the basic text is set in a serifed face, a related sanserif is frequently useful for other elements, such as tables, captions or notes. In complicated texts, such as dictionary entries, it may also be necessary to mix unserifed and serifed fonts on the same line. If you've chosen a family that includes a matched sanserif, your problems may be solved. But many successful marriages between serifed and unserifed faces from different families are waiting to be made.

Frutiger Méridien Univers

Suppose your main text is set in Méridien – a serifed roman and italic designed by Adrian Frutiger. It would be reasonable to look first of all among Frutiger's other creations for a related sanserif. Frutiger is a prolific designer of types, both serifed and unserifed, so there are several from which to choose. Univers is his most widely used sanserif. But another of his unserifed faces – the one to which he gave his own name – is structurally much closer to Méridien and works handsomely as a companion.

Hans Eduard Meier's Syntax is a sanserif much different in structure from either Frutiger or Univers. It is based on serifed Renaissance forms like those of Garamond. It works well with such faces as Stempel or Adobe Garamond, or with Sabon, another descendant of Garamond, designed by Meier's contemporary and countryman, Jan Tschichold.

If your choice falls on a more geometric sanserif, such as Futura, a Renaissance roman will hardly suffice as a serifed companion. Many romans based on the work of Bodoni, however, breathe much the same spirit as Futura. They aspire not to calligraphic motion but to geometric purity.

Gabocse escobaG
Gabocse escobaG
Gabocse escobaG

Syntax and Minion, above; Futura and Berthold Bodoni, center; Helvetica and Haas Clarendon, below.

6.6 MIXING ALPHABETS

6.6.1 *Choose non-Latin faces as carefully as Latin ones.*

Mixing Latin letters with Hebrew or Arabic is, in principle, scarcely different from mixing roman with blackletter or serif with sans. Different though they look, and even though they read in different directions, all these alphabets spring from the same source, and all are written with similar tools. Many structural similarities underlie the obvious differences. A book involving more than one alphabet therefore poses some of the same questions posed by a bilingual or polylingual book set entirely in Latin letters. The typographer must decide in each case – after studying the text – whether to emphasize or minimize the differences. In general, the more closely different alphabets are mixed, the more important it becomes that they should be close in color and in size, no matter how superficially different in form.

The Latin, Greek and Cyrillic alphabets are as closely related in structure as roman, italic and small caps. (And in most Cyrillic faces, the lower case is close in color and shape to Latin small caps.) Random marriages of Latin and Greek, or Latin and Cyrillic, look just as ungainly and haphazard as random combinations of roman, italic and small caps – but excellent sets of related faces have developed, and a few homogeneous polyglot families have been designed.

Plato and Aristotle both quote the line of Parmenides that says πρώτιστον μὲν Ἔρωτα θεῶν μητίσατο πάντων: "The first of all the gods to arise in the mind of their mother was PHYSICAL LOVE."
Греки боготворили природу и завещали миру свою религию, то есть *философию и искусство*, says a character named Shatov in Dostoevsky's novel *Demons*: "The Greeks deified nature and bequeathed to the world their religion, which is *philosophy and art*."

Robert Slimbach's Minion roman, italic and small caps, with upright and cursive Minion Cyrillic and a prototype version of Minion Greek.

The text on this page is set in ITC Mendoza 10/13 with 12 pt GFS Neo Hellenic lower case and 11.5 pt Neo Hellenic caps. On the facing page, the roman and italic are Figural 10/13; the Greek is 10.5 pt GFS Porson. (The original edition of Cornford's book, printed in 1912, was set in the curious combination of Century Expanded and Porson Greek.)

ΦΥΣΙΣ AS THE SOUL / THE SOUL AS ΓΝΩΣΙΣ.

The second proposition of Thales declares that the All is alive, or has Soul in it (τὸ πᾶν ἔμψυχον). This statement accounts for the mobility of φύσις. Its motion, and its power of generating things other than itself, are due to its life (ψυχή), an inward, spontaneous principle of activity. (Cf. Plato, *Laws* 892c: φύσιν βούλονται λέγειν γένεσιν τὴν περὶ τὰ πρῶτα· εἰ δὲ φανήσεται ψυχὴ πρῶτον, οὐ πῦρ οὐδὲ ἀήρ, ψυχὴ Ƌ' ἐν πρώτοις γεγενημένη, σχεδὸν ὀρθότατα λέγοιτ' ἂν εἶναι διαφερόντως φύσει.)...

It is a general rule that the Greek philosophers describe φύσις as standing in the same relation to the universe as soul does to body. Anaximenes, the third Milesian, says: οἶον ἡ ψυχὴ ἡ ἡμετέρα ἀὴρ οὖσα συγκρατεῖ ἡμᾶς, καὶ ὅλον τὸν κόσμον πνεῦμα καὶ ἀὴρ περιέχει. "As our soul is air and holds us together, so a breath or air embraces the whole cosmos."[1]...

The second function of Soul – knowing – was not at first distinguished from motion. Aristotle says, φαμὲν γὰρ τὴν ψυχὴν λυπεῖσθαι χαίρειν, θαρρεῖν φοβεῖσθαι, ἔτι δὲ ὀργίζεσθαί τε καὶ αἰσθάνεσθαι καὶ διανοεῖσθαι· ταῦτα δὲ πάντα κινήσεις εἶναι δοκοῦσιν. ὅθεν οἰηθείη τις ἂν αὐτὴν κινεῖσθαι. "The soul is said to feel pain and joy, confidence and fear, and again to be angry, to perceive, and to think; and all these states are held to be movements, which might lead one to suppose that soul itself is moved."[2] Sense-perception (αἴσθησις), not distinguished from thought, was taken as the type of all cognition, and this is a form of action at a distance.[3]

---

1 Frag. 2. Compare Pythagoras' "boundless breath" outside the heavens, which is inhaled by the world (Arist., *Phys.* 213b22), and Heraclitus' "divine reason," which surrounds (περιέχει) us and which we draw in by means of respiration (Sext. Emp., *Adv. Math.* vii.127).

2 *De anima* 408b1.

3 *De anima* 410a25: Those who make soul consist of all the elements, and who hold that like perceives and knows like, "assume that perceiving is a sort of being acted upon or moved and that the same is true of thinking and knowing" (τὸ Ƌ' αἰσθάνεσθαι πάσχειν τι καὶ κινεῖσθαι τιθέασιν· ὁμοίως δὲ καὶ τὸ νοεῖν τε καὶ γιγνώσκειν).

All such action, moreover, was held to require a continuous vehicle or medium, uniting the soul which knows
to the object which is known. Further, the soul and its object must not only be thus linked in physical contact, but
they must be *alike* or *akin*....

It follows from this principle that, if the Soul is to
know the world, the world must ultimately consist of the
same substance as Soul. Φύσις and Soul must be homogeneous. Aristotle formulates the doctrine with great precision:

ὅσοι δ' ἐπὶ τὸ γινώσκειν καὶ τὸ αἰσθάνεσθαι τῶν ὄντων,
οὗτοι δὲ λέγουσι τὴν ψυχὴν τὰς ἀρχάς, οἱ μὲν πλείους
ποιοῦντες, ταύτας, οἱ δὲ μίαν, ταύτην, ὥσπερ Ἐμπεδοκλῆς
μὲν ἐκ τῶν στοιχείων πάντων, εἶναι δὲ καὶ ἕκαστον ψυχὴν
τούτων, λέγων οὕτως

γαίῃ μὲν γὰρ γαῖαν ὀπώπαμεν, ὕδατι δ' ὕδωρ,
αἰθέρι δ' αἰθέρα δῖαν, ἀτὰρ πυρὶ πῦρ ἀΐδηλον,
στοργῇ δὲ στοργήν, νεῖκος δέ τε νείκεϊ λυγρῷ.

τὸν αὐτὸν δὲ τρόπον καὶ Πλάτων ἐν τῷ Τιμαίῳ τὴν
ψυχὴν ἐκ τῶν στοιχείων ποιεῖ· γιγνώσκεσθαι γὰρ τῷ ὁμοίῳ
τὸ ὅμοιον, τὰ δὲ πράγματα ἐκ τῶν ἀρχῶν εἶναι.

"Those who laid stress on its knowledge and perception of all that exists, identified the soul with the ultimate
principles, whether they recognized a plurality of these or
only one. Thus, Empedocles compounded soul out of all
the elements, while at the same time regarding each one of
them as a soul. His words are,

With earth we see earth, with water water,
with air bright air, ravaging fire by fire,
love by love, and strife by gruesome strife.

"In the same manner, Plato in the *Timaeus* constructs
the soul out of the elements. Like, he there maintains, is
known by like, and the things we know are composed of
the ultimate principles...."[4]

4 *De anima* 404*b*8–18.

The texts on
this and the
facing page are
adapted from
F.M. CORNFORD'S
*From Religion to
Philosophy: A
Study in the Ori-
gins of Western
Speculation*
(London, 1912).
Some of the
Greek quotations
have been ex-
tended, and some
have been moved
from the foot-
notes into the
main text. This
makes Cornford's
prose seem more
pedantic and less
lucid than it
really is, but it
poses a harder
test for the type
and at the same
time permits a
more compact
typographic
demonstration.

These lines
are from §5
of Anna
Akhmatova's
В сороковом
году.

Но я предупреждаю вас,

But I'm warning you,

Что я живу в последний раз.

this is my last existence.

Ни ласточкой, ни кленом,

Not as a swallow, not as a maple,

Ни тростником и ни звездой ...

not as a cat-tail and not as a star ...

The words of Anna Akhmatova in the letters of Vadim Lazurski. The type is Lazurski Cyrillic with its companion roman.

Greek letters, like Greek words, are used for many purposes in non-Greek-speaking countries. Physicists and fraternity members, astronomers and novelists have raided the old alphabet for symbols. Because of their frequent use in mathematics and technical writing, a grab-bag of Greek letters lurks somewhere in nearly every digital typesetting system. α, β, γ, θ, π, Ω (alpha, beta, gamma, theta, pi, cap omega) and their brethren are usually housed, with other mathematical symbols, in a ghetto called the pi font. But setting Greek *text* with such a font is not a thankful task. Pi fonts lack the breathing marks and accents used in the classical language, and even the two simple diacritics (acute and diaeresis) that survive in modern Greek; and some pi fonts include only ten Greek caps – Γ Δ Θ Λ Ξ Π Σ Φ Ψ Ω – because the others – A B E H Z I K M N O P T Y X – have familiar roman forms, though not in every case the same phonetic value.

A text that includes even a single Greek quotation calls for a Greek text font rather than a pi font. A text font will include not only the full alphabet but matching punctuation and all the monotonic (modern) or polytonic (classical) diacritics. It will include two forms of lowercase sigma (ς, used at the ends of words, and σ, used everywhere else), and three iota subscripts, positioned to fit beneath the three long vowels with which they are used (ᾄ, ῇ, ῷ, for example). With luck, the font may also include a sensible kerning table and a rational keyboard layout. This is a lot to ask from an industry in which there is, officially, no culture other than commerce and no purpose except monetary gain. It is a lot to ask, but not by itself enough. In Greek as in any other alphabet, *the face must suit the text*. It must also suit the context, which is likely to be roman and italic.

There may be 50,000 fonts of type for the Latin alphabet now on the market in digital form. These comprise some 6000 families. Perhaps two per cent of them are truly useful for text work – but a hundred families of type is still a very generous number, and the available text faces cover a wide stylistic range. With a little scrounging, one can turn up several dozen digital fonts of Greek – but again, only a small percentage of these have any real potential for text work. It is therefore often best to choose a Greek font *first*, and then a roman and italic to go with it, even when only a few Greek words or a single Greek quotation is present in the text you are going to set.

Two Greek text fonts with eminent credentials – Victor Scholderer's New Hellenic, designed in 1927, and Richard Porson's Porson, designed in 1806 – are shown, in their digital incarnations, on pages 108 & 109. Porson's Greek was first commissioned by Cambridge University Press, but it became in the twentieth century the favorite Greek at Oxford, while Scholderer's New Hellenic became the favorite Cambridge Greek. New Hellenic in particular has an eminent Renaissance pedigree further discussed in chapter 10.

6.6.2 *Match the continuity of the typography to the continuity of thought.*

A text composed in a single dialect may be full of leaps and holes, while a text that hops and skips through several languages and alphabets may in fact be tracing a path that is perfectly smooth. The continuity, or lack of continuity, that underlies the text should as a rule be revealed, not concealed, in the cloth the typographer weaves.

An author who quotes Greek or Hebrew or Russian or Arabic fluently and gracefully in speech should be permitted to do likewise on the page. Practically speaking, this means that when the alphabets are mixed, they should be very closely balanced both in *color* and in *contrast*.

abyohi ἄβγοθι *abyohi*
abyohi ἄβγοθι *abyohi*

abyohi ἄβγοθι *abyohi*

Victor Scholderer's New Hellenic paired with José Mendoza's Mendoza
(above), with Peter Matthias Noordzij's Caecilia (center) and with
Adobe Jenson (below). Mendoza is a face with very low contrast (the
thicks and thins are nearly the same). New Hellenic and Caecilia have an
unmodulated stroke – in other words, no contrast at all. New Hellenic
and Adobe Jenson have stylistic compatibility of a different kind. Both
stem from the work of Nicolas Jenson, who in 1469 cut the father of this
roman and in 1471 the grandfather of this Greek.

Flow and *slope* are other factors to consider, especially when
balancing Latin and Greek. Many Greek text faces (the Porson
and Didot Greeks for example) are structurally comparable to
italics. That is, they are cursive. Some of them are upright
nonetheless (like the Didot), and some (like the Porson) slope.
When roman, italic and Greek are combined on the page, the
Greek may be upright like the roman, or it may harmonize with
the italic in flow and slope. It may also stand aloof, with a gait
and inclination of its own.

6.6.3 *Balance the type optically more than mathematically.*

Two other factors of importance when types sit side by side are
their *torso* (x-height) and *extension*. When a long-limbed Greek is
paired with a short-limbed Latin, the difference will stand out.
Large disparities in x-height are far more obvious still. In metal,
this is a harsh typographic constraint. In the digital medium, it is
easy to match the torso of any Greek face to that of any Latin face
exactly, through microscopic adjustments in size. But an optical,
not mathematical, match is the goal. Classical Greek, beneath its
cloud of diacritics, needs more room to breathe than roman type.
And when setting Greek in footnotes, the minimum practical
size is the size at which the accents are still legible.

abyohi *ἄβγοθι abyohi*

abyohi ἄβγοθι *abyohi*

abyohi ἄβγοϑι *abyohi*

Above: The Greek of Richard Porson paired with W. A. Dwiggins's Electra.
Center: Didot Greek paired with Adobe Caslon. *Below*: The Bodoni Greek
of Takis Katsoulides paired with the Esprit roman and italic of Jovica
Veljović. Electra italic and Porson Greek both have a slope of 10°, while
the Caslon italic slopes at 20°. Porson, with its rationalist axis, also has a
structural kinship to Electra. The Didot Greek, though Neoclassical in
form, is closer in color to Caslon. Katsoulides's more playful Bodoni
Greek is closer both in structure and in spirit to Esprit.

The type on page 109 looked fine when it was first roughed
out, using bald Greek letters identical in x-height to the roman.
When the bald sorts were replaced with accented letters, the
Greek was still mathematically correct but optically too large.
Balance was restored by shrinking the Greek from 11 to 10.5 pt.
The x-height of the type is (as usual in a Neoclassical text face)
only about two fifths of the body size. The difference in x-height
between 10.5 and 11 pt type is accordingly two fifths of half a
point. That is roughly 70 μm, which is less than 0.003 inch. Not
much, but enough to unbalance or balance the page.

6.7 NEW ORTHOGRAPHIES

No writing system is fixed. Even our ways of writing classical
Latin and Greek continue to change, along with our ways of
writing and spelling such rapidly mutating languages as English. But many languages old to speech are new to writing, and
many have not yet decided their literate form.

In North America, for example, Navajo, Hopi, Tlingit, Cree,
Ojibwa, Inuktitut and Cherokee, among others, have evolved
quite stable writing systems, in which a substantial printed literature has accrued. But many Native American languages are still
being written in different ways by every scholar and student who

113

happens by. Some, like Tsimshian and Kwakwala, already possess a considerable written literature, but in cumbersome scripts that even scholars have ceased to use.

Typographers must generally confront these problems piecemeal. Alphabets are often created by fiat, but it is usually in tiny increments that real typographic style evolves.

6.7.1 *Add no unnecessary characters.*

Colonial expansion has carried the Arabic alphabet across the north of Africa and much of southern Asia, Cyrillic script across the north of Asia, and the Latin alphabet around the world. For better or for worse, most of those learning to read and write in newly literate languages are exposed to writing in a colonial language first. For readers and typographers alike, the basic Latin, Cyrillic or Arabic alphabet is therefore often the easiest place to start, and the fewer additional symbols required the better. The dream of a common language, imposed upon many minority cultures, has proven for most to be a nightmare. But in a world where there are hundreds of ancestral and classical languages and literatures instead of one or two, prayers for renewed diversification often entail the dream of a common script.

> Wa'giên sq!ê'ñgua lā'na hîn sā'wan, "K!wa la t!āla'ñ ł
> gia'ḷītc!în."

> Wagyaan sqqinggwa llaana hin saawan, "Kkwa lla
> ttaalang hl gyadliittsin."

A sentence in the Haida language, in the earliest (1901) standard orthography and a more recent, simplified version. In the first, glottalized consonants are marked by exclamations and long vowels by macrons. In the second, both are notated by doubling. (Translation: *Then the one in the bow said, 'Let us take it aboard.'*)

6.7.2 *Add only characters that are visually distinct.*

The texture of the typographic page depends not only on how the type is designed, set and printed, but also on the frequency of different letters. Latin looks smoother than English (and much smoother than German) because it uses fewer ascending and descending letters, no accented characters, and (in the hands of most editors) very few caps. Polynesian languages – Maori and Hawaiian, for example – which are long on vowels and short on consonants, compose into a texture even creamier than Latin, and require an even smaller alphabet.

Most languages need more, not fewer, consonants than the basic Latin alphabet provides. There may be (as in Haida and Tlingit) four forms of *k,* or (as in the Khoisan languages of southwest Africa) 36 different clicks – and if each is lexically significant, each needs a distinctive typographic form.

Vowels are fairly easy to elaborate when need be; except for the *y,* they have no extenders. Navajo, for example, involves twelve forms of a – a, aa, ą, ąą, á, áá, áa, aá, ą́, ą́ą́, ą́ą, ąą́ – all easily distinguished. Typographically, it would be no problem to add another dozen forms.

Consonants are not quite so easy to ramify, precisely because so many of them have extenders. Typographically deficient forms therefore often crop up. Lakota, for example – the language of the Teton Sioux – requires two forms of *h.* Stephen Riggs, who published the first Lakota dictionary and grammar in 1852, chose to mark the second form with an overdot: *ḣ.* This character, which is still used by many native speakers and some scholars, is easily mistaken for *li.* More recent Lakota spelling replaces the dotted *h* with an *x.* This is easier to set, but more importantly, it is harder to misread.

In the Tlingit language, spoken and written in southern Alaska, northern British Columbia and the Yukon, underscores are used to mark uvular consonants, which is fine for k̲ and x̲, but not so fine for g̲. A form like ġ or ǧ or ḡ, though less consistent, is more compact and, once again, harder to misread.

The desire for consistency was not the only factor that led earlier linguists to write g instead of ǧ. The Tlingit alphabet was developed, like many early twentieth-century writing systems, using only the keyboard of a North American typewriter. Recent Tlingit publications are typeset with computers using modified fonts of Palatino or Stone, but the iron metaphor of the typewriter has not yet loosed its hold.

Elsewhere in the world, the mechanical typewriter and letterpress are still economically viable and socially prestigious tools – and this need not prevent new alphabet design. The Pan Nigerian face shown overleaf was cut and cast commercially for hand composition in 1983. Mechanical typewriters using a monospaced version of the font entered production in 1985.

In the Navajo alphabet (*saad bee 'ál'íní*), long vowels are written double and nasal vowels are written with an ogonek. High tone is marked with an acute. Long high vowels carry two acutes, one on each vowel. Long falling vowels carry an acute on the first vowel only, long rising vowels carry an acute on the second vowel only. Glottalized consonants are followed by apostrophes.

àbɓcddɗeəɛ́fghiîíjkƙl
ABʼBCDDʼDEƎÉFGHIIIJKKʼL
MNÒỌPRSSṬTÛŪṾVWYZ
mnòọprsṣtûūṿvwyz

New
Orthogra-
phies

Pan Nigerian alphabet designed in 1983 by Hermann Zapf, in collaboration with Victor Manfredi. This normalizes the missionary orthographies
that have been used for Hausa, Igbo, Yoruba, Edo, Fulfulde and several
other Nigerian languages.

6.7.3 *Avoid capricious redefinition of familiar characters.*

Mayan languages have been written in roman script since the
1550s, but more than one orthography remains in use. Perhaps
the oldest, based on the manuscript tradition of the *Popol Vuh,*
uses the numerals 3 and 4 and the digraphs 4h and 4, [*including
the comma*] to write several glottalized consonants. The Quiché
words for sun and moon, for example, can be written *k'ih* and
ic', or *kkih* and *icc*, or *3ih* and *i4*, and the word for blood can be
written *quit'z* or *quittz* or *qui4,*. In the final case – but not in any
of the others – the comma is part of the word and not a mark of
punctuation.

Though it is not as picturesque as Mayan hieroglyphs, this
alphanumeric script appeals to some scholars and amateurs,
perhaps because of its very strangeness. Typographically, it begs
for clarification, either through the creation of unambiguous
new symbols or through reversion to plain old roman letters
(which is now a common practice).

6.7.4 *Don't mix faces haphazardly when specialized sorts are required.*

ʔaλʼaqə́m is
Upper Chehalis,
meaning
you will emerge;
ɪntə-næʃənļ
fənɛɾɪks
(*international
phonetics*)
is English.

If a text involves setting occasional words such as ʔaλʼaqə́m or
ɪntə-næʃənļ fənɛɾɪks, it is best to plan for them from the beginning. Two standard phonetic alphabets are in use: the international (IPA) and the American. But the extra characters involved
have been cut for only a few faces. (Lucida Sans, Stone and Times
Roman are examples. Stone phonetic – which is used here –
exists in both serifed and unserifed forms.) The typographer
therefore has two choices: to set the entire text in a face for which

116

matching phonetic characters are available, so that phonetic transcriptions can enter the text transparently and at will; or to set the main text in a suitably contrasting face, and switch to the phonetic font (along with its matching text font, if required) each time a phonetic transcription occurs.

If contrasting faces are used for phonetic transcriptions and main text, each entire phonetic word or passage, not just the individual phonetic characters, should be set in the chosen phonetic face. Patchwork typography, in which the letters of a single word come from different faces and fonts, is a sign of typographic failure. Forms such as 'Θraētona' and 'Usaδan,' sometimes used to represent the script of ancient languages such as Avestan, are typographically problematic because they mix two alphabets *within a single word*. Such mixtures rarely succeed unless all the fonts involved have been designed as a single family. (This is the case here, where a unified Latin and Greek are used.)

6.8 BUILDING A TYPE LIBRARY

6.8.1 *Choose your library of faces slowly and well.*

Some of the best typographers who ever lived had no more than one roman font at a time, one blackletter and one Greek. Others had as many as five or six romans, two or three italics, three blackletters, three or four Greeks. Today, the typographer can buy fonts by the thousand on compact discs, and use the telephone to download thousands more: more fonts than any human could use, yet never a complete selection.

With type as with philosophy, music and food, it is better to have a little of the best than to be swamped with the derivative, the careless, the routine.

The stock fonts supplied with software packages and desktop printers are sometimes generous in number, but they are the wrong fonts for many tasks and people, and most of them are missing essential parts (small caps, text figures, ligatures, diacritics and important analphabetics).

Begin by buying one good face or family, or a few related faces, with all the components intact. And instead of skipping from face to face, attempting to try everything, stay with your first choices long enough to learn their virtues and limitations before you move on.

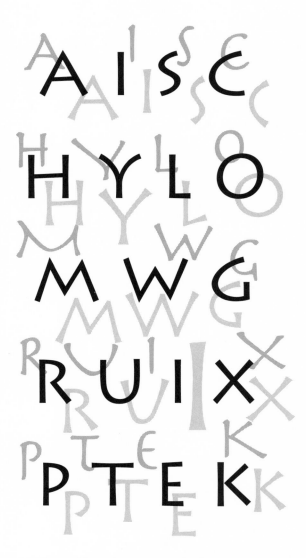

Carol Twombly's Lithos (1988) and Adrian Frutiger's
Herculanum (1990) and Rusticana (1991) are typefaces based on
early Mediterranean inscriptions. In this example, Lithos
is printed solid, Herculanum (upper rows) and
Rusticana (lower rows) are screened.

Printing from movable type was first invented not in Germany in the 1450s, as Europeans often claim, but in China in the 1040s. In preference to Gutenberg, we should honor a scholarly engineer by the name of Bí Shēng (畢昇). The earliest surviving works printed in Asia from movable type seem to date from the thirteenth century, but there is a clear account of the typesetting process, and Bí Shēng's role in its development, by the eleventh-century essayist Shěn Kuò.

The new technology reached Korea before the middle of the thirteenth century and Europe before the middle of the fifteenth. There it intersected the already long and fertile history of the roman letter. And there typesetting flourished as it had failed to do in China, because of the far smaller number of characters European scripts required. Even at the end of the nineteenth century, most printing in China was done by the same method used in the eighth century to make the first printed books: entire pages of text were carved by hand into wooden printing plates. Corrections were made by drilling out the error, installing a wooden plug, and cutting the new characters. It is the same technique used to make the woodcut illustrations that were often combined with printed text.

7.1 THE EARLY SCRIBAL FORMS

The earliest surviving European letterforms are Greek capitals scratched into stone. The strokes are bony and thin, almost ethereal – the opposite of the heavy substance they are carved in. The letters are made primarily from straight lines, and when curved forms appear, they have a very large *aperture*. This means that forms like S and C and M, which can be relatively open or relatively closed, are about as open as they can get. These early Greek letters were drawn freehand, not constructed with compasses and rule, and they have no serifs – neither the informal entry and exit strokes left by a relaxed and fluent writer, nor the symmetrical finishing strokes typically added to letters by a formal scribe.

In time, the strokes of these letters grew thicker, the aperture lessened, and serifs appeared. The new forms, used for in-

Shěn Kuò's account is contained in his *Mèngxī Bǐtán* (夢溪筆談), "Dream Creek Essays." For more information in English, see Denis Twitchett, *Printing and Publishing in Medieval China* (London, 1983), and Thomas F. Carter, *The Invention of Printing in China and Its Spread Westward*, 2nd ed., revised by L. Carrington Goodrich (New York, 1955).

scriptions throughout the Greek empire, served as models for formal lettering in imperial Rome. And those Roman inscriptional letters – written with a flat brush, held at an angle like a broadnib pen, then carved into the stone with mallet and chisel – have served in their turn as models for calligraphers and type designers for the past two thousand years. They have a modest aperture, a *modulated* stroke (a stroke whose thickness varies with direction), and they have lively but full and formal serifs.

A B C S P Q R

Trajan, designed by Carol Twombly in 1988, is based on the inscription at the base of Trajan's Column, Rome, carved in AD 113.

Between the Roman inscriptions and Gutenberg's time, there were many further changes in European letterforms. Narrow rustic capitals, wide uncials and other forms evolved. Writing spread to the farthest corners of Europe, and many regional scripts and alphabets arose. Monastic scribes – who were designers, copyists and archivists as well – kept many of the older letterforms alive. They used them for titles, subheads and initials, choosing newer and more compact scripts for running text. Out of this rich multiplicity of letters, a basic dichotomy evolved: *majuscules* and *minuscules*: large formal letters and smaller, more casual ones: the upper and lower case, as we call them now.

C A R O L U S   M A G N U S
Caroline or Carolingian means of the time
of the Emperor Charlemagne: «Big Charles».

Carol Twombly's Charlemagne (above), Gudrun Zapf-von Hesse's Alcuin (center) and Gottfried Pott's Carolina (below) are typefaces based on Carolingian majuscules and minuscules from ninth- and tenth-century European manuscripts.

Many of the old scribal conventions survive in typesetting today. Titles are still set in large, formal letters; large initials mark the beginnings of chapters or sections; small capitals mark an opening phrase. The well-made page is now what it was then: a window into history, language and the mind: a map of what is being said and a portrait of the voice that is silently speaking.

In the later Middle Ages and the early Renaissance, a well-trained European scribe might know eight or ten distinct styles of script. Each was defined as precisely as a typeface, stored like a font in the human memory, and each had certain uses. Sacred scriptures, legal documents, romance literature, business and personal letters all required different scripts, and particular forms evoked specific languages and regions.

Historical Interlude

When the technology of movable type arrived, Europe was rich with Gothic, Byzantine, Romanesque and humanistic hands, and with a wealth of older letters. They are all still with us in some way, but the humanistic hand, based on the Carolingian minuscule, has become the central form: the roman lower case, evolving into a thousand variations, sports and hybrids, like the willow or the rose.

7.2 THE TYPOGRAPHIC LATIN LETTER

Several systems are in use for classifying typefaces. Some of them use fabricated terms such as 'garalde' and 'didone.' Others rely on familiar but vague labels such as 'old style,' 'modern' and 'transitional.' All these systems work to a certain extent, but all leave much to be desired. They are neither good science nor good history.

Rigorously scientific descriptions and classifications of typefaces are certainly possible, and important research has been under way in this field for several years. Like the scientific study of plants and animals, the infant science of typology involves precise measurement, close analysis, and the careful use of technically descriptive terms.

But letterforms are not only objects of science. They also belong to the realm of art, and they participate in its history. They have changed over time just as music, painting and architecture have changed, and the same historical terms – Renaissance, Baroque, Neoclassical, Romantic, and so on – are useful in each of these fields.

The art history of Latin letterforms is treated in greater detail in an incomplete series of essays in *Serif* magazine, issues 1–5 (1994–97).

This approach to the classification of letterforms has another important advantage. Typography never occurs in isolation. Good typography demands not only a knowledge of type itself, but an understanding of the relationship between letterforms and the other things that humans make and do. Typographic history is just that: the study of the relationships between type designs and the rest of human activity – politics, philosophy, the arts, and the history of ideas. It is a lifelong pursuit, but one that is informative and rewarding from the beginning.

7.2.1 *The Renaissance Roman Letter*

Renaissance roman letters developed among the scholars and scribes of northern Italy in the fourteenth and fifteenth centuries. Their translation from script to type began in Italy in 1465 and continued for more than a century. Like Renaissance painting and music, Renaissance letterforms are full of sensuous

abcefgnopj
abcefgnopj
abcefgnopj
abcefgnopj

Four twentieth-century reconstructions of Renaissance roman typefaces. Centaur (top) was designed by the American typographer Bruce Rogers, Boston, c.1914, after Nicolas Jenson, Venice, 1469. Bembo (second) was cut by Monotype, London, in 1929, based on the design of Francesco Griffo, Venice, 1499. Adobe Garamond (third) was designed by Robert Slimbach, San Francisco, 1988, after Claude Garamond, Paris, c. 1540. DTL Van den Keere (bottom) is Frank Blokland's reconstruction of a font cut for Christophe Plantin by Hendrik van den Keere, Antwerp, in 1575.

and unhurried light and space. They have served as typographic benchmarks for five hundred years.

The earliest surviving roman punches or matrices may well be Garamond's, cut in Paris in the 1530s. For earlier type, we have no evidence beyond the printed books themselves. The basic structure and form of these early typefaces is clear beyond dispute, but in their subtlest details, all the existing replicas of fifteenth-century Italian type are hypothetical reconstructions.

Like Roman inscriptional capitals, Renaissance roman lowercase letters have a modulated stroke (the width varies with direction) and a *humanist* axis. This means that the letters have the form produced by a broadnib pen held in the right hand in a comfortable and relaxed writing position. The thick strokes run NW/SE, the axis of the writer's hand and forearm. The serifs are crisp, the stroke is light, and the contrast between thick strokes and thin strokes is generally modest.

In summary, the characteristics of the early Renaissance roman letter are these:

- *stems vertical*
- *bowls nearly circular*
- *modulated stroke*
- *consistent humanist axis*
- *modest contrast*
- *modest x-height*
- *crisp, oblique head serifs (on letters such as* b *and* r *)*
- *abrupt, flat or slightly splayed bilateral foot serifs (on letters such as* r, l *and* p *)*
- *abrupt, pen-formed terminals on* a, c, f *and* r
- *rising crossbar in* e, *perpendicular to the stroke axis*
- *the roman font is solitary (there is no italic or bold)*

In later Renaissance forms (from 1500 on), the letterforms grow softer, smoother and more self-contained in subtle ways:

- *head serifs become more wedge-shaped*
- *foot serifs become adnate (flowing smoothly into the stem) instead of abrupt*
- *terminals of* c, f *and* r *become less abrupt and more lachrymal (teardrop-shaped)*
- *crossbar of* e *becomes horizontal*

Rome is located in the midst of Italy. Why is roman type a category separate from italic? It seems a question to which typographers might possess the answer. But the question and the answer both have as much to do with politics and religion as with calligraphy and typography.

Roman type consists of two quite different basic parts. The upper case, which does indeed come from Rome, is based on Roman imperial inscriptions. The lower case was developed in northern Europe, chiefly in France and Germany, in the late Middle Ages, and given its final polish in Venice in the early Renaissance. Nevertheless, it too is Roman in the larger sense. While the roman upper case is a legacy of the Roman Empire, the lower case is a legacy of the Holy Roman Empire, the pagan empire's Christianized successor. It acquired its fundamental form at the hands of Christian scribes, many of them employed during the late eighth century as administrators and teachers by the Holy Roman Emperor Charlemagne.

Italic letterforms, on the other hand, are an Italian Renaissance creation. Some early italics come from Rome, others from elsewhere in Italy, and when they were first converted to type, italics were still full of local flavor and freshness. But the earliest italic fonts, cut between 1500 and 1540, consist of lower case only. They were used with upright roman caps but not in conjunction with the roman lower case.

abcefgnopxyz

abcefgnopxyz

Two revivals of Renaissance italic type. Monotype Arrighi (above) is derived from one of a series of italics designed by Frederic Warde, London and Paris, 1925–29, after Ludovico degli Arrighi, Rome, 1524. Monotype Bembo italic (below) was cut in London in 1929, based on the work of both Arrighi and Giovanantonio Tagliente, Venice, 1524.

The characteristics of the Renaissance italic letter can be summarized as follows:

- *stems vertical or of fairly even slope, not exceeding 10°*
- *bowls generally elliptical*
- *light, modulated stroke*
- *consistent humanist axis*
- *low contrast*
- *modest x-height*
- *cursive forms with crisp, oblique entry and exit serifs*
- *descenders serifed bilaterally or not at all*
- *terminals abrupt or lachrymal*
- *italic lower case paired with small, upright roman capitals, and with occasional swash capitals; italic otherwise fully independent of roman*

Historical Interlude

Early Renaissance italics are known as *Aldine* italics, in honor of the scholar and publisher Aldus Manutius, who commissioned the first italic type from Francesco Griffo in 1499. Strange to say, in 1996, not a single authentic reconstruction of an Aldine italic appears to be available, either in metal or in digital form. Monotype Bembo roman and Monotype Poliphilus are both based on Griffo's work, but their companion italics are not; they come from a different age. The digital italic nearest to an Aldine in design is Giovanni Mardersteig's Dante italic, but even this has sloped instead of upright capitals.

See page 200 for reproductions of two Aldine italics.

equbdaffglopsþz

abefop*abefop*

Two recent typefaces in the Mannerist tradition. Poetica (above) is a chancery italic based on sixteenth-century models. It was designed by Robert Slimbach and issued by Adobe in 1992. Galliard (below), designed by Matthew Carter, was issued by Linotype in 1978. It is based on letterforms cut in the sixteenth century by Robert Granjon.

7.2.3   *The Mannerist Letter*

Mannerist art is Renaissance art to which subtle exaggerations –
of length, angularity or tension, for example – have been added.
Mannerist typographers, working chiefly in Italy and France
early in the sixteenth century, began the practice of using roman and italic in the same book, and even on the same page –
though rarely on the same line. It was also during the Mannerist period that sloped roman capitals were first added to the
italic lower case.

*The
Typographic
Latin
Letter*

   There are many fine sixteenth-century examples of Mannerist typefaces, including roman titling fonts with long, delicate extenders, chancery italics with even longer and often ornamented extenders, and text faces with short extenders but
increased tension in the forms. Digital interpretations of a
number of these faces have recently been made.

abefop*abefop*

abefop*abefop*

abefop*abefop*

abefop*abefop*

Four revivals of Baroque typefaces. Monotype 'Garamond' (top) is based
on fonts cut in France by Jean Jannon, about 1621. DTL Elzevir (second) is
based on fonts cut by Christoffel van Dijck at Amsterdam in the 1660s.
Linotype Janson Text (third) is based on fonts cut by Miklós Kis, Amsterdam, about 1685. Adobe Caslon (bottom), by Carol Twombly, is based on
faces cut by William Caslon, London, in the 1730s.

126

7.2.4 The Baroque Letter

Baroque typography, like Baroque painting and music, is rich with activity and takes delight in the restless and dramatic play of contradictory forms. One of the most obvious features of any Baroque typeface is the large *variation in axis* from one letter to the next. Baroque italics are *ambidextrous*: both right- and left-handed. And it was during the Baroque that typographers first made a habit of mixing roman and italic *on the same line*.

In general, Baroque letterforms appear more modelled and less *written* than Renaissance forms. They give less evidence of the direct trace of the pen. Yet they take many different forms, and they thrived in Europe throughout the seventeenth century, endured through much of the eighteenth, and enjoyed an enthusiastic revival during the nineteenth.

Baroque letterforms generally differ from Renaissance letters in the following ways:

- *stroke axis of the roman and italic lower case varies widely within a single alphabet*
- *slope of italic averages 15° to 20° and often varies considerably within a single alphabet*
- *contrast increased*
- *x-height increased*
- *aperture generally reduced*
- *further softening of terminals from abrupt to lachrymal*
- *roman head serifs become sharp wedges*
- *head serifs of italic ascenders become level and sharp*

7.2.5 The Rococo Letter

The historical periods listed here – Renaissance, Baroque and so on – belong to all the arts, and they are naturally not limited, in typography, to roman and italic letters. Blackletter and script types passed through the same phases as well. But the Rococo period, with its love of florid ornament, belongs almost entirely to blackletters and scripts. Roman and italic type was certainly used by Rococo typographers, who often surrounded their texts with typographic ornaments, engraved medallions, and so on. They produced a good deal of Rococo *typography*, but little or not much Rococo roman and italic *type*.

Several romans and italics that might indeed be classified as

abcefgnopy

CEFOTZ

abcefgnopy

DTL Fleischman. Note the ornate forms of g, y and several of the capitals, and the exaggerated contrast in the o. This exaggerated contrast is typical of the Romantic types cut by Firmin Didot and Giambattista Bodoni after Fleischman's death in 1768. But Romantic types have an obsessively vertical axis. The primary axis of Fleischman's type is oblique. Structurally, these letters belong to the Baroque. But their tendency to ornamentation and exaggeration sets them apart from earlier Baroque types. That is a reason for calling them Rococo.

Rococo were, however, cut in Amsterdam in 1738–39 by the German-born punchcutter Johann Michael Fleischman. Digital versions of these fonts have recently been released by the Dutch Type Library in 's-Hertogenbosch.

7.2.6 *The Neoclassical Letter*

Generally speaking, Neoclassical art is more static and restrained than either Renaissance or Baroque art, and far more interested in rigorous consistency. Neoclassical letterforms follow this pattern. In Neoclassical letters, an echo of the broadnib pen can still be seen, but it is rotated away from the natural writing angle to a strictly vertical or *rationalist* axis. The letters are moderate in contrast and aperture, but their axis is dictated by an idea, not by the truth of human anatomy. They are products of the Rationalist era: frequently beautiful, calm forms, but forms oblivious to the more complex beauty of organic fact. If Baroque letterforms are ambidextrous, Neoclassical letters are, in their quiet way, *neitherhanded.*

abefop*abefop*

abefop*abefop*

abefop*abefop*

Three twentieth-century revivals of Neoclassical letterforms. *Above:*
Monotype Fournier, which is based on types cut by Pierre Simon Fournier,
Paris, about 1740. *Center:* Monotype Baskerville, which is based on the
designs of John Baskerville, Birmingham, about 1754. *Below:* Monotype
Bell, based on the types cut in London in 1788 by Richard Austin for the
typefounder and publisher John Bell.

The first Neoclassical typeface, known as the *romain du roi*
or King's Roman, was designed in France in the 1690s, not by a
typographer but by a government committee consisting of two
priests, an accountant and an engineer. Other Neoclassical faces
were designed and cut in France, England, Italy and Spain during the eighteenth and nineteenth centuries, and some of them
have remained in continuous use throughout all subsequent
changes of style and fashion.

The American printer and statesman Benjamin Franklin
deeply admired the Neoclassical type of his English contemporary John Baskerville, and it is partly due to Franklin's support
that Baskerville's type became more important in the United
States and France than it ever was in Baskerville's native land.
But the connection between Baskerville and America rests on
more than Benjamin Franklin's personal taste. Baskerville's letters correspond very closely to the federal style in American architecture. They are as purely and unperturbably Neoclassical
as the Capitol Building, the White House, and many another
federal and state edifice. (The Houses of Parliament in London
and in Ottawa, which are Neogothic instead of Neoclassical, call
for typography of a different kind.)

In brief, Neoclassical letterforms differ from Baroque letters as follows:

- *predominantly vertical axis in both roman and italic*
- *slope of italic generally uniform, averaging 14° to 16°*
- *serifs generally adnate, but thinner, flatter, more level*

7.2.7   The Romantic Letter

Neoclassicism and Romanticism are not sequential movements in European history. They marched through the eighteenth century and much of the nineteenth side by side: vigorously opposed in some respects and closely united in others. Both Neoclassical and Romantic letterforms adhere to a rationalist axis, and both look more drawn than written, but it is possible to make some precise distinctions between the two. The most obvious difference is one of contrast. In Romantic letters we will normally find the following:

- *abrupt modulation of the stroke*
- *vertical axis intensified through exaggerated contrast*
- *hardening of terminals from lachrymal to round*
- *serifs thinner and more abrupt*
- *aperture reduced*

This remarkable shift in type design – like *all* structural shifts in type design – is the record of an underlying change in handwriting. Romantic letters are forms from which the broadnib pen has vanished. In its place is the pointed and flexible quill. The broadnib pen produces a smoothly modulated stroke whose thickness varies with direction, but the pointed quill performs quite differently. The stroke of a flexible quill shifts suddenly from thin to thick to thin again, in response to changes in pressure. Used with restraint, it produces a Neoclassical flourish. Used with greater force, it produces a more dramatic and Romantic one. Dramatic contrast, which is essential to much Romantic music and painting, is essential to Romantic type design as well.

Romantic letters can be extraordinarily beautiful, but they lack the flowing and steady rhythm of Renaissance forms. It is that rhythm which invites the reader to enter the text and read. The statuesque forms of Romantic letters invite the reader to stand outside and *look* at the letters instead.

abefop*abefop*

abefop*abefop*

abefop*abefop*

abefop*abefop*

Historical Interlude

Four revivals of Romantic letterforms. Monotype Bulmer (top) is based on a series of fonts William Martin cut in London in the early 1790s. Linotype Didot (second), drawn by Adrian Frutiger, is based on fonts Firmin Didot cut in Paris between 1799 and 1811. Berthold Bodoni (third) is based on fonts cut by Giambattista Bodoni at Parma between 1803 and 1812. Berthold Walbaum (bottom) is based on types cut by Justus Erich Walbaum, Weimar, about 1805.

7.2.8 *The Realist Letter*

The nineteenth and twentieth centuries have entertained a be-wildering variety of artistic movements and schools – Realism, Naturalism, Impressionism, Expressionism, Art Nouveau, Art Deco, Constructivism, Cubism, Abstract Expressionism, Pop Art, Op Art, and many more. Virtually all of these movements have raised waves in the typographic world as well, though only a few are important enough to merit a place in this brief survey. One of these movements is typographic Realism.

The Realist painters of the nineteenth century – Gustave Courbet, François Millet and many others – turned their backs on the subjects and poses approved by the academy. They set out instead to paint ordinary people doing their ordinary tasks. Realist type designers – Alexander Phemister, Robert Besley and others, who have not achieved the posthumous fame of the

abcefgnop

abcefgnop

Akzidenz Grotesk (above) is a Realist typeface issued by the Berthold Foundry, Berlin, in 1898. It is the immediate ancestor of Morris Benton's Franklin Gothic (1903) and of Helvetica, issued by the Haas Foundry in 1952. Haas Clarendon (below), designed in 1951 by Hermann Eidenbenz, is a revival of an earlier Realist face, the first Clarendon, cut by Benjamin Fox for Robert Besley, London, 1845.

painters – worked in a similar spirit. They made blunt and simple letters, based on the script of people denied the opportunity to learn to read and write with fluency and poise. Realist letters very often have the same basic shape as Neoclassical and Romantic letters, but most of them have heavy, slab serifs or no serifs at all. The stroke is often uniform in weight, and the aperture (often a gauge of grace or good fortune in typefaces) is tiny. Small caps, text figures and other signs of sophistication and elegance are almost always missing.

7.2.9   *Geometric Modernism: The Distillation of Function*

Early modernism took many intriguing typographic forms. One of the most obvious is geometric. The sparest, most rigorous architecture of the early twentieth century has its counterpart in the equally geometric typefaces designed at the same time, often by the same people. These typefaces, like their Realist predecessors, make no distinction between main stroke and serif. Their serifs are equal in weight with the main strokes or are missing altogether. But most Geometric Modernist faces seek purity more than populism. Some show the study of archaic inscriptions, and some include text figures and other subtleties, but their shapes owe more to pure mathematical forms – the circle and the line – than to scribal letters.

abcefgnop
abcefgnop

Two Geometric Modernist typefaces. Futura (above) was designed in Germany in 1924–26 by Paul Renner. Memphis (below) was designed in 1929 by Rudolf Wolf, art director at the Stempel Foundry. The original design for Futura included text figures and many highly geometric, alternative characters which have never been issued in metal, though The Foundry (London) issued them in digital form in 1994.

Memphis is often but wrongly credited to Emil Rudolf Weiss.

abefop*abefop*
abefop*abefop*
abefop*abefop*
abefop*abefop*

Four neohumanist or Lyrical Modernist typefaces. Spectrum (top) was designed by Jan van Krimpen in the Netherlands during the 1940s and issued by both Enschedé and Monotype in 1952. Palatino (second) was designed by Hermann Zapf, Frankfurt, 1948. Dante (third) was designed by Giovanni Mardersteig, Verona, 1952. Pontifex (bottom) was designed by Friedrich Poppl, Wiesbaden, 1974. All but the last were originally cut by hand in steel, just like Renaissance faces.

133

Another major phase of modernism in type design is closely allied with abstract expressionist painting. Painters in the twentieth century rediscovered the physical and sensory pleasures of painting as an act, and the pleasures of making organic instead of mechanical forms. Designers of type during those years were equally busy rediscovering the pleasures of *writing* letterforms rather than drawing them. In rediscovering calligraphy, they rediscovered the broadnib pen, the humanist axis and humanist scale of Renaissance letters. Typographic modernism is fundamentally the reassertion of Renaissance form. There is no hard line between modernist design and Renaissance revival.

7.2.11 *The Expressionist Letter*

In yet another of its aspects, typographic modernism is rough and concrete more than lyrical and abstract. Rudolf Koch, Vojtěch Preissig and Oldřich Menhart are three designers who explored this path in the early part of the twentieth century. They are in some respect the typographic counterparts of expressionist painters such as Vincent van Gogh and Oskar Kokoschka. More recent painters and type designers, such as Zuzana Ličko, have proven that the genre is still richly productive.

Expressionist designers use many different tools. Koch and Preissig often cut their own letters in metal or wood. Menhart worked with a pen and rough paper. Ličko has exploited the

abcefghijop

abefopabefop

Two Expressionist types: one Modernist and one Postmodern. Preissig was designed in New York in 1924 by the Czech artist Vojtěch Preissig. It was cut and cast in Prague in 1925. Zuzana Ličko's Journal was designed in Berkeley in 1990 and issued in digital form by Emigre.

harsh economies of digital plotting routines, slicing from control point to control point not with a knife, file or chisel but with digitized straight lines.

7.2.12 *Elegiac Postmodernism*

Modernism in type design has its roots in the study of history, the facts of human anatomy, and in the pleasures of calligraphy. Like the Renaissance itself, modernism is more than a phase or fad that simply runs its course and expires. It remains very much alive in the arts generally and in type design in particular, though it no longer seems the final word. In the last decades of the twentieth century, critics of architecture, literature and music – along with others who study human affairs – all perceived movements away from modernism. Lacking any proper name of their own, these movements have come to be called by the single term postmodernism. And postmodernism is as evident in the world of type design as it is in other fields. *Historical Interlude*

   Postmodern letterforms, like Postmodern buildings, frequently recycle and revise Neoclassical, Romantic and other premodern forms. At their best, they do so with an engaging lightness of touch and a fine sense of humor. Postmodern art is for the most part highly self-conscious, but devoutly unserious. Postmodern designers – who frequently are or have been Modernist designers as well – have proven that it is possible to infuse Neoclassical and Romantic form, and the rationalist axis, with genuine calligraphic energy.

abefop*abefop*

abefop*abefop*

Two Postmodern faces. Esprit (above) was designed by Jovica Veljović, Beograd, 1985. Nofret (bottom) was designed by Gudrun Zapf-von Hesse, Darmstadt, 1990. Both types sing, where many Postmodern faces merely screech. But the song is elegiac more than lyrical.

abefop*abefop*

abefop*abefop*

Two Geometric Postmodern faces: Triplex Sans (above) and Officina Serif (below). Triplex italic was designed by John Downer in 1985. Its companion romans – one with serifs, one without – were designed by Zuzana Ličko in 1989–90, and the full *ménage à trois* was issued in 1990 by Emigre. Officina (ITC, 1990) was designed by Erik Spiekermann. It has been issued in both serifed and unserifed versions.

7.2.13 *Geometric Postmodernism*

Some Postmodern faces are highly geometric. Like their predecessors the Geometric Modernist faces, they are usually slab-serifed or unserifed, but often they exist in both varieties at once or are hybrids of the two. They are rarely, it seems, based on the pure and simple line and circle, but almost always on more mannered, often asymmetric forms. And like other Postmodern types, they are rich with nostalgia for something premodern. Many of these faces are indebted to older industrial letterforms, including typewriter faces and the ubiquitous factory folk-art of North American highway signs. They recycle and revise not Romantic and Neoclassical but Realist ideas. To this industrial unpretentiousness, however, they often add not only Postmodern humor but also the fruits of typographic sophistication: text figures, small caps, large aperture, and subtle modelling and balancing of forms.

Postmodern art, like Neoclassical art, is above all an art of the surface: an art of reflections rather than visions. It has thrived in the depthless world of high-speed offset printing and digital design, where modernism starves. But the world of the scribes, in which the craft of type design is rooted, was a depthless world too. It was the world of the Gothic painters, in which everything is present in one plane. In that respect at least, postmodernism and modernism alike confront the basic task with which typography began.

136

7.3.1 *The Linotype Machine*

The Linotype machine, invented in the 1880s by Ottmar Mergenthaler and much modified over the years, is a kind of cross between a casting machine, a typewriter, a vending machine and a backhoe. It consists of a series of slides, belts, wheels, lifts, vises, plungers and screws, controlled from a large mechanical keyboard. Its complex mechanism composes a line of matrices, justifies the line by sliding tapered wedges into the spaces between the words, then casts the entire line as a single metal slug for letterpress printing.

> For a detailed account of the growth of mechanized typesetting, see Richard E. Huss, *The Development of Printers' Mechanical Typesetting Methods 1822–1925* (Charlottesville, Virginia, 1973).

Typeface design for the Linotype was restricted by three basic factors. First, kerning is impossible without special compound matrices. (The basic italic *f* in a Linotype font therefore always has a stunted head and tail.) Second, the em is divided into only 18 units, which discourages subtlety of proportion. Third, the italic and roman matrices are usually paired. In most faces, each italic letter must therefore have the same width as its counterpart in roman.

A number of typefaces designed for the Linotype were artistically successful in spite of these constraints. Hermann Zapf's Aldus and Optima, Rudolph Růžička's Fairfield, Sem Hartz's Juliana, and W. A. Dwiggins's Electra, Caledonia and Falcon were all designed for the Linotype machine. Linotype Janson, adapted by Zapf in 1952 from the seventeenth-century originals of Miklós Kis, is another eminent success. Many Linotype faces have nevertheless been modified in the course of digitization, to make use of the kerning capabilities of digital machines and restore the independent proportioning of roman and italic.

7.3.2 *The Monotype Machine*

In 1887, in competition with Mergenthaler, Tolbert Lanston created a machine that stamped individual letters in cold metal and assembled them into lines. This device was soon abandoned for another – built in 1900 by Lanston's colleague John Bancroft – that cast individual letters from molten metal rather than cold-stamping them. It was soon sold worldwide as the Monotype machine. It is two machines in fact, a terminal and an output device, and in this respect resembles most computer-driven typesetting machines. But the Monotype terminal carries a large mechanical keyboard, including seven full alphabets as well as analphabetics. The keyboard punches holes in a paper tape, like a narrow player-piano roll, by driving pins with compressed air. The output device is the caster, which reads the paper tape by blowing more compressed air through the punched holes, then casts and assembles the letters.

The Monotype em, like the Linotype em, is divided into only 18 units, but italic and roman are independent in width, kerning is possible, and because the type remains in the form of separate letters, typeset lines can be further adjusted by hand. Characters larger than 24 pt are cast individually and left for hand assembly. In fact, the Monotype machine is a portable typefoundry as much as it is a composing machine – and it is increasingly used as such, even though its unit system imposes restrictions on letterform design, and it is incapable of casting in hard metal.

7.3.3 *Two-Dimensional Printing*

From the middle of the fifteenth century to the middle of the twentieth, most roman letters were printed by a technique rooted in sculpture. In this process, each letter is carved at actual size on the end of a steel punch. The punch is then struck into a matrix of softer metal, the matrix is fitted into a mold, and three-dimensional metal type is cast from an alloy of lead, tin and antimony. The cast letters are locked in a frame and placed in a printing press, where they are inked. Their image is then imprinted *into* the paper, producing a tactile and visual image. The color and sheen of the ink join with the smooth texture of crushed paper, recessed into the whiter and rougher fibers surrounding the letters and lines. A book produced by this means is a folding inscription, a flexible sculpture in low relief. The black light of the text *shines out from within* a well-printed letterpress page.

Renaissance typographers reveled in the physical depth and texture they could achieve by this method of printing. Neoclassical and Romantic printers, like Baskerville, often took a different view. Baskerville printed his sheets by letterpress – since he had no other method – but then had them ironed like laundry to remove the sculptural tinge.

With the development of lithography, at the end of the eighteenth century, printing moved another step back toward the two-dimensional world of the medieval scribes. Since the middle of the twentieth century, most commercial printing has been by two-dimensional means. The normal method is offset photolithography, in which a photographic or digital image is etched into a plate, inked, *offset* to a smooth intermediary blanket, and layed flat on the surface of the page.

In the early days of commercial offset printing, type was still set with Linotype or Monotype machines. Proofs were pulled in a letterpress, then cut, pasted and photographed. Type designers saw their work altered by this process. Most letters designed to be printed in three dimensions look weaker when printed in two. But other letters prospered: geometric letters, which evoked the world of the draftsman rather than the goldsmith, and flowing letters recalling the heritage of the scribe.

7.3.4 *Phototype Machines*

Light flashes through the image of a letter carried on glass or photographic film; the size of the letter is altered with a lens; its target location is fixed by a mirror, and it is exposed like any other photographic image onto photosensitive paper or film. Machines that operate on this principle are the natural children of the camera and the offset press. They were designed and patented in the 1890s and in regular use for setting titles and headlines by 1925, though it was not until the 1960s that they came to dominate the trade.

Just as the sophistication and subtlety of handset type seemed at first to be swept aside when composing machines appeared, so the sophistication slowly achieved with Linotype and Monotype machines seemed to be swept aside by this new technological wave. The photosetters were fast, but they knew nothing of subtle changes in proportion from size to size. Their fonts lacked ligatures, text figures and small caps. American-made fonts lacked even the simplest accented characters. The choice of faces was poor. And with the sudden, widespread use of these complex but simplistic machines came the final collapse of the old craft system of apprenticeships and guilds.

Phototypesetting machines and their users had only begun to answer these complaints when digital equipment arrived to replace them. Some excellent faces were designed for phototype machines – from Adrian Frutiger's Apollo (1962) to Bram de Does's Trinité (1982) – but in retrospect, the era of phototype seems only a brief interregnum between hot metal and digital composition. The important innovation of the period was not, after all, the conversion of fonts from metal to film, but the introduction of microcomputers to edit, compose and correct the text and to drive the last generations of photosetting machines.

7.3.5 *Historical Recutting & Twentieth-Century Design*

New typefaces have been designed in vast numbers in the past hundred years, and many old ones have been resuscitated. From 1960 to 1980, most new types and revivals were designed for photosetting, and since 1980, almost all have been planned for digital composition. But most of the older faces now sold in digital form have already passed through another stylistic filter. They were recut in the early twentieth century, either as foundry type or as matrices for the Monotype or Linotype machines. Typography was radically reformed between 1920 and 1950, through the commercial reinvention of typographic history. It is worth looking back at this process to see something of what went on, because its legacy affects us still.

Two separate companies – one based in England, one in America – rose up around the Monotype machine and followed two quite separate development programs. The English company, advised during its heyday by a scholar named Stanley Morison, cut a series of facsimiles based on the work of Francesco Griffo, Giovanantonio Tagliente, Ludovico degli Arrighi and other early designers. It was Morison who conceived the idea of turning independent Renaissance faces into families by mating one designer's roman with another's formerly self-sufficient italic. The fruits of this enterprise included Poliphilus and Blado (one of Griffo's romans mated with an altered version of one of Arrighi's italics), Bembo (a later version of the same roman, paired with an altered version of one of Tagliente's italics), and the brilliantly successful shotgun marriage of Centaur roman (designed by Bruce Rogers) with the Arrighi italic (designed by Frederic Warde). This program was supplemented by commissioning new faces from artists such as Eric Gill, Alfred Fairbank, Jan van Krimpen and Berthold Wolpe.

Lanston Monotype, as the American company was called, made some historical recuttings of its own and issued many new and historically based faces designed by its own advisor, Frederic Goudy. A third campaign to recreate typographic history in marketable form was mounted by Linotype, under the direction of the English master printer George William Jones.

Several of the larger typefoundries – including ATF (American Type Founders) in the United States, Deberny & Peignot in France, Enschedé in the Netherlands, Stempel in Germany and Grafotechna in Czechoslovakia – continued ambitious programs of their own, lasting in some cases into the 1980s. Revivals of faces by Claude Garamond, Miklós Kis and other early designers came from these foundries during the twentieth century, along with important new faces by such designers as Hermann Zapf, Jan van Krimpen, Adrian Frutiger, Oldřich Menhart and Hans Eduard Meier. Zapf's Palatino, which became the most widely used (and most widely pirated) face of the twentieth century, was cut by hand in steel and cast as a foundry type in the ancient way, in 1949–50, while phototype machines and early computers were humming no great distance away.

The earlier history of type design is the history of forms made by individual artists and artisans who began their careers as apprentices and ended them as independent masters and small businessmen. The scale of the industry enlarged in the seventeenth and eighteenth centuries, and questions of fashion increasingly superseded questions of artistry. By the end of the nineteenth century, commercial considerations had changed the methods as well as the taste of the trade. Punches and matrices were increasingly cut by machine from large pattern letters, and calligraphic models were all but unknown.

The twentieth-century rediscovery of the history and principles of typographic form was not associated with any particular technology. It occurred among scholars and artists who brought their discoveries to fruition wherever they found employment: in typefoundries, typesetting-machine companies, art schools and their own small, independent studios.

Despite commercial pressures, the best of the old metal foundries, like the best of the new digital ones, were more than merely market-driven factories. They were cultural institutions, on a par with fine publishing houses and the ateliers of printmakers, potters, weavers and instrument makers. What made them so was the stature of the type designers, living and dead, whose work they produced – for type designers are, at their best, the Stradivarii of literature: not merely makers of salable products, but artists who design and make the instruments that other artists use.

141

7.3.6 Digital Typography

It is much too soon to summarize the history of digital typography, but the evolution of computerized bitmapping, hinting and scaling techniques has proceeded very quickly since the development of the microchip at the beginning of the 1970s. At the same time, the old technologies, freed from commercial duties, have by no means died. Foundry type, the Monotype, the Linotype and letterpress remain important artistic instruments, alongside brush and chisel, pencil, graver and pen.

Typographic style is founded not on any one technology of typesetting or printing, but on the primitive yet subtle craft of writing. Letters derive their form from the motions of the human hand, restrained and amplified by a tool. That tool may be as complex as a digitizing tablet or a specially programmed keyboard, or as simple as a sharpened stick. Meaning resides, in either case, in the firmness and grace of the gesture itself, not in the tool with which it is made.

7.4 THE PLURALITY OF TYPOGRAPHIC HISTORY

Every alphabet is a culture. Every culture has its own version of history and its own accumulation of tradition – and this chapter has dwelt on the recent history of one alphabet only. The Arabic, Armenian, Burmese, Cherokee, Cree, Cyrillic, Devanagari, Georgian, Greek, Gujarati, Hebrew, Japanese, Korean, Malayalam, Tamil and Telugu alphabets and syllabaries – to name only a few – have other histories of their own, in some cases every bit as intricate and long as – or longer than – the history of Latin letterforms. So, of course, has the logographic script of Chinese. These histories have touched at certain points; at other points, they diverge. Here at the beginning of the twenty-first century, an unusual degree of convergence can be seen. But the challenge and excitement of multilingual typography still lies largely in the fact that different typographic histories momentarily share the page. Typographers working with multiple alphabets are multiply blessed: with a chance to learn the cultural history as well as the typographic technicalities of every script concerned.

The histories of Greek and Cyrillic types are taken up more briefly in chapter 10, and the legacies of individual typefoundries are summarized briefly in appendix D, page 309.

A book is a flexible mirror of the mind and the body. Its overall size and proportions, the color and texture of the paper, the sound it makes as the pages turn, and the smell of the paper, adhesive and ink, all blend with the size and form and placement of the type to reveal a little about the world in which it was made. If the book appears to be only a paper machine, produced at their own convenience by other machines, only machines will want to read it.

8.1 ORGANIC, MECHANICAL & MUSICAL PROPORTION

A page, like a building or a room, can be of any size and proportion, but some are distinctly more pleasing than others, and some have quite specific connotations. A brochure that unfolds and refolds in the hand is intrinsically different from a formal letter that lies motionless and flat, or a handwritten note that folds into quarters and comes in an envelope of a different shape and size. All of these are different again from a book, in which the pages flow sequentially in pairs.

Much typography is based, for the sake of convenience, on standard industrial paper sizes, from 35 × 45 inch press sheets to 3½ × 2 inch conventional business cards. Some formats, such as the booklets that accompany compact discs, are condemned to especially rigid restrictions of size. But many typographic projects begin with the opportunity and necessity of selecting the dimensions of the page.

There is rarely a free choice. A page size of 12 × 19 inches, for example, is likely to be both inconvenient and expensive because it is just in excess of 11 × 17, which is a standard industrial unit. And a brochure that is 5 × 9 inches, no matter how handsome, might be unacceptable because it is too wide to fit into a standard business envelope (4 × 9½). But when the realm of practicality has been established, and it is known that the page must fall within certain limits, how is one to choose? By taking whatever is easiest, or biggest, or whatever is the most convenient standard size? By trusting to blind instinct?

Instinct, in matters such as these, is largely memory in disguise. It works quite well when it is trained, and poorly otherwise. But in a craft like typography, no matter how perfectly honed one's instincts are, it is useful to be able to calculate answers exactly. History, natural science, geometry and mathematics are all relevant to typography in this regard – and can all be counted on for aid.

Organic, Mechanical and Musical Proportion

Scribes and typographers, like architects, have been shaping visual spaces for thousands of years. Certain proportions keep recurring in their work because they please the eye and the mind, just as certain sizes keep recurring because they are comfortable to the hand. Many of these proportions are inherent in simple geometric figures – equilateral triangle, square, regular pentagon, hexagon and octagon. And these proportions not only seem to please human beings in many different centuries and countries, they are also prominent in nature far beyond the human realm. They occur in the structures of molecules, mineral crystals, soap bubbles, flowers, as well as books and temples, manuscripts and mosques.

Two useful works on organic form and structure are: D'Arcy Thompson, *On Growth and Form* (rev. ed., Cambridge, 1942) and Peter S. Stevens, *Patterns in Nature* (Boston, 1974).

The tables on pages 148–149 list a number of page proportions derivable from simple geometric figures. These proportions occur repeatedly in nature, and pages that embody them recur in manuscripts and books from Renaissance Europe, Táng and Sòng dynasty China, early Egypt, precolumbian Mexico and ancient Rome. It seems that the beauty of these proportions is more than a matter of regional taste or immediate fashion. They are therefore useful for two purposes. Working and playing with them is a way of developing good typographic instincts, and they serve as useful references in analyzing old designs and calculating new ones.

For comparison, several other proportions are included in the tables. There are several simple numerical ratios, several standard industrial sizes, and several proportions involving four irrational numbers important in the analysis of natural structures and processes. These numbers are $\pi = 3.14159...$, which is the circumference of a circle whose diameter is one; $\sqrt{2} = 1.41421...$, which is the diagonal of a unit square; $e = 2.71828...$, which is the base of the natural logarithms; and $\varphi = 1.61803...$, a number discussed in greater detail on page 155. Certain of these proportions reappear in the structure of the human body; others appear in musical scales. Indeed, one of the simplest of all systems of page proportions is based on the familiar intervals of the diatonic scale. Pages that embody these basic musical proportions have been in common use in Europe for more than a thousand years.

144

Sizing and spacing type, like composing and performing music or applying paint to canvas, is largely concerned with intervals and differences. As the texture builds, precise relationships and very small discrepancies are easily perceived. Establishing the overall dimensions of the page is more a matter of limits and sums. In this realm, it is usually sufficient, and often it is better, if structural harmony is not so much enforced as implied. That is one of the reasons typographers tend to fall in love with books. The pages flex and turn; their proportions ebb and flow against the underlying form. But the harmony of that underlying form is no less important, and no less easy to perceive, than the harmony of the letterforms themselves.

Shaping the Page

The page is a piece of paper. It is also a visible and tangible proportion, silently sounding the thoroughbass of the book. On it lies the textblock, which must answer to the page. The two together – page and textblock – produce an antiphonal geometry. That geometry alone can bond the reader to the book. Or conversely, it can put the reader to sleep, or put the reader's nerves on edge, or drive the reader away.

Arithmetic and mathematics also drive away some readers, and this is a chapter peppered with both. Readers may well ask whether all this is necessary, merely in order to choose where some letters should sit on a piece of paper and where the paper itself should be trimmed. The answer, naturally, is no. It is not in the least necessary to understand the mathematics in order to perform the actions that the math describes. People walk and ride bicycles without mathematical analyses of these complex operations. The chambered nautilus and the snail construct perfect logarithmic spirals without any need of logarithmic tables, sliderules or the theory of infinite series. The typographer likewise can construct beautiful pages without knowing the meaning of symbols like π or φ, and indeed without ever learning to add and subtract, if he has a well-educated eye and knows which buttons to push on the calculator and keyboard.

The mathematics are not here to impose drudgery upon anyone. On the contrary, they are here entirely for pleasure. They are here for the pleasure of those who like to examine what they are doing, or what they might do or have already done, perhaps in the hope of doing it still better. Those who prefer to act directly at all times, and to leave the analysis to others, may be content in this chapter to study the pictures and skim the text.

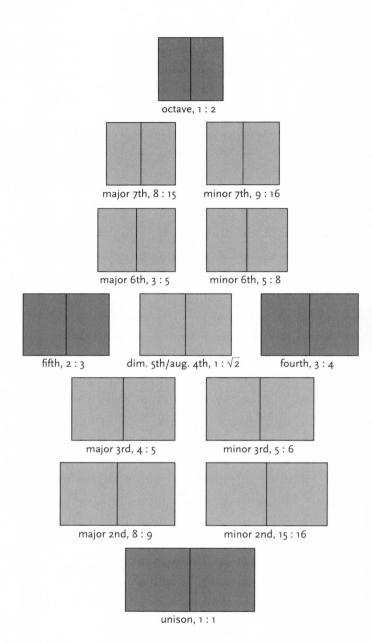

octave, 1 : 2

major 7th, 8 : 15   minor 7th, 9 : 16

major 6th, 3 : 5   minor 6th, 5 : 8

fifth, 2 : 3   dim. 5th/aug. 4th, 1 : √2̄   fourth, 3 : 4

major 3rd, 4 : 5   minor 3rd, 5 : 6

major 2nd, 8 : 9   minor 2nd, 15 : 16

unison, 1 : 1

Page proportions corresponding to the chromatic scale, from unison (at
the bottom) to octave (at the top). The musical correlations are shown
in detail on the facing page.

146

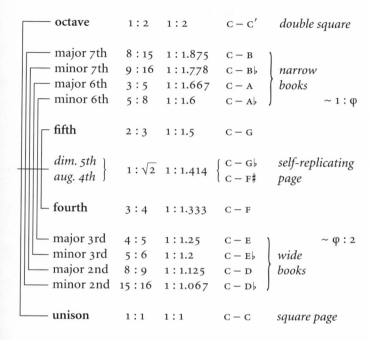

octave	1 : 2	1 : 2	C – C′	*double square*
major 7th	8 : 15	1 : 1.875	C – B	
minor 7th	9 : 16	1 : 1.778	C – B♭	*narrow books*
major 6th	3 : 5	1 : 1.667	C – A	
minor 6th	5 : 8	1 : 1.6	C – A♭	~ 1 : φ
fifth	2 : 3	1 : 1.5	C – G	
dim. 5th / aug. 4th	1 : √2̄	1 : 1.414	C – G♭ / C – F♯	*self-replicating page*
fourth	3 : 4	1 : 1.333	C – F	
major 3rd	4 : 5	1 : 1.25	C – E	~ φ : 2
minor 3rd	5 : 6	1 : 1.2	C – E♭	*wide books*
major 2nd	8 : 9	1 : 1.125	C – D	
minor 2nd	15 : 16	1 : 1.067	C – D♭	
unison	1 : 1	1 : 1	C – C	*square page*

Page shapes derived from the chromatic scale. Two-page spreads that embody these proportions are shown on the facing page.

The perfect intervals (fifth and fourth) coincide exactly with the favorite page shapes of the European Middle Ages, which are still in use today: the page proportions 2 : 3 and 3 : 4. Renaissance typographers made extensive use of narrower pages, corresponding to the larger impure intervals (major and minor sixth, major and minor seventh).

Each page shape has a counterpart with which it alternates. If a sheet whose proportions are 5 : 8 is folded in half, it produces a sheet whose proportions are 4 : 5. If this is folded once again, it produces another sheet whose proportions are 5 : 8. In the same way, the proportion 1 : 2 alternates with the proportion 1 : 1. The proportion 1 : √2̄, corresponding to the diminished fifth and augmented fourth of equal temperament, is the only one that alternates with itself.

In musical terms, these alternating proportions form *harmonic inversions*. (The harmonic inversion of a fifth, for example, is a fourth, and the harmonic inversion of a minor sixth is a major third.) The total of each such pair of intervals is always *one octave*.

The value for the diminished 5th/-augmented 4th is calculated here according to the system of equal temperament. All other intervals are calculated according to the system of just intonation.

		Page & Textblock Proportions		Sample sizes in inches		
octave	A	Double Square	1 : 2	4.5 × 9	5 × 10	5.5 × 11
	B	Tall Octagon	1 : 1.924	4.7 × 9	5.2 × 10	5.7 × 11
major 7th		8 : 15	1 : 1.875	4.8 × 9		
	C	Tall Hexagon	1 : 1.866			5.9 × 11
	D	Octagon	1 : 1.848	4.9 × 9	5.4 × 10	6 × 11
		5 : 9	1 : 1.8	5 × 9		
minor 7th		9 : 16	1 : 1.778		5.1 × 9	
	E	Hexagon = 1 : √3	1 : 1.732	4.9 × 8.5	5.2 × 9	6.4 × 11
	F	Tall Pentagon	1 : 1.701	5 × 8.5	5.3 × 9	6.5 × 11
major 6th		3 : 5	1 : 1.667	5.1 × 8.5		
		Legal Sheet	1 : 1.647			8.5 × 14
	G	Golden Section	1 : 1.618	5.3 × 8.5	5.6 × 9	6.8 × 11
minor 6th		5 : 8	1 : 1.6	5 × 8		
	H	Pentagon	1 : 1.539	5.5 × 8.5	5.9 × 9	7.2 × 11
fifth		2 : 3	1 : 1.5		6 × 9	7.3 × 11
	Z	ISO = 1 : √2	1 : 1.414	6.4 × 9	7.1 × 10	7.8 × 11
		5 : 7	1 : 1.4			
	J	Short Pentagon	1 : 1.376	6.5 × 9	7.3 × 10	8 × 11
fourth		3 : 4	1 : 1.333	6.8 × 9	7.5 × 10	9 × 12
	K	Tall Half Octagon	1 : 1.307	6.9 × 9	7.7 × 10	8.4 × 11
		Letter Sheet	1 : 1.294			8.5 × 11
major 3rd		4 : 5	1 : 1.25	7.2 × 9	8 × 10	8.8 × 11
	L	Half Octagon	1 : 1.207		8.3 × 10	9.1 × 11
minor 3rd		5 : 6	1 : 1.2	7.5 × 9		
	M	Truncated Pentagon	1 : 1.176		8.5 × 10	9.4 × 11
		6 : 7	1 : 1.167	7.7 × 9		
		e : π	1 : 1.156			
	N	Turned Hexagon	1 : 1.155	7.8 × 9	8.7 × 10	9.5 × 11
major 2nd		8 : 9	1 : 1.125	8 × 9	8.9 × 10	9.8 × 11
	O	Tall Cross Octagon	1 : 1.082	8.3 × 9	9.2 × 10	10.2 × 11
minor 2nd		15 : 16	1 : 1.067	8.4 × 9	9.4 × 10	10.3 × 11
	P	Turned Pentagon	1 : 1.051	8.6 × 9	9.5 × 10	10.5 × 11
unison	Q	SQUARE	1 : 1	9 × 9	10 × 10	11 × 11
	R	Broad Pentagon	1 : 0.951	8.9 × 8.5	10 × 9.5	11 × 10.5
	S	Broad Cross Octagon	1 : 0.924	9.2 × 8.5	10 × 9.2	11 × 10.1
major 2nd		9 : 8	1 : 0.889	9.6 × 8.5		11 × 9.8
	T	Broad Hexagon	1 : 0.866	9.8 × 8.5	10 × 8.7	11 × 9.5
	U	Full Cross Octagon	1 : 0.829	10.3 × 8.5	10 × 8.3	11 × 9.1
major 3rd		5 : 4	1 : 0.8	10.6 × 8.5		11 × 8.8
		Landscape Letter	1 : 0.773	11 × 8.5	10 × 7.7	

	Column Proportions		Sample sizes in picas			
a	Quadruple Square	1 : 4	10 × 40	11 × 44	12 × 48	*double octave*
	1 : √15	1 : 3.873	10 × 39			
	4 : 15	1 : 3.75		12 × 45		*major 14th*
	5 : 18	1 : 3.6	10 × 36	12 × 43		
	9 : 32	1 : 3.556	11 × 39			*minor 14th*
	1 : √12	1 : 3.464	11 × 38		15 × 52	
b	Octagon Wing	1 : 3.414		12 × 41		
	3 : 10	1 : 3.333		12 × 40	15 × 50	*major 13th*
	1 : 2φ	1 : 3.236				
	5 : 16	1 : 3.2			15 × 48	*minor 13th*
	1 : √10	1 : 3.162	12 × 38			
	1 : π	1 : 3.142		14 × 44		
c	Double Pentagon	1 : 3.078	12 × 37	14 × 43	16 × 49	
d	Triple Square	1 : 3	12 × 36	14 × 42	16 × 48	*twelfth*
e	Wide Octagon Wing	1 : 2.993				
z	1 : 2√2 = 1 : √8	1 : 2.828				
f	Pentagon Wing	1 : 2.753		16 × 44		
	1 : e	1 : 2.718	14 × 38		18 × 49	
	3 : 8	1 : 2.667		15 × 40	18 × 48	*eleventh*
	1 : √7	1 : 2.646				
g	Extended Section	1 : 2.618				
h	Tall Octagon Column	1 : 2.613			18 × 47	
i	Mid Octagon Column	1 : 2.514				
	2 : 5	1 : 2.5	16 × 40	18 × 45	20 × 50	*major 10th*
j	Short Octagon Column	1 : 2.414				
	5 : 12	1 : 2.4			20 × 48	*minor 10th*
k	Hexagon Wing	1 : 2.309	16 × 37	20 × 46		
m	Double Truncated Pentagon	1 : 2.252				
	4 : 9	1 : 2.25		20 × 45		*major 9th*
	1 : √5	1 : 2.236	17 × 38		21 × 47	
	5 : 11	1 : 2.2		20 × 44	24 × 53	
	15 : 32	1 : 2.133			24 × 52	*minor 9th*
A	Double Square	1 : 2	18 × 36	21 × 42	24 × 48	*octave*

[The musical intervals listed in the right hand column are the *compound intervals* of the chromatic scale. Octave + minor 2nd = minor 9th; octave + major 3rd = major 10th; octave + fifth = twelfth, etc.]

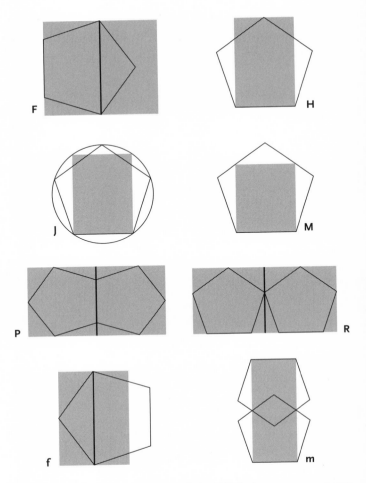

F P, R and f are
shown here as
two-page spreads.
H, J, M and m are
shown as single
pages.

Pages derived from the pentagon: **F** the Tall Pentagon page, 1 : 1.701;
H Pentagon page, 1 : 1.539; **J** Short Pentagon page, 1 : 1.376; **M** the Truncated Pentagon page, 1 : 1.176; **P** Turned Pentagon page, 1 : 1.051; **R** the
Broad Pentagon page, 1 : 0.951; **f** Pentagon Wing, 1 : 2.753; **m** the Double
Truncated Pentagon, 1 : 2.252. The pentagon page differs by 2% from the
North American standard small trade book size, which is half the size of a
letter sheet: 5½ × 8½ inches. A more eminent page proportion, the golden
section, is also present in the pentagon (see page 156). In nature, pentagonal symmetry is rare in inanimate forms. Packed soap bubbles seem to
strive for it but never quite succeed, and there are no mineral crystals with
true pentagonal structures. But pentagonal geometry is basic to many living things, from roses and forget-me-nots to sea urchins and starfish.

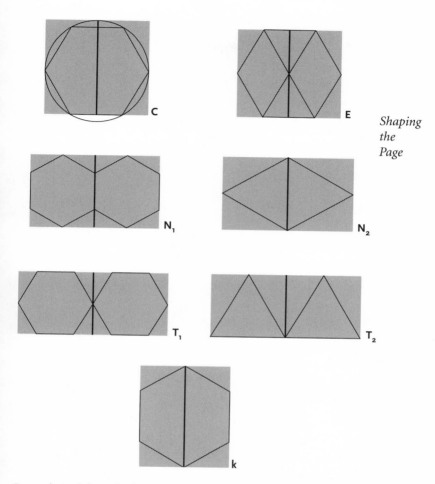

Pages derived from the hexagon: **C** the Tall Hexagon page, 1 : 1.866; **E** Hexagon page, 1 : $\sqrt{3}$ = 1 : 1.732; **N** Turned Hexagon page, 1 : 1.155; **T** Broad Hexagon page, 1 : 0.866; **k** Hexagon Wing, 1 : 2.309. The hexagon consists of six equilateral triangles, and each of these page shapes can be derived directly from the triangle instead. The hexagon merely clarifies their existence as mirror images, like the pages of a book. Hexagonal structures are present in both the organic and the inorganic world – in lilies and wasps' nests, for example, and in snowflakes, silica crystals and sunbaked mudflats. The proportions of the broad hexagon page are within one tenth of one per cent of the natural ratio π/e, while the turned hexagon page (which is the broad hexagon rotated 90°) approximates the ratio e/π. (The hexagon page used in this book is analyzed on page 6.)

All formats on this page are shown as two-page spreads.

*Organic,
Mechanical
and Musical
Proportion*

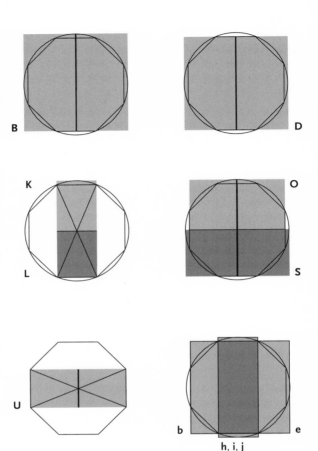

Pages derived from the octagon: **B** the Tall Octagon page, 1 : 1.924;
D Octagon page, 1 : 1.848; **K** Tall Half Octagon page, 1 : 1.307; **L** Half
Octagon page, 1 : 1.207; **O** Tall Cross Octagon, 1 : 1.082; **S** Broad Cross
Octagon page, 1 : 0.924; **U** the Full Cross Octagon page, 1 : 0.829;
b Octagon Wing, 1 : 3.414; **e** Wide Octagon Wing, 1 : 2.993; **h, i, j** Tall,
Middle and Short Octagon Columns, 1 : 2.613, 1 : 2.514 and 1 : 2.414. The
tall half octagon page (**K**), used in Roman times, differs by a margin of
1% from the standard North American letter size. Are proportions derived from the hexagon and pentagon livelier and more pleasing than
those derived from the octagon? Forms based on the hexagon and pentagon are, at any rate, far more frequent than octagonal forms in the
structure of flowering plants and elsewhere in the living world.

152

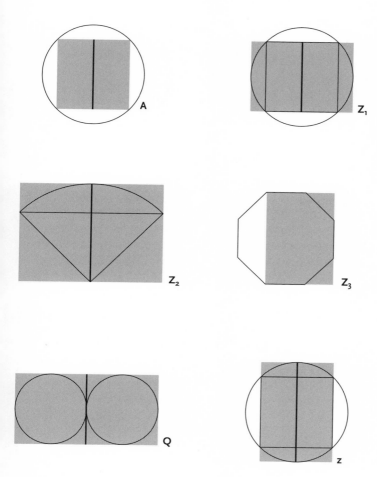

Pages derived from the circle and square: **A** Double Square page, $1:2$; **Z** the Broad Square page, which is the ISO standard, $1:\sqrt{2} = 1:1.414$; **Q** the Perfect Square; **z** Double ISO, $1:2\sqrt{2} = 1:2.828$. The proportion $1:\sqrt{2}$ is that of side to diagonal in a square. A rectangle of these proportions (and no others) can be halved or doubled indefinitely to produce new rectangles of the same proportion. The proportion was chosen for that reason as the basis for ISO (International Organization for Standardization) paper sizes. The A4 sheet, for example, is standard European letter size, 210×297 mm $= 8\frac{1}{4}" \times 11\frac{5}{8}"$. An $8\frac{1}{2}" \times 12"$ book page also embodies this proportion.

The ISO or broad square page is latent not only in the square but in the octagon.

Except for Z_3, all formats on this page are shown as two-page spreads.

153

A O

A2

A1

A4

A3

A5

ISO sheet sizes:
- A0 = 841 × 1189 mm
- A1 = 594 × 841 mm
- A2 = 420 × 594 mm
- A3 = 297 × 420 mm
- A4 = 210 × 297 mm
- A5 = 148 × 210 mm

When a sheet whose proportions are $1 : \sqrt{2}$ is folded in half, the result is a sheet half as large but with *the same proportions*. Standard paper sizes based on this principle have been in use in Germany since the early 1920s. The basis of the system is the A0 sheet, which has an area of $1\ m^2$. Yet precisely because it is *reciprocal with nothing but itself,* the ISO page is, in isolation, the least musical of all the major page shapes. It needs a textblock of another shape for contrast.

The golden section is a symmetrical relation built from asymmetrical parts. Two numbers, shapes or elements embody the golden section when the smaller is to the larger as the larger is to the sum. That is, $a:b = b:(a+b)$. In the language of algebra, this ratio is $1:\varphi = 1:(1+\sqrt{5})/2$, and in the language of trigonometry, it is $1:(2\sin 54°)$. Its approximate value in decimal terms is $1:1.61803$.

Shaping the Page

The second term of this ratio, φ (the Greek letter *phi*), is a number with several unusual properties. If you *add* one to φ, you get its square ($\varphi \times \varphi$). If you *subtract* one from φ, you get its reciprocal ($1/\varphi$). And if you multiply φ endlessly by itself, you get an infinite series embodying a single proportion. That proportion is $1:\varphi$. If we rewrite these facts in the typographic form mathematicians like to use, they look like this:

$$\varphi + 1 = \varphi^2$$

$$\varphi - 1 = 1/\varphi$$

$$\varphi^{-1}:1 = 1:\varphi = \varphi:\varphi^2 = \varphi^2:\varphi^3 = \varphi^3:\varphi^4 = \varphi^4:\varphi^5 \ldots$$

If we look for a numerical approximation to this ratio, $1:\varphi$, we will find it in something called the Fibonacci series, named for the thirteenth-century mathematician Leonardo Fibonacci. Though he died two centuries before Gutenberg, Fibonacci is important in the history of European typography as well as mathematics. He was born in Pisa but studied in North Africa. On his return, he introduced arabic numerals to the North Italian scribes.

As a mathematician, Fibonacci took an interest in many problems, including the problem of unchecked propagation. What happens, he asked, if everything breeds and nothing dies? The answer is a logarithmic spiral of increase. Expressed as a series of integers, such a spiral takes the following form:

$0 \cdot 1 \cdot 1 \cdot 2 \cdot 3 \cdot 5 \cdot 8 \cdot 13 \cdot 21 \cdot 34 \cdot 55 \cdot 89 \cdot 144 \cdot 233 \cdot 377 \cdot 610 \cdot 987 \cdot 1597 \cdot 2584 \cdot 4181 \cdot 6765 \cdot 10{,}946 \cdot 17{,}711 \cdot 28{,}657 \ldots$

Here each term after the first two is *the sum of the two preceding*. And the farther we proceed along this series, the closer

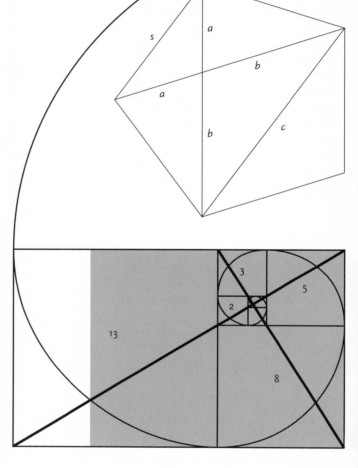

The
Golden
Section

The screened area represents a two-page spread in which each page embodies the golden section. The root of the spiral, which is the navel of the page, lies at the intersection of the diagonals. This is a Renaissance structure: precisely measured and formed, yet open-ended, unconfined. Like Thoreau's vision of the mind (page 66), it is *hypethral*. (Compare the equally elegant but closed, medieval structure on page 173 and the resolutely linear structure on page 154.)

G Golden Section, $1 : \varphi = 1 : 1.618....$ In the pentagon, the side s and the chord c embody the golden section. The smaller is to the larger as the larger is to the whole, or $s : c = c : (s + c)$. When two chords intersect, they divide each other in the same proportion: $a : b = b : c$, where $c = a + b$. Moreover, $b = s$. Thus, $a : s = s : c = c : (s + c) = 1 : \varphi$.

An evolving sequence of figures that embody the golden section also defines the path of a logarithmic spiral. And if the lengths of the sides of the figures are rounded off to the nearest whole numbers, the result is a Fibonacci series of integers.

156

we come to an accurate approximation of the number φ. Thus
5 : 8 = 1 : 1.6; 8 : 13 = 1 : 1.625; 13 : 21 = 1 : 1.615; 21 : 34 =
1 : 1.619, and so on.

In the world of pure mathematics, this spiral of increase,
the Fibonacci series, proceeds without end. In the world of
mortal living things, of course, the spiral soon breaks off. It is
repeatedly interrupted by death and other practical considerations – but it is visible nevertheless in the short term. Abbreviated versions of the Fibonacci series, and the proportion 1 : φ,
can be seen in the structure of pineapples, pinecones, sunflow-
ers, sea urchins, snails, the chambered nautilus, and in the proportions of the human body as well.

If we convert the ratio 1 : φ or 1 : 1.61803 to percentages,
the smaller part is roughly **38.2**% and the larger **61.8**% of the
whole. But we will find the exact proportions of the golden section in several simple geometric figures. These include the pentagon, where they are relatively obvious, and the square, where
they are somewhat more deeply concealed.

The golden section was much admired by classical Greek
geometers and architects, and by Renaissance mathematicians,
architects and scribes, who often used it in their work. It has
also been much admired by artists and craftsmen, including typographers, in the modern age. Paperback books in the Pen-
guin Classics series have been manufactured for more than half
a century to the standard size of 111 × 180 mm, which embodies
the golden section. The Modulor system of the Swiss architect
Le Corbusier is based on the golden section as well.

If type sizes are chosen according to the golden section, the
result is again a Fibonacci series:

(a) 5 · 8 · 13 · 21 · 34 · 55 · 89 …

These sizes alone are adequate for many typographic tasks.
But to create a more versatile scale of sizes, a second or third interlocking series can be added. The possibilities include:

(b) 6 · 10 · 16 · 26 · 42 · 68 · 110 …
(c) 4 · 7 · 11 · 18 · 29 · 47 · 76 …

All three of these series – **a**, **b** and **c** – obey the Fibonacci
rule (each term is the sum of the two terms preceding). Series **b**
is also related to series **a** by simple doubling. The combination

Shaping
the
Page

The golden
section, 1 : φ,
differs by roughly
one per cent from
the interval of the
minor sixth in
the chromatic
scale. The
proportion 5 : 8,
which is the
arithmetic value
of the minor
sixth in music, is
often used in
typography as a
rough approxim-
ation to the
golden section.

of **a** and **b** is therefore a two-stranded Fibonacci series with incremental symmetry, forming a very versatile scale of type sizes:

(d) 6 · 8 · 10 · 13 · 16 · 21 · 26 · 34 · 42 · 55 · 68 ...

The double-stranded Fibonacci series used by Le Corbusier (with other units of measurement) in his architectural work is similarly useful in typography:

(e)

4	6½	10½	17	27½	44½	72	
5	8	13	21	34	55	89	...

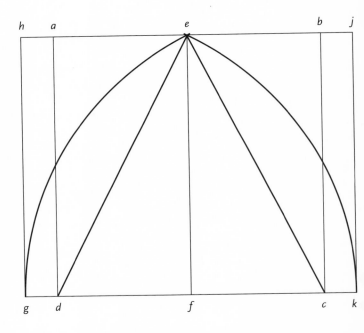

Finding the golden section in the square. Begin with the square *abcd*. Bisect the square (with the line *ef*) and draw diagonals (*ec* and *ed*) in each half. An isosceles triangle, *cde*, consisting of two right triangles, is formed. Extend the base of the square (draw the line *gk*) and project each of the diagonals (the hypotenuse of each of the right triangles) onto the extended base. Now *ce* = *cg*, and *de* = *dk*. Draw the new rectangle, *efgh*. This and its mirror image, *ejkf*, each have the proportions of the golden section. That is to say, *eh*:*gh* = *gh*:(*gh* + *eh*) = *ej*:*jk* = *jk*:(*jk* + *ej*) = 1 : φ. (Contrast this with figure Z₂ on page 153.)

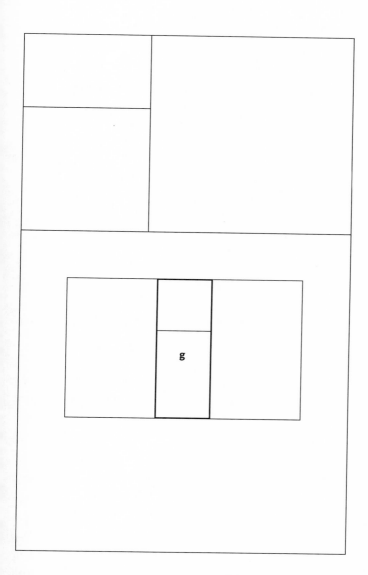

The relationship between the square and the golden section is perpetual. Each time a square is subtracted from a golden section, a new golden section remains. If two overlapping squares are formed within a golden-section rectangle, two smaller rectangles of golden-section proportions are created, along with a narrow column whose proportions are $1 : (\varphi + 1)$ $= 1 : 2.618$. This is **g**, the Extended Section, from the table on page 149. If a square is subtracted from this, the golden section is restored.

T HIS PARAGRAPH, for example, is indented according to the golden section. The indent is to the remainder of the line as that remainder is to the full text measure. Here the measure is 21 picas, and the indent is 38.2% of that, which is 8 picas.

The amount of *sinkage* (the extra white space allowed at the top of the page) is 7 lines (here equal to 7 picas). Add the extra pica of white space created by the indent itself, and you have an imaginary 8-pica square of empty space in the upper left corner of the textblock.

The size of the elevated cap is related in turn to the size of the indent and the sinkage. Eight picas is 96 pt, and 61.8% of that is 59.3 pt. But the relationship between 59 or 60 pt type and an 8-pica indent would be difficult to perceive, because a 60 pt letter is not visibly 60 pt high. The initial used has an actual 60 pt cap height instead. Depending on the face, such a letter could be anywhere from 72 to 100 pt nominal size; here it is 84 pt Castellar.

8.3 PROPORTIONS OF THE EMPTY PAGE

8.3.1 *Choose inherently satisfying page proportions in preference to stock sizes or arbitrary shapes.*

The proportions of a page are like an interval in music. In a given context, some are consonant, others dissonant. Some are familiar; some are also inescapable, because of their presence in the structures of the natural as well as the man-made world. Some proportions also seem particularly linked to living things. It is true that wastage is often increased when an 8½ × 11 inch page is trimmed to 7¾ × 11 or 6¾ × 11, or when a 6 × 9 book page is narrowed to 5⅝ × 9. But an organic page looks and feels different from a mechanical page, and the shape of the page itself will provoke certain responses and expectations in the reader, independently of whatever text it contains.

8.3.2 *Choose page proportions suited to the content, size and ambitions of the publication.*

There is no one ideal proportion, but some are clearly more ponderous, others more brittle. In general, a book page, like a human being, should not peer down its nose, nor should it sag. The narrower page shapes require a soft or open spine so that the opened book lies flat, and at smaller sizes, narrower pages are suitable only for text that can be set to a narrow measure. At larger sizes, the narrow page is more adaptable.

For ordinary books, consisting of simple text in a modest size, typographers and readers both gravitate to proportions ranging from the light, agile 5 : 9 [1 : 1.8] to the heavier and more stolid 4 : 5 [1 : 1.25]. Pages wider than 1 : √2 are useful primarily in books that need the extra width for maps, tables, sidenotes or wide illustrations, and for books in which a multiple-column page is preferred.

When important illustrations are involved, these generally decide the shape of the page. Typically, one would choose a page somewhat deeper than the average illustration, both to leave extra blank space at the foot of the page, and to permit the insertion of captions. The e/π or turned hexagon page, 1 : 1.16, for example, which is slightly deeper than a perfect square, is useful for square artwork, such as photographs taken with a square-format camera. The π/e or broad hexagon page, 1 : 0.87, is useful for landscape photographs in the 4 × 5 format, and the full cross octagon page, 1 : 0.83, for landscape photos in the wider format of 35 mm. (Uncropped 35 mm transparencies embody the proportion 2 : 3.)

8.3.3 *Choose page and column proportions whose historical associations suit your intended design.*

Early Egyptian scribes (when not writing vertically) tended to write a long line and a wide column. This long Egyptian line reappears in other contexts over the centuries – on Roman imperial writing tablets, in medieval European charters and deeds, and in many poorly designed twentieth-century works of academic prose. It is a sign, generally speaking, that the emphasis is on the writing instead of the reading, and that writing is seen as an instrument of power, not an instrument of freedom.

Early Hebrew scribes generally favored a narrower column, and early Greek scribes a column narrower still. But they, like the Egyptians, were making scrolls instead of bound books. It is difficult, therefore, to compare modern notions of the page directly with theirs. You can open a scroll as wide as you like, exposing one column, two columns, three. This flexible approach to the concept of the page survives to some extent in early codices (bound books). There are early books that are three times taller than wide, others that are close to square, and many shapes between.

In medieval Europe, most books, though certainly not all, settled down to proportions ranging from 1:1.5 to 1:1.25. Paper – once the mills were built in Europe – was commonly made in sheets whose proportions were 2:3 [1:1.5] or 3:4 [1:1.33]. These proportions, which correspond to the acoustically perfect musical intervals of fifth and fourth, also reproduce one another with each fold. If a sheet is 40 × 60 cm [2:3] to start with, it folds to 30 × 40 [3:4], which folds to 20 × 30, and so on. The 25 × 38 inch [roughly 2:3] and 20 × 26 inch [roughly 3:4] press sheets used in North America today are survivors of this medieval tradition.

The page proportion $1:\sqrt{2}$, which is now the European standard, was also known to the medieval scribes. And the tall half octagon page, 1:1.3 (the shape enshrined now in North American letter paper) has a similar pedigree. The British Museum has a Roman wax-tablet book of precisely this proportion, dated about AD 300.

Renaissance typographers continued to produce books in the proportions 1:1.5. They also developed an enthusiasm for narrower proportions. The proportions 1:1.87 (tall hexagon), 1:1.7 (tall pentagon), 1:1.67 [3:5], and of course 1:1.62, the golden section, were used by typographers in Venice before the end of the fifteenth century. The narrower page was preferred especially for works in the arts and sciences. Wider pages, better able to carry a double column, were preferred for legal and ecclesiastical texts. (Even now, a Bible, a volume of court reports or a manual on mortgages or wills is likely to be on a wider page than a book of poems or a novel.)

Renaissance page proportions (generally in the range of 1:1.4 to 1:2) survived through the Baroque, but Neoclassical books are often wider, returning to the heavier Roman proportion of 1:1.3.

8.4.1 *If the text is meant to invite continuous reading, set it in columns that are clearly taller than wide.*

Horizontal motion predominates in alphabetic writing, and for beginners, it predominates in reading. But vertical motion predominates in reading for those who have really acquired the skill. The tall column of type is a symbol of fluency, a sign that the typographer does not expect the reader to have to puzzle out the words.

Shaping the Page

The very long and very narrow columns of newspapers and magazines, however, have come to suggest disposable prose and quick, unthoughtful reading. A little more width not only gives the text more presence; it implies that it might be worth savoring, quoting and reading again.

8.4.2 *Shape the textblock so that it balances and contrasts with the shape of the overall page.*

The proportions that are useful for the shapes of pages are equally useful in shaping the textblock. This is not to say that the proportions of the textblock and the page should be the same. They often were the same in medieval books. In the Renaissance, many typographers preferred a more polyphonic page, in which the proportions of page and textblock differ. But it is pointless for them to differ unless, like intervals in music, they differ to a clear and purposeful degree.

For all the beauty of pure geometry, a perfectly square block of type on a perfectly square page with even margins all around is a form unlikely to encourage reading. Reading, like walking, involves navigation – and the square block of type on a square block of paper is short of basic landmarks and clues. To give the reader a sense of direction, and the page a sense of liveliness and poise, it is necessary to break this inexorable sameness and find a new balance of another kind. Some space must be narrow so that other space may be wide, and some space emptied so that other space may be filled.

In the simple format shown overleaf, a page whose proportions are 1 : 1.62 (the golden section) carries a textblock whose proportions are 1 : 1.8 [5 : 9]. This difference constitutes a primary visual chord which generates both energy and harmony in the page. It is supplemented by secondary harmonies created by the proportions of the margins and the placement of the textblock – not in the center of the page but high and toward the spine.

The textblock itself, in this example, is symmetrical, but it is placed asymmetrically on the page. The lefthand page is a mirror image of the right, but no mirror image runs the other way. The two-page spread is symmetrical horizontally – the direction in which the pages turn, either backward or forward, as the reader consults the book – but it is asymmetrical vertically – the direction in which the page stays put while the reader's eye repeatedly works its way in one direction: down.

This interlocking relationship of symmetry and asymmetry, and of balanced and contrasted shape and size, was not new when this example was designed (in Venice in 1501). The first European typographers inherited some two thousand years' worth of research into these principles from their predecessors, the scribes. Yet the principles are flexible enough that countless new typographic pages and page-spreads wait to be designed.

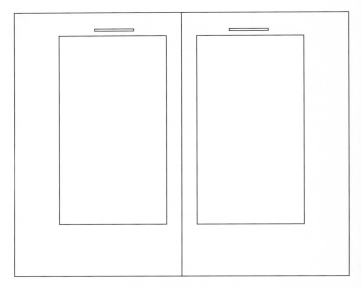

Page spread, probably by Francesco Griffo, Venice, 1501. The text is Virgil's *Aeneid,* set entirely in a crisp, simple italic lower case, 12/12 × 16, with roman small capitals, approximately 5 pt high. The original page size is 10.7 × 17.3 cm.

8.5.1 *Bring the margins into the design.*

In typography, margins must do three things. They must *lock the textblock to the page* and *lock the facing pages to each other* through the force of their proportions. Second, they must *frame the textblock* in a manner that suits its design. Third, they must *protect the textblock,* leaving it easy for the reader to see and convenient to handle. (That is, they must leave room for the reader's thumbs.) The third of these is easy, and the second is not difficult. The first is like choosing type: it is an endless opportunity for typographic play and a serious test of skill.

Perhaps fifty per cent of the character and integrity of a printed page lies in its letterforms. Much of the other fifty per cent resides in its margins.

Shaping the Page

8.5.2 *Bring the design into the margins.*

The boundaries of the textblock are rarely absolute. They are nibbled and punctured by paragraph indents, blank lines between sections, gutters between columns, and the sinkage of chapter openings. They are overrun by hanging numbers, outdented paragraphs or heads, marginal bullets, folios (page numbers) and often running heads, marginal notes and other typographic satellites. These features – whether recurrent, like folios, or unpredictable, like marginal notes and numbers – should be designed to give vitality to the page and further bind the page and the textblock.

8.5.3 *Mark the reader's way.*

Folios are useful in most documents longer than two pages. They can be anywhere on the page that is graphically pleasing and easy to find, but in practice this reduces to few possibilities: (1) at the head of the page, aligned with the outside edge of the textblock (a common place for folios accompanied by running heads); (2) at the foot of the page, aligned with or slightly indented from the outside edge of the text; (3) in the upper quarter of the outside margin, beyond the outside edge of the text; (4) at the foot of the page, horizontally centered beneath the textblock.

The fourth of these choices offers Neoclassical poise but is not the best for quick navigation. Folios near the upper or lower outside corner are the easiest to find by flipping pages in a small book. In large books and magazines, the bottom outside corner is generally more convenient for joint assaults by eye and thumb. Folios placed on the inner margin are rarely worth considering. They are invisible when needed and all too visible otherwise.

It is usual to set folios in the text size and to position them near the textblock. Unless they are very black, brightly colored or large, the folios usually drown when they get very far away from the text. Strengthened enough to survive on their own, they are likely to prove a distraction.

8.5.4 *Don't restate the obvious.*

In Bibles and other large works, running heads have been standard equipment for two thousand years. Photocopying machines, which can easily separate a chapter or a page from the rest of a book or journal, have also given running heads (and running feet, or footers) new importance.

Except as insurance against photocopying pirates, running heads are nevertheless pointless in many books and documents with a strong authorial voice or a unified subject. They remain essential in most anthologies and works of reference, large or small.

Like folios, running heads pose an interesting typographic problem. They are useless if the reader has to hunt for them, so they must somehow be distinguished from the text, yet they have no independent value and must not become a distraction. It has been a common typographic practice since 1501 to set them in spaced small caps of the text size, or if the budget permits, to print them in the text face in a second color.

8.6 PAGE GRIDS & MODULAR SCALES

8.6.1 *Use a modular scale if you need one to subdivide the page.*

Grids are often used in magazine design and in other situations where unpredictable graphic elements must be combined in a rapid and orderly way.

Modular scales serve much the same purpose as grids, but they are more flexible. A modular scale, like a musical scale, is a

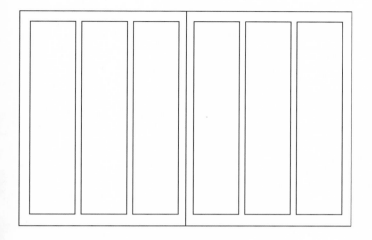

Standard grid for three-column magazine

prearranged set of harmonious proportions. In essence, it is a measuring stick whose units are indivisible and not of uniform size. The traditional sequence of type sizes shown on page 45, for example, is a modular scale. The single- and double-stranded Fibonacci series discussed on pp 157–158 are modular scales as well. These scales can, in fact, be put directly to use in page design by altering the units from points to picas.

It is perfectly feasible to create a new modular scale for any project requiring one, and the scale can be founded on any convenient single or multiple proportion – a given page size, for example, or the dimensions of a set of illustrations, or something implicit in the subject matter. A work on astronomy might use a modular scale based on star charts or Bode's law of interplanetary distances. A book on Greek art might be laid out using intervals from one or more of the Greek musical scales or, of course, the golden section. A work of modernist literature might be designed using something more deliberately arcane – perhaps a scale based on the proportions of the author's hand. Generally speaking, a scale based on two ratios (1 : φ and 1 : 2, for example) will give more flexible and interesting results than a scale founded on just one.

The Half Pica Modular scale illustrated here is actually a miniaturized version of the architectural scale of Le Corbusier, which is based in turn on the proportions of the human body.

See Le Corbusier, *The Modulor* (2nd ed., Cambridge, Mass., 1954).

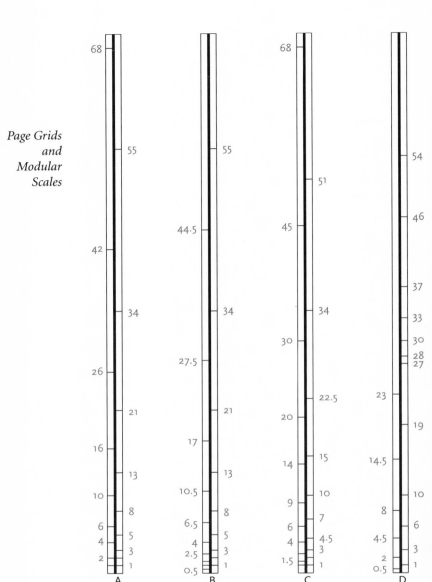

Four examples of modular pica sticks (shown at half actual size). **A** Whole Pica Modular scale. **B** Half Pica Modular scale. These are both two-stranded Fibonacci series, based on the ratios 1 : φ and 1 : 2. **C** Medieval Interval scale, based on the proportions 2 : 3 and 1 : 2. **D** Timaean Scale, a simplified version of the Pythagorean scale outlined in Plato's *Timaeus*.

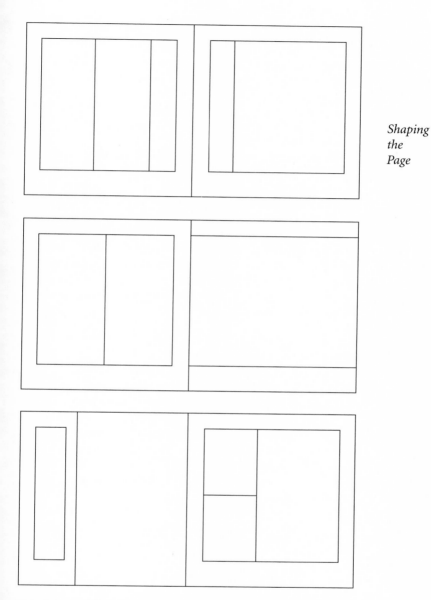

Use of the modular scale. These pages and textblocks have been subdivided using the Half Pica Modular scale. The pages are 52 × 55 picas
(8⅝" × 9⅛"), with margins of 5, 5, 5 & 8 picas. The basic textblock is 42 picas square. Thousands of different subdivisions are possible. (For more
complex examples on similar principles, see Le Corbusier, *The Modulor*.)

Examples

The formula for designing a perfect page is the same as the formula for writing one: start at the upper left hand corner and work your way across and down; then turn the page and try again. The examples on the following pages show only a few of the many kinds of typographic structures that might evolve along the way.

In fact, the weaving of the text and the tailoring of the page are thoroughly interdependent. We can discuss them one by one, and we can separate each in turn into a series of simple, unintimidating questions. But the answers to these questions must all, in the end, fold back into a single answer. The page, the pamphlet or the book must be seen as a whole if it is to look like one. If it appears to be only a series of individual solutions to separate typographic problems, who will believe that its message coheres?

In analyzing the examples on the following pages, these symbols are used:

Proportions:	P = page proportion: h/w
	T = textblock proportion: d/m
Page size:	w = width of page (trim-size)
	h = height of page (trim-size)
Textblock:	m = measure (width of primary textblock)
	d = depth of primary textblock (excluding running heads, folios, etc)
	λ = line height (type size plus added lead)
	n = secondary measure (width of secondary column)
	c = column width, where there are even multiple columns
Margins:	s = spine margin (back margin)
	t = top margin (head margin)
	e = fore-edge (front margin)
	f = foot margin
	g = internal gutter (on a multiple-column page)

Page and textblock proportions (P and T in the examples) are given here as single values (1.414, for example). To find the same values in the table on page 148, look up the corresponding *ratio* (1 : 1.414, for example).

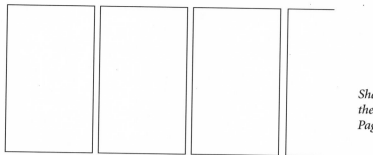

P = variable; T = 1.75. Margins: *t* = *h*/12; *f* = 1.5*t*; *g* = *t*/2 or *t*/3. Text columns from Isaiah Scroll A, from Qumran Cave 1, on the Dead Sea. The column depth is 29 lines and the measure is 28 picas, giving a line length of roughly 40 characters. Elsewhere in the scroll, column widths range from 21.5 to 39 picas. Paragraphs begin on a new line but – in keeping with the crisp, square Hebrew characters – are not indented. (Palestine, perhaps first century BC.) Original size: 26 × 725 cm.

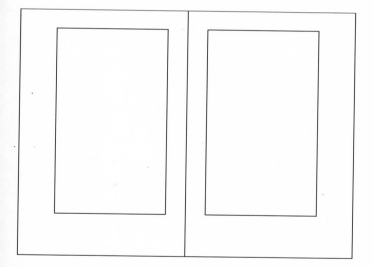

P = 1.5 [2 : 3]; T = 1.7 [tall pentagon]. Margins: *s* = *t* = *w*/9; *e* = 2*s*. The text is a fantasy novel, Francesco Colonna's *Hypnerotomachia Poliphili*, set in a roman font cut by Francesco Griffo. (Aldus Manutius, Venice, 1499.) Original size: 20.5 × 31 cm.

Examples

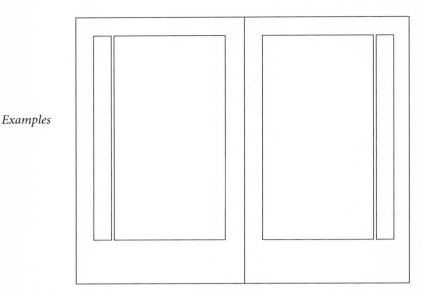

P = 1.62 [golden section]; T = 1.87 [tall hexagon]. Margins: *s = w*/9; *t = s*; *e* = 2*s*. Secondary column: *g = w*/75; *n = s*. The text is in Claude Garamond's 14 pt roman; the sidenotes are 12 pt italic. The gutter between main text and sidenotes is tiny: 6 or 7 pt against a main text measure of 33.5 picas. But the differences in size and face prevent any confusion. The text is a history of the Hundred Years' War. (Jean Froissart, *Histoire et chronique*, Jean de Tournes, Paris, 1559.) Original size: roughly 21 × 34 cm.

This grid is analyzed on the facing page.

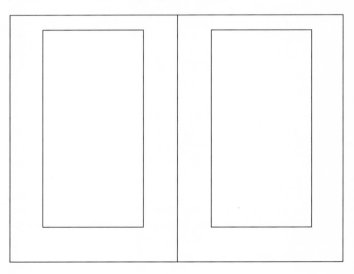

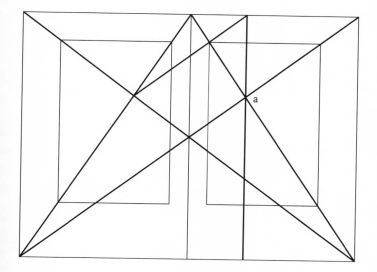

P = T = 1.5 [2 : 3]. Margins: $s = w/9$; $t = h/9$; $e = 2s$; $f = 2t$. The margins are thus in the proportion $s : t : e : f = 2 : 3 : 4 : 6$. A sound, elegant and basic medieval structure, which will work for any proportion of page and textblock, so long as the two remain in unison. Spine and head margins may be ninths, tenths, twelfths or any other desired proportion of the page size. Twelfths, of course, give a fuller and more efficient page, with less white space. But if the page proportion is 2 : 3 and the spine and head margins are ninths, as shown here, the consonance of textblock and page is considerably deepened, because $d = w$, which is to say, the *depth* of the textblock matches the *width* of the page. Thus $m : w = d : h = w : h = m : d = s : t = e : f = 2 : 3$. Point **a**, where the half and full diagonals intersect, is one third of the way down and across the textblock and the page. Jan Tschichold, 1955, after Villard de Honnecourt, France, *c.* 1280. See Tschichold's *The Form of the Book* (1991).

FACING PAGE: P = 1.5 [2 : 3]; T = 2 [double square]. Margins: $s = e = w/5$; $t = s/2$. The text is a book of poems, set throughout in a chancery italic with roman capitals. The designer and publisher of this book was a master calligrapher, certainly aware of the tradition that the inner margins should be smaller than the outer. He followed that tradition himself with books of prose, but in this book of poems he chose to center the textblock on the page. The text throughout is set in one size. Titles are set in the capitals of the text font, letterspaced about 30%. There are no running heads or other diversions. (Giangiorgio Trissino, *Canzone*, Ludovico degli Arrighi, Rome, *c.* 1523.) Original size: 12.5 × 18.75 cm.

Scribes employing this format often designed their pages so that the line height was an even factor of the spine margin. If $\lambda = s/3$, the depth of the textblock will be 27 lines. If $\lambda = s/4$, the depth of the textblock will be 36 lines.

Examples

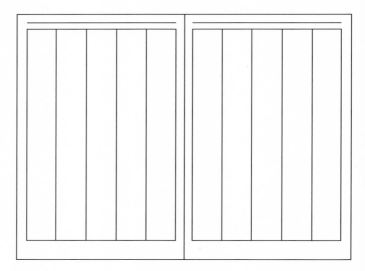

P = 1.5 [2 : 3]; T = 1.54 [pentagon textblock]. Margins: $s = w/20$; $t = s = h/30$; $e = w/15 = 4s/3$; $f = 2t$. This is the format used for the index to the fifth edition of the *Times Atlas of the World* (London, 1975). The page is a standard medieval shape. The text is set in 5.5 pt Univers leaded 0.1 pt on a 12-pica measure, in five subdivided columns per page. Columns are separated by thin vertical rules. Keywords and folios, at the top of the page, are in 16 pt Univers semibold. (Because of their prominence, these running heads are included here in calculating the size and shape of the textblock.) The text is 204 lines deep, yielding an average of 1000 names per page for 217 pages. This index is a masterpiece of its kind: a potent typographic symbol, an efficient work of reference, and a comfortable text to browse. Original size: 30 × 45 cm.

This grid is analyzed on the facing page.

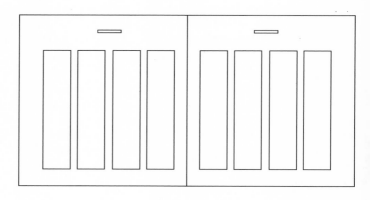

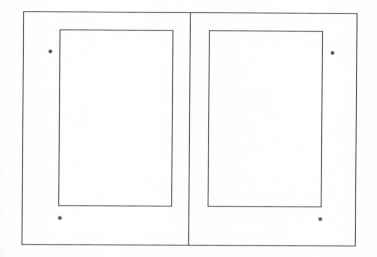

P = 1.414 [$\sqrt{2}$]; T = 1.62 [φ, the golden section]. Margins: $s = t = w/9$ and $e = f = 2s$. This is a simple format for placing a golden-section textblock on an ISO page, locking the two together with margins in the proportions 1 : 2. Two possible locations for folios are shown: in the upper outside margin and (as an alternative) underneath the lower outside corner of the textblock. There is also ample room for sidenotes in the fore-edge if required. If the spine and top margins on these pages are increased to $w/8$, while the textblock and page are held at their original proportion, the relationship of the margins becomes $e = f = φs$, another golden section.

FACING PAGE: P = 1.1; T = 0.91; $c = w/6$. Margins: $s = w/14$; $e = 2s$; $t = 3s$; $f = 3s/2$; $g = m/20$. The proportions of the textblock are the *reciprocal of the proportions of the page*: 0.91 = 1/1.1, which is to say that the textblock is the same shape as the page, rotated 90°. But if the gutters are removed from the textblock and the four columns closed up solid, the textblock collapses to the same shape *in the same orientation* as the page. In other words, the textblock has been expanded from the same shape to the reciprocal shape of the page *entirely by the addition of white space*. The text is the Greek Bible, lettered in uncials, about 13 characters per line. There are no spaces between the words, but there is some punctuation, and the text has a slight rag, with line breaks carefully chosen. This subtle piece of craftsmanship was produced in Egypt in the fourth century. It is the Codex Sinaiticus, Add. Ms. 43725, at the British Library, London. Original size: 34.5 × 38 cm.

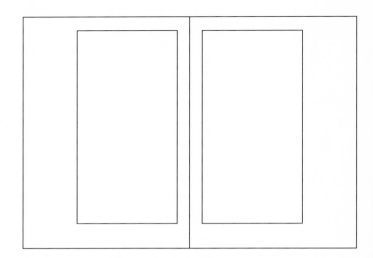

P = 1.414 [$\sqrt{2}$]; T = 2 [double square]. Margins: $s = w/12$; $f = 2t = h/9$; $e = w/3$. The wide fore-edge of this manuscript book had a purpose: it was deliberately left free for sidenotes to be added by the owner. The text is a sequence of short poems by the Roman poet Horace, written in Caroline minuscule. (Ms. Plut. 34.1, Laurentian Library, Florence; tenth century.)

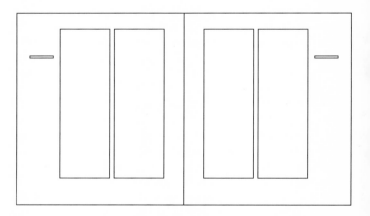

P = 1.176 [truncated pentagon page]; T = 1.46. Margins: $s = h/11$; $t = 5s/6$; $e = 5s/2$; $f = 3s/2$. Columns: $c = 3w/10$; $g = s/4$. The text (set in Friedrich Poppl's Pontifex, 11/13 × 17 R R) is a series of essays on twentieth-century art, published in Canada in 1983, with many full-page illustrations. Original size: 24 × 28 cm.

8.8.1 *Improvise, calculate, and improvise some more.*

Numerical values – used by all typographers in their daily work – give an impression of exactness. Careful measurement and accurate calculation are indeed important in typography, but they are not its final purpose, and moments arise in every project when exactness bumps its head against approximation. On the mechanical side, paper expands and contracts, and printing presses, folding machines and trimming knives – not to speak of typesetting hardware and software – all have their margins of error. The typographer can rarely profit from these variations and cannot entirely prevent them. On the planning side, however, imprecision can often be put to better use.

Shaping the Page

Some typographers prefer to design by arithmetic from the outset, in a space composed of little invisible bricks called points and picas. Others prefer to work in the free two-dimensional space of a sketchpad, converting their layouts afterward to typographic measure. Most work involves a combination of these methods, with occasional collisions between the two. But the margins of inexactness that crop up in the rounding of units, in conflicts between optical and arithmetic spacing and centering, in combining proportions, and in translating from one form of measurement to another should be welcomed as opportunities, not as inconsistencies to be ignored, glossed over or begrudged. The equal temperament of the typesetting machine and the just intonation of the sketchpad should be used to test and refine one another until the final answer sings.

8.8.2 *Adjust the type and the spaces within the textblock using typographic increments, but rely on free proportions to adjust the empty space.*

Proportions are more flexible than picas, and it is usually convenient and appealing to work in even units. A margin of 5.32 picas, for example, begs to be altered to 5 or 5¼ or 5½. But picas per se are less important than proportions, and the system of typographic sizes and units serves the interrelations of letterforms better than it serves the interrelations of empty space. As a general rule, it is better to make incremental jumps in the textblock first and to readjust the margins thereafter – paying more attention in the latter case to absolute proportion than to convenient units of measurement. When space is measured purely in points, the temptation to rearrange it into even picas is miraculously lessened.

8.8.3 *Keep the page design supple enough to provide a livable home for the text.*

Architects build perfectly proportioned kitchens, living rooms and bedrooms in which their clients will make, among other things, a mess. Typographers likewise build perfectly proportioned pages, then distort them on demand. The text takes precedence over the purity of the design, and the typographic texture of the text takes precedence over the absolute proportions of the individual page.

If, for instance, three lines remain at the end of a chapter, looking forlorn on a page of their own, the design must flex to accommodate them. The obvious choices are: (1) running two of the previous spreads a line long (that is, adding one line to the depth of two pairs of facing pages), which will leave the final page one line short; (2) running half a dozen of the previous spreads a line short, thereby bumping a dozen lines along to the final page; or (3) reproportioning some non-textual element – perhaps an illustration or the sinkage, if any, at the head of the chapter.

Spacious chapter heads stand out in a book, as they are meant to. Reproportioning the sinkage is therefore a poor option unless all chapter heads can be reproportioned to match. And running six spreads short is, on the face of it, clearly a greater evil than running two spreads long.

If there are only a few pages to the document, the whole thing can, and probably should, be redesigned to fit the text. But in a book of many pages, widow lines, orphaned subheads, and the runt ends of chapters or sections are certain to require reproportioning some spreads. A rigid design that demands an invariant page depth is therefore inappropriate for a work of any length. Altering the leading on short pages to preserve a standard depth (vertical justification, as it is sometimes called) is not a solution. Neither is stuffing extra space between the paragraphs. These antics destroy the fabric of the text and thus strike at the heart of the book.

The state of the art has more by far to do with the knowledge and skill of its practitioners than with the subtleties of their tools, but tools can constrain that skill or set it free. The limitations of the tools are therefore also of some interest. They are of special interest now, because they are subject to rapid change.

9

9.1 THE SIXTY THOUSAND CHARACTER ALPHABET

It is often said that the Latin alphabet consists of 26 letters, the Greek of 24 and the Arabic of 28. If you confine yourself to one case only, a narrow historical window and the dialect in power, this abstraction can come true. If you include both caps and lower case, accented letters and continental consonants and vowels – á à â ǎ å ã ä ą ă ā æ ç ć č ċ đ é ł ñ and all the rest – the Latin alphabet is not 26 letters long after all; it is at least 260 and able to increase at any time. The alphabet that classicists now use for classical Greek, with its long parade of vowels and diacritics – ά ὰ ᾶ ἀ ἄ ἂ ἆ ἁ ἅ ἃ ἇ and so on – is modest by comparison: no more than 200 glyphs altogether.

To the 260-character European alphabet, mathematicians, grammarians, chemists and even typographers are prone to make additions: arabic numerals, punctuation, technical symbols, letters borrowed from Hebrew and Greek, and, where the letterforms require or invite them, a few typographic ligatures and alternates as well. There is no hope at this stage of counting the number of sorts or glyphs precisely, but it is easy to hit 300, and not hard to hit 500.

At the end of the eighteenth century, an English-speaking hand compositor's standard lower case had 54 compartments, holding roman or italic *a* to *z*, arabic numerals, basic ligatures, spaces and punctuation. The upper case had another 98, containing caps and analphabetics. That total, 98 + 54 = 152, is the English-speaking hand compositor's minimum basic allotment. When more sorts are required, as they very often are, supplementary cases are used. Two pair give 304 compartments; three pair give 456; four pair give 608. This has been the ordinary typographic ballpark for some time. How Gutenberg's cases were arranged we do not know, but we know how big they were. He

Printing enthusiasts sometimes speak of *the lay of the case* as if it were universal law – but the lay of the case is as localized as the lay of the land. Hand compositors often set not from paired but from single cases. These have been reduced to as few as 89 compartments but sometimes contain 400 or more.

179

used not 26 but 290 different sorts, in one face and one size, in an unaccented language, to set his 42-line Bible. The Monotype machine, built five centuries later, with 255 (later 272) positions in a standard matrix case, had fallen only a little ways behind.

Simple computers and e-mail links are, by comparison, victims of linguistic, intellectual and typographic poverty. The alphabet they use is the basic character set defined by the American Standard Code for Information Interchange, or ASCII. Each character is limited to seven bits of binary information, so the maximum number of characters is $2^7 = 128$. Thirty three of those are normally subtracted for control codes, and one represents an empty space. The remainder, 94, is not enough to handle even basic text in Spanish, French or German. The fact that such an alphabet was long considered adequate tells us something about the cultural narrowness of American civilization, or American technocracy, in the midst of the twentieth century.

The extended ASCII alphabet, now in general use, is made from eight-bit characters. This gives $2^8 = 256$ glyphs altogether, though conventional typesetting software often limits the working selection to 224 or even fewer at a time. The upper register of this alphabet – wholly invisible on a normal computer keyboard – is usually filled out with characters selected from the Latin 1 Character Set established by ISO: the International Organization for Standardization, Geneva. (The full range of ISO characters is illustrated and discussed in appendix A, page 271.)

The allotment of 256 or even 224 characters is adequate for basic communication in the so-called major (i.e., familiar) languages of Western Europe, but this limit ignores the needs of mathematicians, linguists and other specialists, and of millions of normal human beings who use the Latin alphabet for Czech, Hausa, Hungarian, Latvian, Navajo, Polish, Rumanian, Tlingit, Turkish, Vietnamese and other languages. The extended ASCII character set in its usual form is the alphabet not of the UN General Assembly but of NATO: a technological memento of the them-and-us mentality that thrived in the Cold War.

Good and affordable software that will handle thousands of characters efficiently has been readily available for years, but a common industrial standard and typographic resources to match have been slow in coming. Typographically sectarian and culturally underdeveloped software is the rule.

Earlier typographers were free at any time to cut another punch and cast another character. The freedom to do likewise

Many computer keyboards have over 100 keys, but only 47 are tied to characters. (This odd number is made even by the spacebar.) Each character key has, at minimum, a plain and a shift position, reaching 94 characters in all: ordinarily the 94 basic ASCII characters. But the keys can be remapped and can easily be coded to reach four characters each instead of two. (An example of such a keyboard is shown on page 92.) When more than $47 \times 4 = 188$ characters are needed at one time, more than one keyboard map is in order as well. Function keys are normally used to jump from one map to another: Latin to Greek to Cyrillic to Hebrew for example.

exists with the computer. But finding room for all these letters in a shared standard alphabet involves, in the digital world, a shift from eight-bit to sixteen-bit characters. When we make this change, the alphabet increases to $2^{16} = 65,536$ characters. The first version of a standard set of characters this size – known as Unicode – was roughed out at the end of the 1980s and published in the early 1990s. It is, like any standard, far from perfect, but it does provide a working protocol for a generous Latin alphabet and a base for the technological coexistence of Latin, Arabic, Greek, Hebrew, Cyrillic, Devanagari, Thai and many other alphabets, together with the large standard character sets of Chinese, Japanese and Korean. In its latest published form (version 3.0, issued in spring 2000), Unicode defines 49,194 characters, allocates 6400 for private use, and leaves 7,827 free for future allocation. The remaining 2048 characters are a new extension mechanism. They function in pairs to yield an extra $1024^2 = 1,048,576$ characters, intended to be used when the first 60,000 and some have run out.

See *The Unicode Standard,* Version 3.0 (Reading, Mass., 2000).

Few compositors may need (or want to memorize and keep track of) all 50,000 or 60,000 characters – though the prospect is not, in fact, implausible. Typographers who work with Han Chinese routinely handle 20,000 characters. But authors, editors, typographers and ordinary citizens who just want to be able to spell Dvořák, Miłosz, Mạ'ii or al-Fārābī, or to quote a line of Sophocles or Pushkin, or the Vedas or the Sutras or the Psalms, or write $\varphi \neq \pi$, are incidentally potential beneficiaries of a system this inclusive. So is everyone who wants to send a message via e-mail in an alphabet other than Latin or a language other than English.

There may never be a font of type containing 60,000 well-made characters designed by one designer. But good fonts with well over ten thousand characters, keyed to the Unicode system, are already on the market. There are even a few computer operating systems that support them. More importantly, perhaps, fonts for particular symbol sets and alphabets can be linked and tuned to one another by adjusting weight, letterfit and scale. That task is made more feasible with a new species of fonts, discussed later in this chapter – and when fonts are linked in this way, Unicode can serve as a coordinating mechanism.

These new resources will be much more useful, of course, when ordinary composition software and communication links have managed to catch up.

9.2.1 *Glyphs & Characters*

Typographers are frequently surprised to learn that small caps, text figures, swashes and other things they need and use are nowhere to be found in the lengthening Unicode catalog. But Unicode lists textual, not typographic, symbols. Its aim is to embrace all linguistically meaningful signs, not all their typographically desirable forms and permutations. Because of inconsistencies in its original design, and because it has absorbed inconsistent ISO standards, Unicode does now include many typographic ligatures and other compound characters. In theory, nonetheless, authors, editors and denizens of Unicode think and transmit elemental signs (f + f + i, for instance, rather than *ffi*), and typographers transform these underlying abstract entities into their endlessly varying outward manifestations.

This mode of thinking about text transmission and typography has proven very fruitful, especially in relation to non-Latin scripts. And it has prompted type designers and founders to distinguish with some care between a character set and a *glyph palette*. The plain and swash forms of *z* in Arrighi or Poetica, for example, are different glyphs (different sorts, a hand compositor would say) that correspond to a single character.

In the early days of letterpress, punchcutters frequently cut multiple versions of common letters and other characters (such as the hyphen), so that their subtle, often subliminal, variations would invigorate the page. A hand compositor reaching into the typecase for an *e* might then come up with any of several similar but not identical forms. Few readers may have consciously noticed the difference, yet each of these slyly variant letters contributed its mote of vitality to the page. After five hundred years on the library shelf, that vitality remains. It comes in part from the artistry of the cutters, and in part from the use of a system that lets the glyphs outnumber the characters.

For the origins of Sophia, see Stanley Morison, *Politics and Script* (Oxford, 1972): 98–103, and the review of Sophia and Mantinia in *Print* 48.2 (New York, 1994): 121–122.

Matthew Carter's Sophia, to take a more recent example, is a digital face consisting only of capitals, yet it includes multiple glyphs for many characters. There are four forms of T, three forms each of E, F and R, two forms of A, C, G, H, I, K and many other letters. Some of the variant forms are independent; others are components used in custom-building ligatures. Sophia's stake in the character set is relatively small, because it

THE INTELLECT OF MAN

IS FORCED TO CHOOSE +

PERFECTION °F THE LIFE

OR °F THE WORK ✠

+ + AND IF IT TAKE THE

SECOND MUST REFUSE +

A HEAVENLY MANSION,

RAGING IN THE DARK+

WILLIAM · BUTLER · YEATS

Matthew Carter's Sophia (Carter & Cone, 1993) is a face with alternate
glyphs for many characters. Many of these alternates form ligatures.

has no lower case, but its glyph palette is large (and Carter has been urged to make it larger).

Apart from special cases like Sophia and Poetica, most fonts of Latin type are limited at present to only one glyph for most characters, and a few additional glyphs like *ff* and *ffi*. At the level of the *family* there are several glyphs per character: a, *a*, A, **a**, **a** and sometimes many more. But in English the rules for choosing among these glyphs are editorial as much as typographic. In the Arabic alphabet, by contrast, multiple glyphs are essential in every font, and the choice of glyph is governed by purely scriptorial or typographic rules. There are no capitals, small caps or italics in Arabic script, but ligatures are frequent, and a normal font of type contains about a hundred basic glyphs for the 28 Arabic letters, because most letters have four different forms: initial, medial, final and free-standing.

9.2.2 *Manual, Random and Programmed Variation*

The text is a string of characters; the font is a palette of glyphs – along with all the information (width tables, kerning tables and so on) needed for stringing the glyphs to match the characters. If we think about typography in these terms, it is clear that every font could offer the typographer a different range of choices and pose a different challenge for the composition software. Systems that insert the basic five *f*-ligatures automatically have been with us now for years – but if every font can have a slightly different set of glyphs, it is pointless to expect the composition software by itself to choose effectively among them. Three possibilities remain: (1) the choice of glyphs can be left to the typographer, who picks them and inserts them each by hand; (2) where there are variant forms of single letters, the choice can be left to chance; or (3) the rules for choosing glyphs can be embedded in the font itself.

The first of these options has been the normal practice with foundry type for centuries. Poetica, Sophia and Zapf Renaissance are all masterful examples of digital design, but in the technical sense, they are revolutionary chiefly in that they offer digital typographers the same degree of freedom (and require in return the same investment of skill and attention) that hand compositors have known since the days of Johann Gutenberg.

The second option – letting the designer's chosen variants assert themselves at random – is an old and distinguished

The Multidimensional Font

Lexical ligatures (æ, œ, ß, etc) are those whose usage is defined by lexicographers and grammarians. Typographic ligatures (ff, fi, ﬅ, etc) are those whose usage is primarily a matter of typographic style. The distinction is by no means absolute.

184

method too. Francesco Griffo and Simon de Colines are two of many early masters who cut multiple forms of letters. Some alternates (with forms like ⁀ʋ and ⁀ɴ) were used selectively at the beginnings and endings of words, in contexts where their extra width was useful to the line. Others, which differed among themselves scarcely enough to reach the threshold of visibility, could serve – and did serve – to enliven the text at random.

The computer is, on the face of it, an ideal device for reviving the old luxury of random variations in design at the threshold of perception. But conventional typesetting software focuses instead on the suicidal notion of absolute control – and has been hamstrung in the past by the idea of a single glyph per character. The few digital fonts produced to date that do make use of random forms have been forced to work against the grain of the composition software. They have been plagued, as a result, by problems that discourage their extended or frequent use.

David Pye discusses the importance of *the threshold of visibility* in his perceptive book *The Nature and Art of Workmanship* (Cambridge, UK, 1968).

eeeeeeeee eeeeeeeee eeeeeeɛee

Beowolf (FontShop, 1990) is at root a statuesque text roman drawn by Erik van Blokland. The letterforms are sent to the output device through a subroutine, devised by Just van Rossum, that provokes distortions of each letter within predetermined limits in unpredetermined ways. Three degrees of randomization are available. Within the specified limits, every letter is a surprise.

In Sophia, where there are many empty slots in the character set and alternate glyphs are inserted by hand, it is easy to disguise the extra forms so they will not confuse the operating system. Sophia's four capital T's, for example, are known to the keyboard as T, t, u and \. But in the typeface that Erik van Blokland and Just van Rossum christened Kosmik (FontShop, 1993), every letter, both uppercase and lower, has three forms. Three fonts are then required, and the printer-driver leaps from font to font with each repetition of each letter. This reduces many systems to a state of nervous collapse after setting a few lines.

The same designers' Beowolf and BeoSans rely on the output device to create truly random perturbations from a single set of letterforms instead of making random or rotating choices from a stock of alternate glyphs.

A host of richer possibilities arises from the third option mentioned above: making the rules for choosing glyphs a working part of the font itself. This requires real cooperation from the operating system – but when that cooperation is achieved, it is possible to make the font itself a complex piece of active software: not just a set of glyphs, but a decision-making system that can govern how the glyphs are used.

The Multi-dimensional Font

One of the first steps toward an adaptable font of this kind was taken by Adobe Systems, with their multiple master (MM) series, introduced in 1991. An MM font is, in effect, a set of fonts with a built-in editor, inviting the user to alter and interpolate the letterforms within certain bounds and along certain axes predetermined by the designer. These axes can include, for example, width, weight, optimal size, extender length, terminal shape or serif formation. Within the confines of the composition software and operating systems of the early 1990s, MM fonts, though highly versatile, are tedious to use. Each weight or width must be created as an independent font, dynamic in size (like any PostScript font) but static in every other regard. With newer operating systems, these fonts become dynamic along whatever axis or axes the designer has allowed.

aaaaaaaaaa

In Adobe's terminology, the size axis is called *optical*, not optimal size. What is at issue, however, is physical scale, which is visceral as much as optical.

Adobe Jenson MM is scalable both for weight and for optimal size. Here one letter *of uniform weight* is scaled from 6 to 72 pt optimal size. The forms are then resized to the same x-height so their shapes and effective weights can be compared. If each letter is set at the size intended, optical balance is achieved.

For typographic purposes, the axis of optimal size is usually of paramount importance. Handcut punches inevitably vary in weight, proportion and sharpness of detail from one size to another. A 7 pt font has a darker stroke, *looser dressing* (wider inherent character spacing) and often a larger torso than the 12 pt font. The 24 and 48 pt fonts will be still lighter in the stroke, more tightly fitted, more sharply detailed, and often (though not always) smaller in the eye. Titles, text and footnotes set on the same page in the same face then look balanced in color and form. This kind of subtlety grew rare at the end of the nineteenth century, when many founders gave up cutting punches and began engraving matrices directly by machine in many different sizes from a single set of patterns. Phototype machines, which use a single pattern for type of every size, from 6 pt to 360 pt, leave no vestige whatsoever of the punchcutter's visceral grasp of absolute scale. A sense of respect for changing proportion reappeared momentarily in early digital types, when every font was bitmapped at a predetermined size. But since the early 1980s, digital type has meant type in scalable form, with one mathematical template for all sizes. Multiple master fonts give no control over the palette of glyphs per se, but they do – or rather, they *can* – help to restore a form of typographic harmony that was brought to great refinement in the 1530s, in the workshop of Simon de Colines.

A simpler but likewise significant example of an adaptable font is Zuzana Ličko's Mrs Eaves (Emigre, 1996). There are five basic members of the family: roman, italic, bold roman, and two sizes of small caps. The roman, italic and bold are each equipped with a supplementary battery of 71 ligatures, some subtle, some distinctly cheeky. A supporting piece of software – engineered, once again, by Just van Rossum – lets the compositor decide which ligatures to use, then implants them automatically wherever the equivalent string of characters appears. This is how most systems for handling optional ligatures ought to work – and how, perhaps, one day, they will.

bpfi

Above: 6 pt, 8 pt and 12 pt Monotype metal Centaur, enlarged to 24 pt size. *Below*: the actual 24 pt type.

bpfi

æ ǽ ćky ee ffy ffr gg ggy gi ip it ky oe œ ŝp ſs ſs Th tt tty ty
ae æ ćky ćt ee fb ff ffy ffr ft ggy gi gy ip it ky oe œ Œ ŝp ſs ŝt py tt tty ty tw

Some of the ligatures in Zuzana Ličko's typeface Mrs Eaves. There are 30 ligatures for the caps, 40 for the lower case, and one hybrid (Th). Each of these exists in three forms: roman, italic and bold. The face (though not its complement of ligatures) is based on John Baskerville's roman and italic. It is named for Sarah Ruston Eaves (Mrs Richard Eaves), who for sixteen years was Baskerville's resident housekeeper and lover, and for another eleven years (after the death of her first husband) was his lawful wedded wife.

How many ligatures is a lot? There are only 10 or 11 nowadays (æ, œ, Æ, Œ, ß, fi, fl, ff, ffi, ffl; sometimes fj) in a normal Latin text font, but there are 36 in the font for Gutenberg's 42-line Bible (*c.* 1455), 45 in Robert Granjon's second civilité (*c.* 1570), 55 in Robert Slimbach's Poetica (1992), 70 in Francesco Griffo's first italic (1499), and 352 in Claude Garamond's Royal Greek (*c.* 1541).

9.2.3 *Contextual Intelligence*

For a font of type to qualify as intelligent, it is not enough that it should put alternate glyphs or ligatures where it is told. It must be able to learn to put them where they belong and omit them otherwise. To be durably intelligent, it must be able to keep learning, not only from its maker but from its users too. Fonts that can be taught to behave in different ways in different contexts have been under development since the late 1980s, but the first working versions were publicly released only in 1995.

Fonts with contextual intelligence need support from both the composition software and the operating system – and the pace of such development depends on opportunities for monetary profit more than on disinterested devotion to science and art. Major software manufacturers ignored the first generation of intelligent fonts (known as GX or *graphic extension* fonts). In the year 2000, they are just beginning to support the second generation of such fonts, known as OpenType. A typical GX or OpenType font includes some or all of the following features:

- large character sets, including (for example) roman, italic and small caps, with text and titling figures, superior and inferior letters and figures, and the full range of accented characters, all accessible at once on a single font;
- automated changes in letterfit or scale in tandem with changes in size;
- multiple glyphs for many characters, with contextual rules prescribing when a given glyph is used (e.g., *z* before *f, g, j, p, y, comma* or *semicolon*; *ʒ* before *hard return* or *period + hard return*; *z* otherwise);
- automatic optical repositioning of glyphs in certain contexts (permitting, for example, automatic hanging punctuation and smoother marginal alignments of roman and italic);
- multiple discretionary ligatures, with automatic insertion;
- contextual kerning, applying different values to the same pair of letters in the midst of different sequences.

The latter feature has several basic uses. When roman and italic are combined on a single font, it can solve the nagging problem of faulty spacing before and after italicized words in a line of roman type. (Hand compositors learn early to put a slightly smaller space in front of an *italicized phrase* and a larger

188

one at the end. Keyboard compositors rarely take the time to do the same.) Within a single alphabet, contextual kerning means, for instance, that everyone's initials – even T.A.V.A. Smith's and V.V.T.V. Jones's – can be well spaced once and for all.

If all this sounds as urgent as diamond earrings for the dog, it is well to remember two things. First, these features are essential for setting decent type in many alphabets other than Latin. Second, Latin letters need these features less now than Arabic or Tibetan only because the Latin alphabet, after centuries under a heavy industrial cloud, has evolved a rather stark, puritanical form. There is evidence enough that it will move in other directions when it can. I am thinking of sophisticated calligraphic faces like Poetica, Ex Ponto and Zapf Renaissance; informal scripts like Roger Excoffon's Mistral; celebrations of pure geometry like the early version of Paul Renner's Futura and the later incarnation of Herb Lubalin's Avant Garde; and of complex inscriptional faces such as Mantinia and Sophia, as well as of indulgent new creations such as Mrs Eaves.

9.3 SCRIBAL JUSTIFICATION

It is a guiding principle of this book not to favor any particular kind of composition software or computer platform, nor even to favor computers at all, except by an acceptance of the fact that they are now the primary means of setting type. As an example of the crabwise and ultimately circular progress of typographic method, however, I will focus momentarily on one particular bundle of software which is not now and never was for sale to individual typographers – and whose maker was a firm no longer in business.

In 1993, URW in Hamburg announced a new approach to computer justification, developed in collaboration with Hermann Zapf. This proposal, called the HZ program, was actually several separate bundles of code, offered for sale to developers of composition software. The system evidently now belongs primarily to history, like the Monotype and Linotype and Lasercomp machines, yet it was never really used by anyone except its own developers, and its legacy has yet to be absorbed.

The avowed inspiration for the HZ program was not, for once, Nicolas Jenson's edition of Eusebius nor Aldus's edition of Bembo or Colonna, but Johann Gutenberg's 42-line Bible. And the focus was not on the type in which that book is set, but on

Details can be found in *The Seybold Report on Publishing Systems* 22.11 (1993): 3–9, and in URW's own publication, *hz-program: Micro-typography for Advanced Typesetting* (Hamburg, 1993).

Two blocks of
newspaper
copy.

The upper
block of text
has been
justified line-
by-line by
altering the
spaces be-
tween words.
These spaces
now range
from M/3 to 3
ems.

The lower
block of text
has passed
through all but
the final stage
of the HZ
program. The
spaces be-
tween words
are still fixed at
M/5. They can
be adjusted
now, to take up
the little slack
that remains.

Dieses beinhaltet im wesentlichen
auch die Festlegungen und die
Klärungen solcher Begriffe wie
zum Beispiel typographische
Schriftzeichen, Satz oder Text,
Sachdarstellungen über Schutzgegenstand, die Schutz-
bestimmung, Grundbedingung
auch für einen umfassenden
Schutz sowie weitere wichtige
schriftbezogene Besonderheiten.
Mit Inkrafttreten des Schriftgesetzes, das sich auf das Wiener Ab-

Dieses beinhaltet im wesentlichen
auch die Festlegungen und die Klärungen solcher Begriffe wie zum Beispiel typographische Schriftzeichen,
Satz oder Text, Sachdarstellungen
über Schutzgegenstand, die Schutz-
bestimmung, Grundbedingung auch
für einen umfassenden Schutz sowie weitere wichtige schriftbezogene
Besonderheiten. Mit Inkrafttreten
des Schriftgesetzes, das sich auf das
Wiener Abkommen über besonde-
ren Rechtsschutz typographischer
Schriftzeichen sowie deren interna-

the impeccable evenness of the margins and the word spacing Gutenberg achieved, though his book is set throughout in narrow columns. (The measure is 21 picas, and the type is 18 pt. On average, there are only about 36 characters per line, yet only about one line in four ends with a hyphen.)

These were the components of the HZ program:

- optical alignment of characters at the left and right margins, with half-hung punctuation;
- kerning on the fly from an algorithmic matrix rather than a table, so that kerning varies automatically not only with type size but also with the tightness of the line;
- microscopic expanding and condensing of the *counters* (but not the *strokes*) of individual letters;
- H&J (hyphenation and justification) calculations based on the net benefit to the *paragraph* instead of line-by-line.

Composition systems with paragraph- rather than line-based H&J exist and have existed for some time. The HZ program was unique in combining this approach with other solutions.

These solutions were applied in order, and word space was adjusted only at the end. The system was supported by a scheme for scaling the strokes and counters of digital fonts according to optimal scale. In other words, the program included a procedure along the lines of Adobe's multiple master system, but applicable in theory directly to any scalable digital typeface.

Several of these features reappeared in other forms in 1995, in the early GX fonts. Where and when the others will resurface remains to be seen. Functioning in concert, they gave superb results. The marginal alignment and evenness of spacing produced through the HZ program was better than anything I have found except the slowest, most painstaking hand composition.

The third major element in the HZ program – altering the widths of certain letters – is routine in Hebrew and Arabic typography. It is therefore sometimes known as 'Semitic justification.' The first typographer to do it, however, was Gutenberg, who had learned it from the European scribes.

9.4 DIGITAL BALING WIRE AND CHEWING GUM

The recent history of the typefounding industry, both digital and metal, in Europe and North America, is a litany of corporate fire sales, raids, blind mergers and foreclosures. This degree of financial and managerial turbulence, coupled with the loss of the old system of master and apprentice on the shop floor, has scarred several old and famous names and obliterated others. When the most knowledgeable employees have fled, basic technical and aesthetic decisions, as well as financial and marketing decisions, are made by those with minimal exposure to the craft. At the other extreme are the newest and smallest foundries. Some of these are owned and run by experts, others by those who are only beginning to learn.

A shiny new CD full of digital type may, in consequence, turn out to be an electronic artefact crafted just as subtly as the finest anonymous early manuscript or inscription. Or it may need quick first aid. If alterations are required, they may be as simple as revising a few kerning pairs, or as complex as building missing letters or altering the size and revising the alignment of half the glyphs on the font.

One simple example will suffice. Most of the Monotype digital revivals I have tested in recent years have serious flaws in the kerning tables. The problem occurs with Monotype Arrighi, Baskerville, Blado, Centaur, Dante, Fournier, Gill Sans, Poliphilus, Van Dijck and other masterworks in the Monotype collection. These are well-tried faces of superb design – yet in defiance of tradition, the maker's kerning tables call for a large space (as much as M/4) to be added whenever the *f* is followed by a word space. The result is a large white blotch after every word ending in *f* unless a mark of punctuation intervenes.

Is it east of the sun
and west of   the moon — or
is it west of the moon
and east of the sun?

Monotype digital Van Dijck, before and after editing the kerning table. As issued, the kerning table adds 127 units (thousandths of an em) in the roman, and 228 in the italic, between the letter *f* and the word space. The corrected table adds 6 units in the roman, none in the italic. Other, less drastic refinements have also been made to the kerning table used in the second two lines.

*Digital
Baling Wire
and
Chewing
Gum*

Kerning instructions, character widths and other data can be read as plain text from the AFM file of a fully formed Type 1 PostScript font. With TrueType fonts (and with PostScript fonts that are lacking AFM files), a font editor is needed to decode the information, because the character metrics and kerns are present only in binary form.

Professional typographers may argue about whether the added space should be zero, or ten, or even 25 thousandths of an em. But there is no professional dispute about whether it should be on the order of an eighth or a quarter of an em. An extra space that large is a prefabricated typographic error – one that would bring snorts of disbelief and instantaneous correction from Stanley Morison, Bruce Rogers, Jan van Krimpen, Eric Gill and others on whose expertise and genius the Monotype heritage is built. Happily, it is an easy error to fix. The kerning table can be edited for good with a simple font editor or repaired temporarily from within most typesetting systems and some word processors.

9.5 PIXELS, PROOFS & PRINTING

9.5.1 *If the text will be read on the screen, design it for that medium.*

Like a forest or a garden or a field, an honest page of letters can absorb – and will repay – as much attention as it is given. Much type now, however, is composed not for the page but for the screen of a computer. That screen can be alive with flowing color, but the best computer monitors have dismal resolution (about 100 dpi: one sixth of the current norm for laser printers and less than 5% of the norm for professional digital typesetting). When the text is crudely rendered, the eye goes looking for distraction, which the screen is all too able to provide.

The screen mimics the sky, not the earth. It bombards the eye with light instead of waiting to repay the gift of vision. It is not simultaneously restful and lively, like a field full of flowers, or the face of a thinking human being, or a well-made typographic page. And we read the screen the way we read the sky: in quick sweeps, guessing at the weather from the changing shapes of clouds, or like astronomers, in magnified small bits, examining details. We look to it for clues and revelations more than wisdom. This makes it an attractive place for advertizing and dogmatizing, but not so good a place for thoughtful text.

The screen, in other words, is a reading environment even more fugitive than the newspaper. Intricate, long sentences full of unfamiliar words stand little chance. At text size, subtle and delicate letterforms stand little chance as well. Superscripts and subscripts, footnotes, endnotes, sidenotes disappear. In the

Some typesetting systems and word processors substitute a word space of their own for the word space on the font. When this occurs, there is nothing to correct, because the defective kerning instruction cannot be executed in the first place.

harsh light and coarse resolution of the screen, such literate accessories are difficult to see; what is worse, they dispel the essential illusion of speed. So the links and jumps of hypertext replace them. All the subtexts then can be the same size, and readers are at liberty to skip from text to text like children switching channels on TV. When reading takes this form, both sentences and letterforms retreat to blunt simplicity. Forms bred on newsprint and signage are most likely to survive. Good text faces for the screen are therefore as a rule faces with low contrast, a large torso, open counters, sturdy terminals, and slab serifs or no serifs at all.

If it has anything significant to say, a text that scrolls across the screen still needs the typographer's attention, just like any printed text. It may be that the reader, not the typographer, will actually choose the typeface. The typographer may still have some control over other factors of typographic rhythm – type size, measure, leading. Most importantly, the typographer shapes the virtual page, determining the form and frequency of heads, the orientation and placement of illustrations, the disposition of lists and paragraphs. The typographer gives outward and visible form to the text's intrinsic, invisible order. This determines, in large part, who will read the text and how.

9.5.2 *Check the type at every stage.*

Digital letterforms can be printed directly on paper with laser printers; they can be typeset onto photosensitive paper, negative film or positive film, from which lithographic printing plates, letterpress blocks or serigraphic stencils are then made; or they can be etched directly onto printing plates that run on an offset press. Each of these electrostatic and photographic transformations provides an opportunity for overexposing or underexposing the type.

Check for accurate color and sharpness in the letterforms at every stage, and check for consistency throughout. Inconsistent exposure is often encountered when the work is set a section at a time, or when corrected pages are rerun. But even when all the work is run at once on one machine, inconsistencies can occur. If, for instance, two shelf lots of film or photosensitive paper are inadvertently mixed, the same machine settings will give two different results.

Mechanical errors are also not unknown in the superficially

sanitized, high-tech world of computerized type. Many a finely tooled page has been spoiled in the end by a loose roller or unlubricated ratchet. Check the output against a grid to make sure the leading is consistent, multiple columns align as they should, and the textblock is not trapezoidal unless it is meant to be.

9.5.3 *Follow the work to the printer.*

All typographic decisions – the choice of the type, the choice of size and leading, the calculation of margins and the shaping of the page – involve assumptions about the printing. It is well to find out in advance whether these assumptions stand any chance of being fulfilled. Good printers have much else to teach their clients, and the best typographer can always find something to learn. But the path from the editor's desk to the pressroom floor remains a journey often fraught with danger and surprise. The reason is that it is frequently a journey between economic realms. On the one side, a singular thing, a manuscript, moves slowly through the hands of individual human beings – author, editor, typographer – who make judgements and decisions one by one, and who are free (for a time at least) to change their minds. On the other side, an immensely expensive commodity (blank paper) passes at great speed and irreversibly through an immensely expensive machine.

Digital methods have helped to bring editing, typography and type design back, in some respects, to the close relationship they enjoyed in the golden age of letterpress. But everything the writer, type designer, editor and typographer do is still contingent on the skills and methods of the printer – and while typography, for many, has returned to cottage scale, printing has enlarged to the dimensions of heavy industry. The freedom afforded by cheap and standardized typesetting hardware and software also comes at a price. That price is the danger of weary sameness and thinness in all the work the typographer does. The use of standard industrial papers, inks, presses and binding machinery can easily erase whatever remains of the typographer's personal touch. Yet printing is what typography is usually thought to be for.

If only by default, it falls to the typographer more than to anyone else to bridge this gap between a world focused on the perfect final proof and the world of its industrial replication. No one else works as close to that frontier as the typographer, and no one has a greater need to understand what happens on both sides.

The margins of books cannot be calculated correctly until the binding method is chosen, and they cannot be right in the end unless the chosen method is followed. The type cannot be chosen without coming to some decision about the kind of paper it will be printed on, and cannot look right in the end if that decision is later betrayed. A change of one eighth inch in the folding pattern or trim size will ruin a precisely measured page.

Yet another way to undercut the type is to print it with the wrong ink. Color control is important whether or not color is used, for there are many hues of black, some veering toward red, some veering toward blue. Redder blacks are acceptable on ivory paper. If the paper is closer to gray or white, the black of the ink should move closer to blue. But it will be process black by default – and the density of the type will be at the mercy of the press foreman's final color adjustments – if the text and process-color illustrations are printed in one go.

Ink gloss is rarely a problem on uncoated paper. On coated stock, the sheen of the ink is frequently out of control. For the sake of legibility in artificial light, inks that are used for printing text on a coated sheet should have *less* reflectivity than the paper, rather than more.

9.6 MAINTAINING THE SYSTEM

9.6.1 *Consult the ancestors.*

Typography is an ancient craft and an old profession as well as a constant technological frontier. It is also in some sense a trust. The lexicon of the tribe and the letters of the alphabet – which are the chromosomes and genes of literate culture – are in the typographer's care. Maintaining the system means more than merely buying the newest fonts from digital foundries and the latest updates for typesetting software.

The rate of change in typesetting methods has been steep – perhaps it has approximated the Fibonacci series – for more than a century. Yet, like poetry and painting, storytelling and weaving, typography itself *has not improved*. There is no greater proof that typography is more art than engineering. Like all the arts, it is basically immune to progress, though it is not immune to change. Typography at its best is sometimes as good, and at its worst is just as bad, as it ever was. The speed of certain processes has certainly increased; some old, hard tricks have come to seem easy, and some new ones have been learned. But the quality of typography and printing, their faithfulness to themselves, and the inherent grace and poise of the finished page, is not greater now than it was in 1465. In several respects, digital typography still lags far behind the methods and resources of Renaissance compositors and medieval scribes.

Maintaining the system means openness to the surprises and gifts of the future; it also means keeping the future in touch with the past. This is done by looking with equal eagerness at the old work and the new. Reproductions, of course, are fine as far as they go, but you will never know what a fifteenth-century manuscript or printed book is like until you touch one, smell one, hold one in your hands.

9.6.2 *Look after the low- as well as the high-technology end.*

A computer typesetting system is now likely to consist of three basic pieces of hardware: the computer itself (including processor, keyboard and monitor), a proofing device in the form of a low- or medium-resolution laser printer, and a high-resolution digital output device, which is often separately owned. Inside this hardware there are likely to be five interdependent pieces of software. These are the text editor or word processor, the composition and page make-up system, a library of digital fonts, a font manager, and a font editor. There may also be an assortment of electronic drawing tools and a type manipulation program for curving the baseline, shadowing, texturing, warping and other effects designed to blur the ancient boundary between text and illustration. Outside the hardware, but no less essential to the system, more primitive tools are still required: a pica stick, a sketch pad, a drawing board and instruments, and a library of reference works and examples of fine typography for discussion and inspiration. It is the latter, low-technology end of most typesetting systems that is usually in the most urgent need of upgrading.

Decisions concerning the choice of hardware and software should be made case by case – and can only be made moment by moment, given the current rate of technological change. But at least two basic principles seem clear.

The first is the principle of versatility. Fonts intended for text work should include a wide range of characters and diacritics. (For the Latin alphabet, this might mean all those listed in appendix A.) Composition systems should permit ready access to this full range of characters, and to an open set of special glyphs, whether found on additional fonts or specially made. The composition system should also permit any diacritic or combination of diacritics to be easily superimposed, at any height, upon any letter. At the compositor's discretion, it should substitute any specified ligature for any keyed sequence of letters. And of course, it should permit any line or block of text, or any character, to be conveniently placed in any position: right, left, indented, outdented, centered or justified. In short, a computerized typesetting system should not be more restrictive than hand composition.

Alternatively, fonts themselves may soon provide these basic capabilities. Digital typographers, like those who set by hand, may soon do all their micro-typographic work directly with the font, using 'typesetting programs' only for the larger-scale tasks of shaping pages, drawing boxes and causing the text to flow from box to box.

The second principle is one of quality. One good typeface is better and more useful than an infinity of poor ones. Here as always, good means several things. It means that the letterforms themselves are clearly envisioned, lucidly rendered and, beyond all that, convincing. It means they make mute, irrefutable sense to both body and mind. It means that the fabric in which these letterforms are held is well made too. If the type is metal, it means that the metal is well cast – hard, sharp, free of bubbles or sags – and evenly dressed. If the type is digital, it means that the glyphs are correctly aligned and consistently sized, with accurate widths and sensitive kerning instructions, and that the printer fonts and screen fonts match. A GX font in particular is – or it can be – an electronic artefact of immense sophistication: not only a masterpiece of design but an intangible piece of craftsmanship enriched by many skilled and often uncredited eyes and minds.

Some observers are dismayed and some excited by the complexity of the equipment most typographers now use. Some are excited and others unnerved by the evident power of that equipment and the ease of its operation. Yet inside that complexity, typography persists as what it is: the making of meaningful, durable, abstract, visible signs. When the system crashes, the craft, its purposes, its values and all its possibilities remain.

Type is idealized writing – yet there is no end of typefaces, as there is no end to visions of the ideal. The faces discussed in this chapter cover a wide historical range – Renaissance, Baroque, Neoclassical, Romantic, Modern and Postmodern. They also constitute a wide stylistic variety – formal, informal, fluid, crisp, delicate and robust. The emphasis, however, is on types I like to read and to reread. Each face shown seems to me of both historical and practical importance, and each seems to me one of the finest of its kind. Each also has its limitations. I've included some very well-known types, such as Baskerville and Palatino; some others, like Fairbank italic and Trajanus, that are undeservedly forgotten; and several that are new enough they have not yet had time to establish themselves. Some, like Photina and Vendôme, are well-known in Europe but scarce in North America; others, like Deepdene, have had just as unbalanced a reception the other way round.

I take for granted that most readers of this book will have access to font vendors' specimen books and manufacturers' catalogues. This chapter is no substitute for them. On the contrary, I hope, by pointing out some prominent landmarks and interesting hidden features, to make it easier to navigate at will through the dense fog of conflicting advertisement that gathers on the sea of letters.

Almost all faces listed in this chapter now exist in digital form, though a few are still missing essential components – text figures, for example – in their digital incarnations. Most shortcomings of this sort will soon be remedied if serious typographers make their wishes known. At the same time, some digital foundries are certain to continue making faces in abbreviated, deformed or pirated form. The presence of a typeface in this list is by no means an endorsement of any and every marketed version. (I have noted the few instances in which a font I wanted to include seemed first to require serious editing.)

Buyers of type should be aware that they are always buying a copy of someone's original design. Licensed copies are preferable to unlicensed copies for two important reasons. First, if the designer is still alive, the license implies that the fonts are being sold with the designer's permission and that royalties from the

Candido, leggiadretto, & caro guanto;
Che copria netto auorio, & fresche rose;
Chi vidi al mondo mai si dolci spoglie?
Cosi hauess'io del bel velo altretanto·
O inconstantia de l'humane cose·
Pur questo e' furto; & vie, ch'io me ne spoglie·

stro, & domino Iesu Christo. Gratias ago deo meo semper pro
uobis de gratia dei, quæ data est uobis per Christu Iesum, quod
in omnibus ditati estis per ipsum, in omni sermone, & omni co-
gnitione (quibus rebus testimonium Iesu Christi confirmatu fuit
in uobis) adeo, ut nõ destituamini in ullo dono, expectãtes reue

Nuda latus Marti, ac fulg
Thermodoontiaca munita

Le génie étonnant qui lui donna naissance.
Toi qui sus concevoir tant de plans à la fois,
A l'immortalité pourquoi perdre tes droits?

Many thousands of types, including thousands of copies of earlier
foundry types, are currently for sale. This page shows four of the thousands of excellent types that are *not* for sale. None of these fonts now exists in original form – and to the best of my knowledge, no reasonably
faithful metal copies or digital translations have been made. From top to
bottom, these faces are:

For more about
Colines, see Kay
Amert, "Origins
of the French Old
Style: The Types
of Simon de
Colines," *Printing
History* 26/27
(1992): 17–40,
and Fred
Schreiber, *Simon
de Colines* (Provo,
Utah, 1995).

1 The Petrarca Italic: a 12 pt Aldine italic designed and cut by Francesco
Griffo in 1503 for Gershom Soncino, who printed with it at Fano, on the
Adriatic coast, east of Florence.

2 The Froben Italic: a 12 pt Aldine italic cut for Johann Froben by the
unidentified Master of Basel (possibly Peter Schoeffer the Younger).
Froben started using this type in 1519.

3 The Colines St Augustin Italic [enlarged]: a 13 pt italic designed and cut
by Simon de Colines, Paris. Colines had cut several romans by the time
he finished this type, in 1528, but it may have been his first italic.

4 Firmin Didot Italic N° 1: a 12 pt Neoclassical italic cut by the 19-year-old
Firmin Didot in his father's shop in Paris, 1783.

sale are being paid. Second, the license gives some hope – though rarely a guarantee – that the fonts are not being sold in truncated or mutilated form.

10.1 NOMENCLATURE & SYNONYMY

Only one guiding principle is stated in this chapter:

10.1.1 *Call the type by its proper name if you can.*

Even the best of the older types usually come to us without distinctive names and with only meager clues to who designed them. Setting this record straight, establishing the chronology, and giving credit where credit is due is the chief work of typographic history. People who admire the old types like to talk about them too. For that purpose they need names. These are bestowed for pure convenience, but out of pure affection.

Newer types, and copies of the old ones, need names too. As objects of commerce, they are almost always named by those who sell them, with or without the designer's cooperation. Early in his career, Hermann Zapf designed a type that he called Medici. After some consultation between founder and designer, that name was scrapped. When the first fonts were advertised for sale, they were known as Palatino.

That, however, is not the end of the story. A decade after its release as a foundry and Linotype machine face, Palatino became the object of commercial envy among the manufacturers of fonts for phototype machines. Zapf's design – or rather, his two quite different designs, one for the Linotype, one for the foundry – were then copied right and left, and the copies were sold under names like Pontiac, Patina, Paladium and Malibu. A more recently plagiarized version is sold as Book Antiqua. Max Miedinger's Helvetica has been another object of widespread commercial envy, copied to this day under names such as Vega, Swiss and Geneva. Zapf's Optima is plagiarized as Oracle; Friedrich Poppl's Pontifex is plagiarized as Power, and so on.

The problem is not new. Nicolas Jenson's roman and Greek types were copied by other printers in the 1470s. So were Griffo's types, and Caslon's and Baskerville's and Bodoni's in their days. So are they now; though now, with these artists safely dead and their work in the public domain, we are free both to make the copies honest and to give them honest names.

The name Palatino alludes to the 16th-century Italian calligrapher Giovanni Battista Palatino, but the type is not based on any alphabet Palatino himself designed. The ultimate source of the name is the Mons Palatinus – the Palatine hill in Rome, site of a major temple of Apollo and of several imperial palaces.

Part of the problem is that, in most jurisdictions, type designs themselves are not effectively protected as intellectual property. Courts have not learned to distinguish between typographic artistry and typographic plagiarism. Names, however, can easily be registered as trademarks. Competitors who plagiarize designs can then be forced to give their copies different names. In the literary world, the law works the other way around. It is the substance and the text, not the title, of a story, poem or book that is protected by copyright legislation.

Other complications sometimes spring from this anomaly in the law. The first sizes and weights of Paul Renner's Futura were issued by the Bauer Foundry, Frankfurt, in 1927. The type was a commercial as well as artistic success, and other founders soon copied the design. Sol Hess at Lanston Monotype redrew the face and called it Twentieth Century; ATF sold its own imitation as Spartan. But the Futura that the Bauer Foundry had issued was a timid incarnation of Renner's original design. Renner drew many alternate characters; Bauer issued, for each letter, only the single most conventional of Renner's several forms. In 1993, when David Quay and Freda Sack at The Foundry, London, made a digital translation of Renner's original design, the conventions of the trade prevented them from calling it Futura. Their version – artistically the earliest known version of Futura, though commercially the last to be produced – is sold instead under the trade name Architype Renner. Though it was not Renner's choice, this is a serviceable name to the serious typographer, because it plays no invidious tricks and it plainly acknowledges the originating designer.

Classifying types for science and naming them for commerce are not one in the same, and they are not perhaps entirely compatible activities. There has however been at least one genuine attempt to do both at the same time. The Bitstream digital foundry, established by enthusiastic, knowledgeable people in the early days of digital typography, undertook to rationalize the naming of all its digital faces – most of which were digital reincarnations of types that already existed in other forms. Bitstream denied the cheerful fiction that digital or photographic replicas are equivalents for metal type, and so insisted that digital fonts deserved new names. Its version of Gill Sans was therefore released as Humanist 521, its version of Syntax as Humanist 531, and its version of Frutiger as Humanist 777. Méridien it catalogued as Latin 725, Metro as Geometric 415, Electra as

Transitional 521, and Perpetua as Lapidary 333. In this system, Palatino is Zapf Calligraphic 801, while Optima is Zapf Humanist 601, and Melior is called Zapf Elliptical 711. Reading the Bitstream catalogue can, as a result, be a challenging and useful exercise in typeface identification.

The balance of this chapter is a litany of names. At the beginning of each entry, the original form of the font is indicated by a simple code:

H = originally a metal type for hand composition
M = originally for machine composition in metal
P = originally designed for photosetting
D = originally designed in digital form

cordia uale

Enlargement from a 16 pt serifed type cut in central Italy in 1466–67, probably by Konrad Sweynheym. This is the second type used by Sweynheym and his partner Arnold Pannartz, who printed books with it at Rome from 1467 to 1473. Like Gudrun Zapf-von Hesse's Alcuin type, designed five centuries later, it is rooted in the Carolingian scriptorial tradition, which precedes any division between roman and italic.

10.2 SERIFED TEXT FACES

abcefghijop 123 AO *abcefghijop*

Albertina P A fine text family designed in 1965 by the Belgian calligrapher Chris Brand and issued by Monotype, not in metal but as one of their first proprietary faces for photocomposition. The forms are quiet and alert, the width economical, and the axis is that of the humanist hand. The crisp italic, with its subtly elliptical dots, slopes at a modest 5°. Albertina was designed as a multilingual family, including Latin, Cyrillic and Greek alphabets, but Monotype issued only the Latin forms. The type was issued anew in digital form by DTL in 1996, complete with its requisite text figures and both roman and italic small caps. There is a full range of weights. The Greek and Cyrillic companion faces have also been promised for future release.

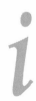

Digital translations of Aldus (on the left) and Palatino (on the right). These are two related faces designed in 1948–53 by Hermann Zapf. Selected letters are shown here for comparison at 72 pt. The basic roman alphabets (Aldus above, Palatino below) are also shown at 18 pt. (Note that neither of these cuts was ever intended to be seen at the 72 pt size. Display sizes of foundry Palatino are far more delicate than this, and Aldus is a text face for which no display sizes were designed. But the enlargements facilitate comparison.)

aa bb cc

ee ff gg

nn oo tt

CC HH

abcdefghijklmnopqrstuvwxyz
abcdefghijklmnopqrstuvwxyz
1 2 3 4 5 6 7 8 9 0
1 2 3 4 5 6 7 8 9 0
A B C D E F G H I J K L M N
A B C D E F G H I J K L M N
O P Q R S T U V W X Y Z
O P Q R S T U V W X Y Z

AO abcdefghijklmnopqrstuvwxyz

Alcuin ᴅ A strong and graceful Carolingian face designed in 1991 by Gudrun Zapf-von Hesse and issued by ᴜʀᴡ. As a genuine Carolingian, Alcuin is really neither roman nor italic, and it neither has nor needs a companion face. It is rooted in handwritten scripts that predate by 600 years the separation of roman and italic. There is, however, a full range of weights with text figures and small caps. This is everything needed for setting excellent text. The face should not be used where editorial inflexibility requires an italic. (See also pp 120, 203.)

abcefghijop 123 AO *abcefghijop*

Aldus ᴍ Roman and italic, designed in 1953 by Hermann Zapf as a text-size Linotype companion for his new foundry face, Palatino. Aldus is narrower than Palatino and has a lower midline (smaller x-height). It is a crisply sculptured and compact text face, rooted in Renaissance scribal tradition. Small caps and text figures are essential to the spirit of the face, but it needs no ligatures. Digital Aldus preserves the Linotype equality of set-width in roman and italic. Palatino, Michelangelo and Sistina are the allied titling faces, and Palatino bold can be used when a bold companion is required. Enge Aldus, a narrower version of the face produced for Linotype in 1959, does not exist in digital form. (See also pp 52, 64, 104, 226.)

abcefghijop 123 AO *abcefghijop*

Baskerville ʜ Roman and italic, designed by John Baskerville in the 1750s and cut for him by John Handy. This is the epitome of neoclassicism and eighteenth-century rationalism in type, and the face was far more popular in Republican France and the American colonies than in eighteenth-century England, where it was made.

Many of the digital faces sold under Baskerville's name are passably faithful to his designs, but small caps and text figures, often omitted, are essential to the spirit of the original, and to an even flow of text. The digital version shown above is Monotype Baskerville. At least two Cyrillic versions also exist: one produced by Monotype and one produced by ParaGraph under license from ɪᴛᴄ. (See also pp 13, 56, 77, 84, 97, 129.)

abcefghijop 123 AO *abcefghijop*

Bell ʜ The original Bell type was cut in London in 1788 by Richard Austin for a publisher named John Bell. It was warmly greeted there and in the usa and was widely used at Boston and Philadelphia in the 1790s. It remains useful for period design work, as an alternative to Baskerville. Monotype cut a facsimile in 1931, and this version has been digitized. Bell has more variation in axis than Baskerville, but it too is an English Neoclassical face. The serifs are very sharp, but the overall spirit is nevertheless closer to brick than to granite, evoking Lincoln's Inn more than St Paul's, and Harvard Yard more than Pennsylvania Avenue. Bell numerals are three-quarter height, neither hanging nor fully ranging. (See also pp 47, 129.)

abcefghijop 123 AO *abcefghijopy*

Bembo ʜ Bembo was produced by Monotype in 1929, based on a roman cut at Venice by Francesco Griffo in 1495. The fifteenth-century original had no italic, and Monotype tested two possibilities as a companion face. One was Fairbank italic; the other was the softer Bembo italic shown here. This italic is in essence a revision of Blado (the italic cut for Poliphilus), with sidelong reference to a font designed in Venice in the 1520s by Giovanni Tagliente. Bembo roman and italic are quieter and farther from their sources than Centaur and Arrighi. They are nevertheless serene and versatile faces of genuine Renaissance structure, and they have in some measure survived the transition to digital composition and offset printing. Text figures and small caps are essential. The bold fonts are irrelevant to the spirit of the face. (See also pp 51, 122, 124, 228.)

Bembo is named for the Venetian poet and historian Pietro Bembo (1470–1547), because the roman on which it is based was first used in Bembo's book *De Aetna*, published by Aldus Manutius in 1496.

abcefghijop 123 AO *abcefghijop*

Berkeley ʜ ɪᴛᴄ Berkeley is a revision of Frederic Goudy's 1938 University of California Oldstyle. The original was one of Goudy's masterpieces. The ɪᴛᴄ version, drawn by Tony Stan and issued in 1983, retains many virtues of the original type but lacks much of its character. It also lacks the text figures and small caps required by the design. Several more faithful digital revivals have been issued. These include ꜰʙ Californian, digitized by David Berlow for the Font Bureau. (See also p 208.)

abcefghijopy! AO *abcefghijopy*

Berling H Designed by the Swedish typographer and calligrapher Karl-Erik Forsberg. This face was issued in 1951 by the foundry from which it takes its name, the Berlingska Stilgjuteriet in Lund, Sweden. It is a neohumanist design, with vigorous modulation of the stroke. Ascenders and descenders are even more frequent in Swedish than in English, and Forsberg's extenders are designed to give minimal interruption to the flow of the text. They are also designed to require no ligatures. The face has a Scandinavian sharpness and clarity, with sharply beaked f, j, y and ! in the roman. The titling figures are well formed, but the text figures (seemingly omitted from all available digital cuts) are better. (See also p 84.)

abcefghijop 123 AO *abcefghijop*

Bodoni H Giambattista Bodoni of Parma, one of the most prolific of all type designers, is also the nearest typographic counterpart to Byron and Liszt. He is typography's arch-romantic. His hundreds of faces, designed between about 1765 and his death in 1813, embrace considerable variety, and more than 25,000 of his punches are in the Bodoni Museum in Parma. The revivals issued in his name reflect only a tiny part of this legacy, and many are simply parodies of his ideas. The typical features of Bodoni revivals are abrupt hairline serifs, ball terminals, vertical axis, small aperture, high contrast, and exaggerated modulation. In the absence of any true copies of Bodoni's types, many typographers prefer the Bodoni cut by Louis Hoell for the Bauer Foundry, Frankfurt, in 1924, and the Berthold Foundry version, produced in 1930. Both have now been issued in digital form. Small caps and text figures are available for both the Bauer and Berthold fonts, and they are essential to these designs. The version shown is Berthold's. (See also pp 13, 131.)

The ITC Bodonis, digitized in 1994–5 under the direction of Sumner Stone, are closest of all the revivals to Bodoni's mature style. There are three versions, based on 6, 12 and 72 pt originals.

abcefghijop 123 AO *abcefghijop*

Bulmer H William Martin of Birmingham was the brother of Robert Martin, Baskerville's chief assistant. He may have learned to cut punches from Baskerville's punchcutter John Handy and may have got his first lessons in type design from Baskerville himself. He moved to London in 1786 and in the

FB Californian (on the left) and ITC Berkeley (on the right) are both derived from Frederic Goudy's University of California Old Style. To facilitate comparison, these two cuts are shown here at slightly different sizes: 74 pt (FB Californian) and 77 pt (ITC Berkeley). Both fonts are shown at 18 pt (Californian above and Berkeley below) in the lower half of the page.

aa bb cc

ee ff gg

nn oo tt

AA HH

abcdefghijklmnopqrstuvwxyz

abcdefghijklmnopqrstuvwxyz

1234567890

1234567890

ABCDEFGHIJKLMN

ABCDEFGHIJKLMN

OPQRSTUVWXYZ

OPQRSTUVWXYZ

early 1790s started cutting types full of Baskervillean shapes yet considerably harsher than Baskerville's. The serifs were abrupt and the contrast much increased. This was the inception of English Romantic typography. Martin's types were sponsored and promoted by the printer William Bulmer, to whose name they became attached. They were copied in 1928 by Morris Benton for ATF, and then by Monotype and Intertype. Several digital versions now exist. The most comprehensive of these is the one released by Monotype in 1994.

abcefghijop 123 AO *abcefghijop*

Caecilia D Designed by Peter Matthias Noordzij and issued by Linotype in 1991. Caecilia Metella was the fourth wife of the Roman general Lucius Cornelius Sulla (*c.*138–78 BC). Sulla led the army that sacked Athens in 86 BC. On his return from that campaign, he led the winning side in the Roman civil war of 82. From 82 to 79 he held the official title of Dictator. In 81 BC, his wife Caecilia was stricken with an unidentified disease – caught, some Romans claimed, from Sulla himself. As Caecilia lay dying, her husband divorced her and had her carried out of the house to avoid contamination. A later Caecilia, also a native of Rome, is revered in the Christian tradition as the patron saint of music. The type that shares the name of these two women is a graceful, sturdy, unpretentious face, useful for text of many kinds. It is a neohumanist slab-serif, perhaps the first of its kind, with a slab-serifed true italic to match. The italic is built to Renaissance parameters, sloping at a modest 5°. Small caps and text figures are intrinsic to the design, and the face is issued in a range of weights. Licensed versions are sold as PMN Caecilia. There is no face called Sulla. (See also p 112.)

abcefghijop 123 AO *abcefghijop*

Californian H The ancestor of this face is Frederic Goudy's University of California Old Style, designed as a proprietary typeface in 1938. Lanston Monotype issued the face for general sale in 1956 under the name Californian. The digital version shown here is FB Californian, made by David Berlow and issued by the Font Bureau in Boston. It is useful to compare this with ITC Berkeley, a good yet more pasteurized version of the same original, first issued as a photocomposition face in 1983.

abcefghijop 123 AO *abcefghijop*

Caslon H William Caslon designed and cut a large number of romans, italics and non-Latin faces between 1720 and his death in 1766. His work is the typographic epitome of the English Baroque and is remarkably well preserved. He published thorough specimens, and a large collection of his punches is now in the St Bride Printing Library, London. There is not much doubt that Caslon was the first great English typecutter, and in the English-speaking world his type has long possessed the semi-legendary, unexciting status of the pipe and slippers, good used car and favorite chair. Typographic opportunists have therefore freely helped themselves to Caslon's reassuring name, and many of the faces sold as Caslons now are merely parodies. Adobe Caslon, drawn by Carol Twombly in 1989, is shown here. It is a well-made version, equipped not only with text figures and small caps, but with optional swash caps, ornaments and other antiquarian accessories. (See also pp 12, 51, 52, 66, 113, 126.)

abcefghijop 123 AO *abcefghijop*

Centaur & Arrighi H Centaur roman was designed by Bruce Rogers in 1912–14, based on the roman type cut at Venice by Nicolas Jenson in 1469. In 1928, the face was mildly sanitized in the course of transposition to the Monotype machine. Frederic Warde drew the Arrighi italic in 1925, based on a chancery font designed by the calligrapher Ludovico degli Arrighi in the 1520s. In 1929, after several revisions, Rogers chose Warde's face as the companion italic for Centaur, provoking more revisions still. The fonts are used both separately and together.

William Morris's Golden Type, cut in 1890, was the first modern attempt to recreate Jenson's roman. A more successful version was the Doves Roman, drawn by Emery Walker and cut by Edward Prince in 1900. But Walker's type has vanished just like Jenson's own. After using it for sixteen years, Thomas Cobden-Sanderson threw it surreptitiously into the Thames from Hammersmith Bridge.

Printed letterpress, Centaur and Arrighi are unrivalled in their power to re-evoke the typographic spirit of the Venetian Renaissance. In the two-dimensional world of digital composition and offset printing, this power is easily lost. The problem is aggravated by weaknesses in the digitization of Arrighi, destroying the balance achieved when the faces were married in metal.

Morris Benton's Cloister Old Style (ATF, 1913–25), George Jones's Venezia (Shanks, 1916; Linotype 1928), Ernst Detterer's Eusebius (Ludlow, 1924), Ronald Arnholm's Legacy (ITC, 1992) and Robert Slimbach's Adobe Jenson (Adobe, 1996) are other significant attempts to do some justice to the same original. (See also pp 12, 16, 67, 79, 84, 105, 122, 124, 223.)

AO abcdefghijklmnopqrstuvwxyz

Clarendon **H** Clarendon is the name of a whole genus of Victorian typefaces, spawned by a font cut by Benjamin Fox for Robert Besley at the Fann Street Foundry, London, in 1845. These faces reflect the hearty, stolid, bland, unstoppable aspects of the British Empire. They lack cultivation, but they also lack menace and guile. They squint and stand their ground, but they do not glare. In other words, they consist of thick strokes melding into thick slab serifs, fat ball terminals, vertical axis, large eye, low contrast and tiny aperture. The original had no italic, as the face had nothing of the fluent hand or sculpted nib left in its pedigree. (Stephenson Blake did however issue a sloped roman version of Besley's original Clarendon – known to them as Consort – in foundry metal in 1953.)

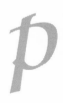

Hermann Eidenbenz drew a revival Clarendon for the Haas Foundry in Münchenstein, Switzerland, in 1951, and in 1962 the foundry finally added the light weight that transformed the series, paring it down from premodern ponderousness to postmodern insubstantiality. In this guise, as a kind of nostalgic steel frame from which all the Victorian murk has been removed, the face has many genuine uses. Monotype Clarendon lacks the presence of Haas Clarendon, which is the version shown. A related face is Morris Fuller Benton's Century Schoolbook, issued by ATF in 1924 and in machine form by Monotype in 1928. This too is now available in a light weight and in digital form. (See also pp 106, 132.)

abcefghijop 123 AO *abcefghijop*

Comenius **P** The seventeenth-century Czech theologian Jan Ámos Komenský, or Comenius, is remembered for his efforts to establish universal public education throughout Europe and for his insistence that there is no incongruity between sacred and secular learning. The typeface aptly named for him is distinguished by its lucid blend of humanist and rationalist forms. It was designed by Hermann Zapf and first released by Berthold in 1980. The axis in the roman varies, and the bowls are asymmetrical. The result is a face alive with static energy. The italic is consistent in its axis and full of vibrant motion. There are two bold weights, both graceful and dramatic in their contrast. No text figures or small caps have been issued.

Diotima roman (on the left) and the normal weight of Nofret roman (on the right): two related faces designed more than thirty years apart by Gudrun Zapf-von Hesse. Diotima was designed as a foundry face for letterpress printing. Nofret was designed for the digital medium. They are shown here for comparison at 72 pt and 18 pt, both in digital form.

aa bb cc

ee ff gg

nn oo tt

AA HH

abcdefghijklmnopqrstuvwxyz

abcdefghijklmnopqrstuvwxyz

1 2 3 4 5 6 7 8 9 0

1 2 3 4 5 6 7 8 9 0

ABCDEFGHIJKLMN

ABCDEFGHIJKLMN

OPQRSTUVWXYZ

OPQRSTUVWXYZ

abcefghijop 123 AO *abcefghijop*

Dante H Roman and italic, designed by Giovanni Mardersteig and cut by hand in steel in 1954 by Charles Malin. Monotype adapted the face for machine setting in 1957 and in the early 1990s produced a digitized version. In its foundry form, Dante is one of the great achievements of twentieth-century typography: a finely tooled and stately neohumanist roman coupled with a very lively and lucid italic. Mardersteig was the greatest modern scholar of Francesco Griffo's work, and his Dante – though not in fact a copy of any of Griffo's types – has more of Griffo's spirit than any other face now commercially available. Used with a reduced size of the upright roman capitals, Dante italic is also the nearest modern counterpart to a true Aldine italic – but the Monotype digital version is considerably coarser than its metal antecedents. Small caps and text figures are, of course, quintessential to Mardersteig's design. (See also p 133.)

abcefghijop 123 AO *abcefghijop*

Deepdene M This may be the gentlest and most lyrical of Frederic Goudy's many book faces. The aperture is larger than usual with Goudy, the x-height is modest, the axis is serenely neohumanist, and the drawing is graceful and even. Goudy drew the roman in 1927, naming it after his house in Marlborough, New York. (The house was named in turn for Deepdene Road on Long Island.) The italic – which slopes at only 3° – was completed the following year, when the face was issued by Lanston Monotype. Light as it is, the italic also has the strength to function as an independent text face. Small caps and text figures (included in the Lanston digital version) are requirements of the design. The swash characters available on supplementary fonts are less an asset than a dangerous temptation.

The baseline alignment and character fit of Lanston digital Deepdene have been edited to produce the font used here.

abcefghijop 123 AO *abcefghijop*

Diotima H Designed by Gudrun Zapf-von Hesse and cut by the Stempel Foundry, Frankfurt, in 1953. Diotima is now issued by Linotype-Hell in digital form. The roman is wide and the italic markedly narrow. There are small caps but no bold weights. The face is named for the earliest woman philosopher on record: Diotima of Mantinea, whose metaphysic of love is recited in Plato's *Symposium* by her former student, Socrates. Diotima is part of a family of faces by the same designer that has accrued over more than thirty years. Its relatives include the Nofret series, Ariadne (a font of swash initials) and the handsome inline titling face, Smaragd. (See also p 212.)

abcefghijop 123 AO *abcefghijop*

Documenta D A sturdy, plain and open text face designed by Frank Blokland and issued by the Dutch Type Library in 1993. Small caps and text figures are supplied for the full range of weights. An unserifed companion face has been designed and is scheduled for future release. (In the meantime, Gerard Daniëls's Caspari, produced by the same foundry, makes an excellent companion for Documenta.)

abcefghijop 123 AO *abcefghijop*

Electra M Several early twentieth-century book faces are creative variations on Neoclassical and Romantic form. This makes them seem, in retrospect, significant precursors of postmodern design. Three were created in the USA for the Linotype machine and became immediate staples of American publishing. One is Rudolph Růžička's Fairfield, issued in 1940. The others are W. A. Dwiggins's Electra, issued in 1935, and his Caledonia, issued in 1938. In their original Linotype form, Electra was the liveliest of the three, though in digital form this is not necessarily so. Electra was first issued with a sloped roman in lieu of an italic, but in 1940 Dwiggins himself replaced this sloped roman with the simple, crisp italic now normally used. Small caps and text figures are inherent in the design. (See also p 113.)

abcefghijop 123 AO *abcefghijop*

Elzevir H Elzevir, issued in 1993, is the Dutch Type Library's digital revival of the work of Christoffel van Dijck, based on fonts he designed and cut at Amsterdam in the 1660s. It is issued in a series of weights, with optional Baroque swash characters and ornamental ligatures. As a face designed for the digital medium, it possesses some of the force that Monotype Van Dijck – an earlier revival – possesses in metal but has lost in its digital translation. (See also p 126.)

abcefghijop 123 AO *abcefghijop*

Esprit **p** Designed by Jovica Veljović in Beograd and issued through ITC, New York, in 1985. A sharply serifed roman and italic of variable axis, large x-height and small aperture. The strokes and bowls of the lower case are full of oblique lines and asymmetric curves which add further energy to the basically rowdy Neobaroque structure. A related but somewhat simpler face is the same designer's earlier Veljović. Small caps and text figures are implicit in the design. The italic text figures, drawn long ago, have yet to be released. (See also pp 113, 135.)

AO abcdefghijklmnopqrstuvwxyz

Fairbank Italic **M** English calligrapher Alfred Fairbank designed this face in 1928 and offered it to Monotype. The corporation considered it at first as a possible companion for Monotype Bembo roman. It is narrow and has a slope of only 4°, but it is full of tensile strength, and in the estimation of Monotype's typographical advisor, Stanley Morison, even after modification by Monotype draftsmen, it overpowered the dignified, soft-spoken roman to which it was betrothed. A new and milder italic – the present Bembo italic – was cut to replace it, and Fairbank has remained a distinguished typographic loner. It can in fact be used with Bembo roman. It also functions happily alone. The italics from which it descends were used for setting extended texts, not as helpmeets to roman faces. Fairbank has the same potential – and Bembo roman caps and small caps can be used with the Fairbank lower case in the Aldine manner. It has, inexplicably, never yet been digitized. (The face is often misdescribed – against its designer's explicit wishes – as 'Bembo Condensed Italic.')

abcefghijop 123 AO *abcefghijop*

Fairfield **M** A text face designed by Rudolph Růžička for the Linotype machine and issued in 1939. Fairfield has a rationalist axis, like the Electra of Růžička's friend and colleague W.A. Dwiggins, and it remained, like Electra, a standard text face in American publishing for roughly forty years. Alex Kazcun digitized Fairfield in 1991, replacing the narrow Linotype italic *f* and *j* with kerning characters and narrowing the set of the italic. He also increased the contrast of the face (thereby delicately tilting it from a pre- to a postmodern design), added additional weights to the range, and included Růžička's alternate italic, oddly rechristened the 'caption font.'

abcefghijop 123 AO *abcefghijop*

Serifed
Text
Faces

Figural ʜ Designed by Oldřich Menhart in 1940 and finally cut and cast by the Grafotechna Foundry, Prague, in 1949. A digital version was created by Michael Gills and issued by Letraset in 1992. Menhart was the master of Expressionism in type design, and Figural is among his finest creations: a rugged but graceful roman and italic, deliberately preserving the expressive irregularity of pen-written forms. The same designer's Manuscript is similar in character but rougher, and his Monument is a congenial titling face for use with either Manuscript or Figural. Digital Figural lacks the marvellous abrasiveness of the original. It is nonetheless a fine text face for use at modest size. And for the moment, this is still the only digital incarnation of any of Menhart's faces. (See also p 109.)

abcefghijop 123 AO *abcefghijop*
C F G I T · *C F G I ℐ O Q T*

Fleischman ʜ This is a digital family based on a set of roman and italic fonts designed and cut by Johann Michael Fleischman in Amsterdam in 1738–9. Fleischman was a prolific punchcutter and typefounder, whose work, like Bodoni's, covers considerable range. In the late 1730s, he and his competitor Jacques-François Rosart both cut text fonts that are truly Rococo. The architecture of these fonts is fundamentally Baroque, but exaggerated contrast is found in the roman and italic *o* and *g*, and in all the round uppercase letters. The serifs on the caps are ostentatious and abrupt. The digital version, which includes text figures, small caps, and a large range of ornamental ligatures, was issued by ᴅᴛʟ in 1995. (See also p 128.)

abcefghijop 123 AO *abcefghijop*

Fournier ʜ The typefaces of Pierre-Simon Fournier come from the same historical period – and much the same rationalist spirit – as Baskerville's designs and Richard Austin's Bell. Yet these types are by no means all alike. Fournier's faces are as French as Bell and Baskerville are English, and Fournier's type is Fournier's, speaking subtly of the man himself.

Fournier is also famous for his use of ornaments. Like Mozart, he moves between pure, and surprisingly powerful, Neoclassicism and airy Rococo. His letters have more variation of axis than Baskerville's, his romans are a little narrower, and his italics are sharper. Late in his life, he cut some of the first condensed roman faces. And like Mozart, he delights in sliding backward from the Neoclassical forms he pioneered to the older forms of the Baroque.

In one important respect, however, Fournier turned his back on the Baroque. He cut his romans and italics as coequal, independent fonts which differ quite deliberately in x-height. In 1925, Monotype cut two separate series based on his work. These were issued in metal as Monotype Fournier and Monotype Barbou. Only the former has been digitized, but both series preserve Fournier's disparate proportioning of roman and italic. Modern editorial convention is still stuck in the Baroque and often demands that roman and italic be mixed on a single line. But Fournier should be used, I think, in Fournier's fashion, or else it should be recut. (See also p 129.)

abcefghijop 1 2 3 AO *abcefghijop*

Galliard P Galliard was once the name of a type size – 9 pt – as well as a dance and its musical form. The family of type now known by this name was designed by Matthew Carter, issued by Mergenthaler in 1978, and later licensed by ITC. It is a crisp, formal but energetic roman and italic, based on the designs of the sixteenth-century French typecutter Robert Granjon. Enough of Granjon's work survives, both in steel and in print, to prove that he was one of the finest punchcutters who ever lived. Galliard is Carter's homage to the man as well as to his work. It is also the preeminent example of a Mannerist revival typeface. Text figures and small caps are implicit in the design. For period typography, sets of Mannerist ligatures and swash capitals are available. The best of the several digital versions appears, not surprisingly, to be Carter's own, released in 1992 by Carter & Cone. The obvious titling face is Carter's Mantinia, another homage to an artist of extraordinary intellect, precision and exemplary technical skill. (See also p 125.)

Garamond ʜ Claude Garamond (or Garamont), who died in 1561, was one of several great typecutters at work in Paris during the early sixteenth century. His teacher, Antoine Augereau, and his gifted contemporaries are remembered now only by scholars, while Garamond suffers posthumous fame. Many of his punches and matrices survive in museum collections, and

his style is not hard to learn to recognize. This has not prevented people from crediting him with type he could not possibly have designed and would not, perhaps, have admired.

Garamond's romans are stately High Renaissance forms with humanist axis, moderate contrast and long extenders. He cut several beautiful italics as well, with some of the first sloped capitals, but he took no apparent interest in the radical new idea of pairing italics with romans. Revivals of his roman faces are often mated instead with italics based on the work of his younger colleague Robert Granjon. Three Garamond and Garamond/Granjon revivals worthy of serious consideration are:

1 Stempel Garamond, issued by the Stempel foundry in 1924 and later digitized by Linotype;
2 Granjon, drawn by George William Jones and issued by Linotype in 1928 – now also in the Linotype digital library – and
3 Adobe Garamond, drawn by Robert Slimbach, issued in digital form by Adobe in 1989.

Jan Tschichold's Sabon, listed separately on page 231, is also closely based on Garamond's originals. Small caps and text figures are available for all of these versions and are quintessential to the designs.

18 pt Stempel
Garamond

18 pt Linotype
Granjon

18 pt Adobe
Garamond

abcefghijop 123 AO *abcefghijop*

abcefghijop 123 AO *abcefghijop*

abcefghijop 123 AO *abcefghijop*

Stempel Garamond is the only one of these in which the italic as well as the roman is based on a genuine Garamond. (The model used, Garamond's *gros romain* italic, is reproduced on page 74.) The rhythm and proportions of the Stempel italic are, however, much changed from the original.

An entirely separate strain of designs, based on the work of Jean Jannon, is also sold under the name Garamond. These are discussed in the following entry. (See also pp 101, 122, 220.)

Jannon H Jean Jannon, born in 1580, was the earliest of the great typographic artists of the European Baroque. He was also a French Protestant, printing illegally in a Catholic regime, and the type he cut and cast during the early seventeenth century was seized in 1641 by agents of the French crown. (Jannon may later have been reimbursed.) After two centuries in storage, it was revived and misidentified as the work of Claude Garamond. The surviving punches are still at the Imprimerie Nationale, Paris.

Prowling the Specimen Books

Jannon's type is elegant and disorderly: of widely varying axis and slope, sharply serifed and asymmetrical. The best revivals of these lovely, distinctly non-Garamondian letters are:

1 ATF 'Garamond,' drawn by M.F. Benton and issued in 1918–20;
2 Lanston's 'Garamont,' which was drawn by Frederic Goudy and issued in 1921;
3 Monotype 'Garamond,' issued in 1922; and
4 Simoncini 'Garamond,' drawn by Francesco Simoncini and issued in metal by the Simoncini Foundry, Bologna, in 1958.

Monotype has been particularly thorough in Jannon's case, issuing two different cuts of italic, both in metal and in digital form. Monotype 156, in which the slope of the caps varies rambunctiously, is closer to Jannon's originals. Monotype 176 was the corporate revision: an attempt to bring the unrepentant French typecutter, or at least his italic upper case, back into line. But irregularity lies at the heart of the Baroque, and at the heart of Jannon's letters, just as it may lie at the heart of his refusal to conform to the state religion of his day. I prefer Monotype 156 italic (called 'alternate' in digital form) for that reason.

abcefghijop 123 AO *abcefghijop*
abcefghijop 123 AO *abcefghijop*

18 pt Monotype 'Garamond'

18 pt Simoncini 'Garamond'

Yet another version of Jannon's type is sold as 'Garamond 3.' This is the ATF 'Garamond' of 1918 as adapted in 1936 for the Linotype machine, now re-revised for digital composition. It is perfectly serviceable as a text face, but it lacks both the slightly disheveled grace of Monotype 'Garamond' and the more carefully combed and erect grace of the Simoncini version.

As issued, Simoncini Garamond lacks text figures and small caps. They have been added to the version shown here.

ITC 'Garamond,' designed in the 1970s by Tony Stan, also has nothing to do with Garamond's type. It is a radically distorted form of Jannon's: distant from the spirit of the Baroque and the Renaissance alike. (See also pp 101, 126, 220.)

Stempel Garamond roman (on the left) is indeed based on the work of Claude Garamond. Monotype 'Garamond' (on the right) is based on the work of Jean Jannon. These two excellent types come from different centuries and spirits as well as different hands and surely merit different names. They are shown here side by side, the Stempel at 70 pt and the Monotype at 78 pt, and one above the other, both at 18 pt.

aa dd ee

ff oo *oo*

rr *kk* xx

AA HH

abcdefghijklmnopqrstuvwxyz
abcdefghijklmnopqrstuvwxyz
1 2 3 4 5 6 7 8 9 0
1 2 3 4 5 6 7 8 9 0
ABCDEFGHIJKLMN
ABCDEFGHIJKLMN
OPQRSTUVWXYZ
OPQRSTUVWXYZ

abcefghijop 123 AO *abcefghijop*

Haarlemmer **M** This is a Bible type – which is to say, a plain face with large x-height – designed by Jan van Krimpen for Monotype in 1938 to fulfill a private commission. It was translated to digital form and issued by the Dutch Type Library in 1996. In essence, it is big-eyed Spectrum. Frank Blokland recently designed an unserifed companion face which is now in private use and scheduled for release in 1998.

abcefghijop 123 AO *abcefghijop*

Hollander **D** Few things are more useful in the typographic world than plain, sturdy, unpretentious and good-natured fonts of type. Hollander is one of several families of such type designed by Gerard Unger. It was completed in 1983, issued in 1986 by Rudolf Hell and is now manufactured by Elsner + Flake. The same designer's Swift (1985) and Oranda (1992) are similar. Hollander has greater bulk than Swift but also sharper serifs. It therefore suffers more from harsh commercial treatment (low resolution, low-grade presswork, low-grade paper).

Jannon See p 219.

Janson See *Kis*, p 223.

abcefghijop 123 AO *abcefghijop*

Jenson **H** Many types of many kinds claim to be inspired by the roman cut at Venice in 1469 by Nicolas Jenson. Some of these derivatives are masterpieces; others are anything but. Bruce Rogers's Centaur is deservedly the best known recreation of Jenson's roman, but Monotype's digital Centaur is a two-dimensional ghost of Rogers's three-dimensional homage to the original Jenson type. Adobe Jenson, drawn by Robert Slimbach and issued in 1995, retraces Rogers's steps and also Frederic Warde's. The italic is based on the same model as Warde's Arrighi italic – a separate design later revised to serve as Centaur's italic. When only the digital fonts are compared, it is clear – to me at least – that Adobe Jenson has better balance between roman and italic and is generally more tolerant of the fundamental flimsiness of two-dimensional printing, though it is otherwise when the two are printed letterpress (using polymer plates for Adobe Jenson). Other families of type with which these should be compared are M.F. Benton's Cloister and Ronald Arnholm's Legacy. (Adobe Jenson and Cloister are closer than Adobe Jenson and Centaur in some interesting respects.) Adobe Jenson is a multiple-master face, scalable both for weight and optical size. Small caps and text figures are essential. There is also a swash italic. (See also pp 16, 112, 223.)

Serifed Text Faces

abcefghijop 123 AO *abcefghijop*

Joanna **H** Designed by the English artist Eric Gill and cut by the Caslon Foundry, London, in 1930. The Monotype version was produced in 1937. This is a face of spartan simplicity, with flat serifs and very little contrast but considerable variation in stroke axis. The italic has a slope of only 3° and is full of roman forms, but it is sufficiently narrower than the roman to minimize confusion. Text figures are essential to Gill's design. Gill Sans is an obvious and very satisfying companion face.

abcefghijop 123 AO *abcefghijop*

Journal **D** A rough and eminently readable face designed by Zuzana Ličko, issued in 1990 by Emigre. Text figures and small caps are part of the design. There is a wide version known as Journal Ultra as well as a range of weights. (See also p 134.)

abcefghijop 123 AO *abcefghijop*

Kennerley **H** This was Frederic Goudy's first successful typeface, designed in 1911. (Goudy was 46 at the time, but his career as a type designer was just beginning.) By his own account, the designer wanted a new type with some of the flavor of Caslon – and Kennerley has Caslon's homey unpretentiousness, though it has returned to Renaissance forms for its underlying architecture and many of its structural details. The italic was drawn seven years after the roman, but Goudy had found his style; the two mate well. The text figures and small caps required by the design are included in Lanston's excellent digital version.

(The spelling 'Kennerly' appears in some type catalogues, but the face was commissioned by and named for the American publisher Mitchell Kennerley, 1878–1950.)

abcefghijop 123 AO *abcefghijnop*

Kis ʜ The Hungarian Miklós Kis is a major figure in Dutch typography, as well as that of his own country. He spent most of
the 1680s in Amsterdam, where he learned the craft and cut
some wonderfully toothy and compact Baroque type. But for
many years Kis's work was incorrectly ascribed to the Dutch
punchcutter Anton Janson. Commerce has no conscience, and
to this day, Kis's type is sold, even by people who know better,
under Janson's name.

Some of Kis's original punches and matrices found their
way to the Stempel Foundry in Frankfurt, and Stempel Janson
is in consequence Kis's actual type, with German sorts (ä, ß, ü,
etc) added by other hands. Linotype Janson was cut in 1954,
based on the Kis originals, under the supervision of Hermann
Zapf. Monotype Janson and Monotype Erhardt are also adapted – less successfully, I think – from Kis's designs. Linotype
Janson Text (1985) likewise seems to me the most successful
digital version. It was prepared under the supervision of Adrian
Frutiger, based on Kis's originals and on Zapf's excellent Linotype machine version. (See also p 126.)

abcefghijop (;!) 123 AO *abcefghijop*

17 pt ɪᴛᴄ Legacy

abcefghijop (;!) 123 AO *abcefghijop*

20 pt Monotype
Centaur & Arrighi

abcefghijop (;!) 123 AO *abcefghijop*

20 pt Adobe
Jenson

Legacy ᴅ Ronald Arnholm's Legacy (ɪᴛᴄ, 1992) is, I think, the
blandest of the many twentieth-century attempts to give new,
two-dimensional life to the old three-dimensional type of the
master typographer Nicolas Jenson. Blandness is not always a
disadvantage in a printing type, however, and Legacy is of interest on other grounds. It marries a redrawing of Jenson's roman
with a redrawing of one of Garamond's italics, rather than one
of Arrighi's, and it is the only revival of Jenson's roman that exists in both unserifed and serifed forms. The model underlying
the roman is reproduced here on page 16 and the model underlying the italic on page 74. Legacy has a substantially larger eye
than either, and in this respect it violates both Jenson's and
Garamond's sense of proportion. It is nevertheless a family with
many merits and uses. (See also p 243.)

abcefghijop 123 AO *abcefghijop*
abcefghijop 123 AO *abcefghijop*
bpbpbpbpbpbpbpbpbpbpbpbp

Lexicon D Designed by Bram de Does in 1992 and issued in digital form by the Enschedé Font Foundry. Lexicon was commissioned, as the name suggests, for a new Dutch dictionary. It was therefore designed to be as compact as a Bible type but to function in a range of sizes and to allow many shades and degrees of emphasis. There are six weights of roman and italic, with roman and italic small caps in every weight. Each weight of roman and italic also exists in separate forms, known as Lexicon 1 and 2. The former has short extenders, the latter extenders of normal length. Lexicon 2A (the light weight with normal extenders) makes an excellent text face for a variety of uses, and Lexicon 1B (the second weight with short extenders) an excellent companion face for notes and other compact matter.

abcefghijop 123 AO *abcefghijop*

LinoLetter D A full family designed by André Gürtler and colleagues and issued in 1991 by Linotype-Hell. The merits of this face are its bony plainness and the presence of all its parts. Fonts of every weight and form (roman, italic and small caps) are sold with the text figures in position, ready for work. Only the currency signs are peculiarly large, as if money mattered most. Like Gürtler's earlier Egyptian 505 (released in film form in 1966), LinoLetter mates heavy, blunt serifs with a modulated stroke. It brings a touch of grace to a sturdy old structure – the Victorian slab-serif – and is useful for setting much plain text.

abcefghijopz 123 AO *abcefghijop*

Manuscript H Designed by Oldřich Menhart in the midst of World War II and issued by Grafotechna, Prague, in 1951. Manuscript is even rougher than the same designer's Figural, but its rough forms are painstakingly chosen and juxtaposed. The roman and italic are perfectly balanced with each other and within themselves. The numerals are large, but their heights are uneven. The family – still, alas, undigitized – includes a Cyrillic companion face.

abcefghijop 123 AO *abcefghijop*

Mendoza D Designed by José Mendoza y Almeida, Paris, and released by ITC in 1991. This is a forceful and resilient neohumanist text face with low contrast and a spartan finish, closer in some ways to the tough and lovely text romans and italics of sixteenth-century Paris than anything else now to be found in digital form. Mendoza prospers under careful handling but is robust enough to survive printing conditions lethal to other text faces. Small caps and text figures are implicit in the design, but the ligatures are best forgotten. There is also an extensive range of weights. (See also pp 52, 101, 108, 112.)

abcefghijop 123 AO *abcefghijop*

Méridien H This was Adrian Frutiger's first text face, designed in 1954 and cut by Deberny & Peignot, Paris, for hand composition. The serifs are triangular and abrupt but subtly inflected. The eye of the face is large, but the italic has impeccable balance and flow. The roman caps, which have unusual authority and poise, make an excellent titling face in themselves. The same designer's Frutiger makes a useful sanserif companion. There is a range of weights, but there are no small caps or text figures. These and a less bashful roman *f* would be welcome additions to this strong and beautiful face. (See also pp 58, 101, 105.)

abcefghijop 123 AO *abcefghijop*

Minion D Designed by Robert Slimbach, San Francisco, and issued by Adobe in 1989. In 1991, it was reissued in multiple master form. Minion is a fully developed neohumanist text family. It is also, in the typographic sense, remarkably economical to set. That is to say that it gives, size for size, a few more characters per line than most text faces without appearing squished or compressed. Small caps and text figures are essential to the design, and these are available across the range: in roman and italic of several weights. The family includes a font of typographic ornaments, swash characters, and a Cyrillic. Upright and cursive Minion Greek exists in trial form but has not yet been released. Slimbach's chancery italic, Poetica, is another useful companion face. (Minion is the face in which this book is set. See also pp 106, 107, 263.)

abcefghijop 123 AO *abcefghijop*

e

Nofret D Designed by Gudrun Zapf-von Hesse and issued by Berthold in 1987. This is a text family related to, but more varied than, the same designer's Diotima and Carmina. Nofret is substantially narrower than Diotima in the roman lower case, but of similar width in the italic. There is a range of weights, and even the heaviest of these retain their grace.

In the nineteenth century, dark, abruptly serifed (and distinctly unfeminine) faces were commonly called egyptians. Twentieth-century faces with similar structure have been given names like Memphis, Cairo and Karnak. Nofret, which is named for Nefertiti, is a queenly face, though not in the typographic sense really an egyptian. Small caps and text figures are readily available and implicit in the design. (See also p 135.)

abcefghijop 123 AO *abcefghijop*

e

Officina D Designed by Eric Spiekermann and colleagues, and issued in 1990 through ITC. This is a narrow and plain yet robust text face, inspired by the typewriter and useful for setting much matter that would, in an earlier age, have stayed in typescript form. It is sturdy enough to withstand rough treatment (low-grade laser printing, for example) yet sufficiently well-built to prosper under better printing conditions. There is a sanserif counterpart. Cyrillic versions of Officina Serif and Sans alike were designed in 1994 by Tagir Safaev and issued in digital form by ParaGraph.

48 pt foundry Palatino, reduced

abcefghijop 123 AO *abcefghijop*

18 pt Linotype digital Palatino

abcefghijop 123 AO *abcefghijop*

18 pt Linotype digital Aldus

abcefghijop 123 AO *abcefghijop*

Palatino H/M Designed in 1948 by Hermann Zapf. Palatino roman was first cut by hand by August Rosenberger at the Stempel Foundry, Frankfurt, then adapted by its designer for the Linotype machine. In photo and digital form, it has become the most widely used of all neohumanist faces, among typographic professionals and amateurs alike. As the most universally admired of Zapf's designs, it is also the most heavily pirated. In its authentic incarnations, Palatino is a superbly balanced, powerful and graceful contribution to typography – but its close relative, Aldus, which was designed expressly for text setting, is often a better choice for that purpose, in company with Palatino as a display face. There is a bold weight, designed in 1950. A bold italic was added, evidently to combat existing forgeries, nearly thirty years later. The extended Palatino family includes two sets of display capitals (Michelangelo and Sistina), a text Greek (Heraklit) and Greek capitals (Phidias). Small caps and text figures are essential to the face.

Because it was first designed as a display face for handsetting in metal, then adapted for use in text sizes on the Linotype machine, there are two fundamentally different yet authentic versions of Palatino italic. There is a wide version, originally matching the roman letter-for-letter in set-width, as required by the Linotype machine, and a narrower, more elegant version intended for hand composition. The Linotype italic (actually the first to be issued) has better readability in sizes of 10 pt and below, but the best digital fonts for larger sizes – in both roman and italic – are based on the large foundry designs. (See also pp 15, 59, 77, 97, 104, 133, 201, 204, 238.)

abcefghijop 123 AO *abcefghijop*

Photina P A text face with predominantly rationalist axis, small aperture and narrow set-width but unmistakable calligraphic energy. It was designed by José Mendoza y Almeida and first issued by Monotype in 1972 for photocomposition. There is a range of weights, and the bold versions are gracefully designed. Photina's proportions are deliberately close to those of Univers, which makes an excellent sanserif companion. This is one of the first and one of the finest postmodern text faces. It was of little use in digital form until the text figures and small caps it requires became available at last, in the year 2000.

AO 123 AO *abcdefghijklmnopqrstuvwxyz* *eaqbabefeghghijklnop QUA stym*

Poetica D A chancery italic designed by Robert Slimbach and issued by Adobe in 1992. The basic family consists of four variations on one italic, with varying amounts of swash. There are

Bembo (on the left) and Poliphilus (on the right): two attempts at reproducing a fifteenth-century Venetian type in twentieth-century terms. Both of these types are based on the same original lower case, but on two different sets of original capitals. They are shown here at 74 pt and at 18 pt. (Poliphilus, of course, was never meant to be seen in public enlarged to this degree. The largest available size in metal matrix form is 16 pt.)

aa bb cc

ee ff gg

nn oo tt

AA CC

abcdefghijklmnopqrstuvwxyz
abcdefghijklmnopqrstuvwxyz

1 2 3 4 5 6 7 8 9 0

1 2 3 4 5 6 7 8 9 0

A B C D E F G H I J K L M N
A B C D E F G H I J K L M N
O P Q R S T U V W X Y Z
O P Q R S T U V W X Y Z

228

also five fonts of swash capitals, two of alternate lowercase letters, two fonts of lowercase initials, two of lowercase terminals, two sets of small caps (ornamented and plain), a font of fractions and standard ligatures, another of ornamental ligatures, one font of analphabetic ornaments, and one font entirely of ampersands. The basic face is a plain neohumanist italic, well suited for extended text. The supplementary fonts permit any desired amount of ostentation. (See also p 125.)

abcefghijop 123 AO *abcefghijop*

Poliphilus & Blado **H** Poliphilus means 'Multiple Love.' This is the name of the lead character in Francesco Colonna's fantasy novel *Hypnerotomachia Poliphili*, "The Dream-Fight of Poliphilus," which Aldus Manutius printed in 1499 using a newly revised roman type by Francesco Griffo. In 1923, Monotype attempted to copy this font for use on their machine. The result was Monotype Poliphilus. It was an early experiment in the resuscitation of Renaissance designs, and the Monotype draftsmen copied the actual letterpress impression, including much of the ink squash, instead of paring back the printed forms to restore what the punchcutter had carved. The result is a rough, somewhat rumpled yet charming face, like a Renaissance aristocrat, unshaven and in stockinged feet, caught between the bedroom and the bath. A second experiment in the same direction produced a very different result: Monotype Bembo, which is based on an earlier state of the same original: the same lower case with an earlier set of capitals. The differences between lowercase Monotype Bembo and Poliphilus, great as they are, are entirely differences of interpretation, not of design.

Blado, the italic companion to Poliphilus, is based not on one of Griffo's own superb italics but on a font designed by Ludovico degli Arrighi about 1526. (Arrighi died soon after finishing this type – probably his sixth italic – and it was acquired by the typographer Antonio Blado of Rome. No type called Arrighi existed when the 1923 revival was made, but Monotype chose nonetheless to name it for its printer, not its designer.)

abcefghijop 123 AO *abcefghijop*

Pontifex **P** Designed by Friedrich Poppl in Wiesbaden and issued in 1976 by Berthold in Berlin. Pontifex is one of several eminent twentieth-century faces built on Mannerist lines. The others include Adrian Frutiger's Méridien, Georg Trump's Trump Mediäval, and Matthew Carter's Galliard. These are four quite different faces, designed by four quite different artists for three different typographic media, but they share several structural presumptions. All have a humanist axis in the roman but an unusually large x-height, a tendency toward sharpness, angularity and tension in the conformation of individual letters, and a considerable slope – 12° to 14° – in the italic. These are features inherited from French Mannerist typecutters such as Jacques de Sanlecque, Guillaume Le Bé and Robert Granjon. Galliard is in fact a revival of Granjon's letters, while Pontifex, Trump and Méridien are independent modern creations sympathetic in spirit to the earlier Mannerist work. Together, these faces demonstrate the considerable range and depth of what one could call the neomannerist aspect of the Modernist tradition. (See also pp 78, 133.)

abcefghijop 123 AO *abcefghijop*

Romanée н Designed by Jan van Krimpen and cut in steel by Paul Helmuth Rädisch at the Enschedé Foundry in Haarlem, Netherlands. The roman owes much to the spirit of Garamond. Van Krimpen designed it in 1928 as a companion for an italic cut in the middle of the seventeenth century by another of Garamond's admirers, Christoffel van Dijck. But Van Krimpen remained dissatisfied with the relationship between the two faces, cut in the same land three hundred years apart. In 1948 he designed an italic of his own to go with Romanée roman. The new italic is distinguished by its prominent descenders, serifed on both sides, and it has much less slope than the italic of Van Dijck. Like the italics of the early sixteenth century – and unlike the italics of both Garamond and Van Dijck – it mates a cursive lower case with upright capitals.

"United they fall, apart they stand as fine designs," said Van Krimpen's younger colleague, Sem Hartz. And it is true that Romanée italic stands very well on its own. Perhaps these faces are best used in the Renaissance manner – not the manner of Van Dijck but the manner of Garamond, his predecessors and colleagues – with the italic set in separate passages rather than laced into the midst of roman text. Digital Romanée, though it has now existed for years, is still awaiting commercial release.

abcefghijop 123 AO *abcefghijop*

Sabon H/M Designed by Jan Tschichold. The foundry version was issued by Stempel in 1964, followed by Monotype and Linotype machine versions in 1967. The series consists of a roman, italic, small caps and semibold, based broadly on the work of Claude Garamond and his pupil Jacques Sabon, who was once employed, after Garamond's death, to repair and complete a set of his teacher's punches. The structure of the letterforms is faithful to French Renaissance models, but Tschichold's face has a larger eye than any but the tiniest sizes cut by Garamond. The type was intended as a general-purpose book face, and it serves this purpose extremely well, though it is bland in comparison with Garamond's originals. (See also pp 52, 104.)

abcefghijop 123 AO *abcefghijopy*

Scala D A crisp, neohumanist text face with sharp serifs and low contrast, designed by Martin Majoor in the 1980s for the Vredenburg concert hall in Utrecht. (This may explain why it is named after an opera house in Milan.) It was publicly issued by FontShop International, Berlin, in 1991. This face has many of the merits of Eric Gill's Joanna – not to mention several merits distinctively its own – without Joanna's eccentricities. Small caps and text figures are implicit in the design – and the basic licensed fonts of FF Scala come pre-equipped with text figures and a full set of ligatures, as if they were really meant for setting type instead of merely typing. There is also an unserifed branch of the family. (See also pp 246, 248–249.)

AO abcdefghijklmnopqrstuvwxyz

Silica D One of the typographic achievements of the late twentieth century is the humanization of the slab-serif letter, which was condemned in the nineteenth century to use in brutal advertising alone. Among the newer and more livable slab-serifed faces are Gerard Unger's Oranda, Matthias Noordzij's Caecilia, and this face, the Silica of Sumner Stone, issued by the Stone Foundry in 1993. The head serifs of Silica are angled like those of a Renaissance roman. There are, however, no text figures, no small caps and no italic. It is a purist face in its way: a solitary alphabet made in many weights.

231

abcefghijop 12369 AO *abcefghijop*

Spectrum H/M Designed in the 1940s by Jan van Krimpen and issued by both Enschedé and Monotype in 1952. This was Van Krimpen's last general text face, and it is now the one most widely used. The roman and italic are reserved, elegant and well matched. The axis is humanist, the aperture large, and the serifs simultaneously sharp and flat (a feature neither unwelcome nor contradictory in typography). Small caps and the distinctive Spectrum text figures, with their very short extenders, are essential to the design. A semibold was added by Sem Hartz and cut by Monotype in 1972. (See also p 133.)

abcefghijop 123 AO *abcefghijop*

Stone Serif D Designed by Sumner Stone, issued in digital form by Adobe in 1987, and in 1989 through ITC. Stone is an extended family, consisting of serifed roman and italic, unserifed roman and italic, and a so-called 'informal' roman and italic, all in a wide range of weights. Informal in this case means that the contrast is reduced, the serifs are flattened, thickened and shortened, a few serifs are amputated entirely from the upper case, and cursive forms of *a* and *g* have slipped, like vacationing italics, into the otherwise proper company of the roman.

The structural dissonances between the basic text face (known as Stone Serif) and Stone Informal, make it questionable whether the two can function usefully together without a differential in size, but the two remaining permutations – Serif plus Sans, or Informal plus Sans – cause no such interference. Their structural similarities hold them together, while their differences in finish make it easy to tell them apart.

The foreshortened terminals on *a, f* and *r,* and the abnormally large x-height, give the roman a rather Edwardian tone, not dispelled by its sharp detailing. In Stone Informal, this premodern aura is reinforced by the blunted serifs. Given the large eye and general absence of humanist spirit, the face can function without text figures and small caps, but these are part of the original design and have now been manufactured and released. A matching set of phonetic characters, designed by John Renner and issued by Adobe, makes the Stone family useful for a range of academic work – and this makes the small caps and text figures more useful as well. (See also p 247.)

abcefghijop 123 AO *abcefghijop*

Swift D Designed by Gerard Unger and first issued in 1987 by Rudolf Hell in Kiel. Swift is avowedly a newspaper type, but it has many additional uses. The eye is large and the set is narrow, but the letters are crisp and open, with chisel-tipped, wedge-shaped terminals and serifs. The axis is humanist and the aperture large. The italic is taut and fluent, with a slope of 6°. The torso of these letterforms is large enough that Swift can function well without text figures and small caps, but these have now been issued by Elsner + Flake. The same designer's sanserif Praxis, and his erect sanserif italic Flora, make useful companion faces for Swift.

abcefghijop 123 AO *abcefghijop*

Trajanus H/M Designed by Warren Chappell, issued in 1939 as a foundry face by Stempel and in machine form by Linotype. The angular, black forms of Trajanus echo the early humanist scripts of the Renaissance and some of the earliest roman printing types, used in Italy and Germany until they were superseded by the early Venetian whiteletter and then by the Aldine roman and italic. But Trajanus is a remarkably graceful face, and the roman is matched by an equally crisp and fluent italic. The figures are three-quarter height. There is a companion bold face designed by Chappell and a Trajanus Cyrillic designed by Hermann Zapf. Chappell's own sanserif, Lydian, is another related design, slightly darker than Trajanus but of similar angularity. With the industry's conversion to PostScript and TrueType, this robust, handsome face temporarily disappeared. Linotype at last issued a digital version in 1997.

Trinité P A text family designed in 1978–81 by Bram de Does for the Enschedé Foundry in Haarlem. The commission began with a challenge: to create in the elastic and ephemeral world of phototype something as resonant and reserved as the handcut metal types of Jan van Krimpen. The impressive result was issued in film form in 1982 by Bobst/Autologic in Lausanne but never effectively distributed. Trinité was issued again in digital form by the Enschedé Font Foundry in 1991.

There are three weights of wide roman, two weights of narrow roman, two weights of small caps and two weights of italic.

Q ábbbçdddêfffggg O
(hhhijijijkkklllmñòppp)
A qqqrstüvwxyyyž IJ
+ 1234567890 =

Q ábbbbçddddê̂ffffgggg O
{hhhhijijijkkkkllllmñòpppp}
A qqqqrstüvwxyyyž IJ
+ 1234567890 =

Q ábbbçdddêfffggg O
(hhhijijijkkklllmñòppp)
A qqqrstüvwxyyyž IJ
+ 1234567890 =

Trinité roman wide (above), italic (center) and roman narrow (below).
All three ranges of each roman face are shown together, and all four
ranges of the italic. In each range, only the extending letters vary.

All weights and widths of roman and italic come in three ranges: with short, normal and long extenders. The capitals remain the same in height; so does the torso of the lower case, but the extenders range to different depths and altitudes. Both weights of italic are also issued in chancery form (with curved extenders). The ordinary roman (Trinité 2, with the normal extenders, in either the wide or the narrow width) makes a fine text face for conventional use. The wide version is 9% wider than the narrow and keeps the same internal rhythm. (In wide and narrow versions alike, for example, the set-widths of the roman letters *i*, *n* and *m* are in exactly the proportion 1 : 2 : 3.) The roman letters slope at 1°, the italics at 3°.

There are no separate characters for ligatures in Trinité. They construct themselves from parts. The *f* + *i* and *f* + *j*, for instance, combine to form the ligatures *fi* and *fj*. (This is the reason for the dancing dots on *i* and *j* in different versions of the face. In Trinité 1 and 2, the dots meld with the arch of the *f*. In Trinité 3, the tallest version, the dots tuck under the arm of *f* instead.) In its present form, with pi fonts, expert sets and other variants, the full family consists of 81 separate digital fonts. Half a dozen of these would be ample for many normal texts. The technical complexities of the series ought not to obscure the simple beauty of the face, which is rooted in the heritage of Van Krimpen and of Italian Renaissance forms. Even the arithmetical signs in Trinité have a slight scribal asymmetry. This is sufficient to enliven the forms for text use yet not enough to render them disfunctionally ornate. Small caps and text figures are essential components of the family.

abcefghijop 123 AO *abcefghijop*

Trump Mediäval H/M Designed by Georg Trump. This was first issued in 1954 by the Weber Foundry, Stuttgart, as a foundry type and in machine form by Linotype. It is a strong, angular roman and italic with humanist axis but Mannerist torque and proportions. The aperture is moderate; the serifs are substantial and abrupt. The numerals, both in text form and in titling form, are notably well designed. There is a range of weights but only a partial set of ligatures. A number of Georg Trump's excellent script faces – Codex, Delphin, Jaguar, Palomba and Time Script, for example – and his slab-serif, City, are potentially useful as companions. (See also pp 52, 84.)

abcefghijop 123 AO *abcefghijop*

Van den Keere ʜ This is a family of digital romans, modelled on a 21 pt font that Hendrik van den Keere of Ghent cut in 1575 for Christophe Plantin of Antwerp. There are several weights, all with the requisite small caps and other components. But in his long, illustrious career as a punchcutter, Van den Keere did not cut a single italic. The italic paired here with his roman is based on the work of his older friend and colleague François Guyot. The digital versions of these types were produced by Frank Blokland in 's-Hertogenbosch and issued by the Dutch Type Library in 1995–97. (See also p 122.)

abcefghijop 123 AO *abcefghijop*

Van Dijck ʜ The family now called Van Dijck – first issued by Monotype in 1935 – is based on an italic cut about 1660 by Christoffel van Dijck and a roman which is probably also his. (The italic survives; the roman is known only from printed specimens.) These are calm and graceful Dutch Baroque faces, modest in x-height, narrow in the italic and relatively spacious in the roman. A comparison of Van Dijck with Kis shows some of the range of Dutch Baroque typographic tradition. Van Dijck's type has some of the industrious serenity found in the work of his great contemporaries, the painters Pieter de Hooch and Jan Vermeer. The digital version of Monotype Van Dijck has, however, lost much of the power and resiliency of the Monotype metal version. (The Dutch Type Library's Elzevir is another, more recent attempt to rekindle the spirit of Van Dijck in digital form. See also pp 51, 192.)

abcefghijop 123 AO *abcefghijop*

Veljović ᴘ Designed by Jovica Veljović and issued in 1984 by ɪᴛᴄ. Veljović is a lively postmodern face, with much inherent movement wrapped around its rationalist axis, and much prickly energy emerging in the long, sharp, abrupt wedge serifs. There is a wide range of weights. Small caps and text figures, though part of the original design, do not appear to be obtainable from any licensed source. Veljović makes an excellent companion for the same designer's Gamma or Esprit and can be mated with his fine script face Ex Ponto. (See also p 15.)

abcefghijop 123 AO *abcefghijop*

abcefghijop 123 AO *abcefghijop*

16 pt Berthold Walbaum

20 pt Monotype Walbaum

Walbaum H Justus Erich Walbaum, who was a contemporary of Beethoven, ranks with Giambattista Bodoni and Firmin Didot as one of the great European Romantic designers of type. He was the latest of the three, but he may well have been the most original. Walbaum cut his fonts at Goslar and Weimar early in the nineteenth century. His matrices were bought by the Berthold Foundry a century later, and Berthold Walbaum, in its metal form, is Walbaum's actual type. Berthold digital Walbaum is a close and careful translation. Monotype Walbaum, different though it is, is also quite authentic. The Berthold version is based on Walbaum's larger fonts, and the Monotype version on his small text sizes.

The letterfit of Berthold digital Walbaum has been edited extensively to produce the fonts used here.

Each of the major Romantic designers had his own effect on design in the twentieth century. Firmin Didot's ghost is palpable in Adrian Frutiger's Frutiger; Bodoni's ghost in Paul Renner's Futura, and Walbaum's spirit is alive in some of the later work of Hermann Zapf. But each of these instances involves a real creative leap, not imitation. Walbaum is the only Romantic type now sold in something like its original form, yet it too has changed – because we see it in the light of later type which Walbaum's letters helped to cause. (See also p 131.)

abcefghijop 123 AO *abcefghijop*

the qua ſp fghj xyz

Zapf Renaissance D Designed by Hermann Zapf in 1984–85 and issued in 1986 by Scangraphic. This family returns, after forty years, to many of the principles that animated one of Zapf's first typefaces, Palatino. But Zapf Renaissance is designed for the high-technology, two-dimensional world of digital imaging, instead of the slower, more multidimensional world of the artist printer's handpress. The result is a less printerly and sculptural, more scribal and painterly typeface – and one which at the same time is more tolerant of digital typography's capricious, even licentious, freedom with size. The family includes a roman, italic, small caps, semibold and swash italic with a rich assortment of pilcrows and fleurons. (See also p 238.)

Linotype Digital Palatino (on the left) and Zapf Renaissance (on the right). Palatino was first designed as a foundry face, with weight and proportion changing considerably from size to size. Zapf Renaissance was designed as a freely scalable digital face, in which one pattern serves for every size. Both types are shown here at 72 pt and 18 pt.

aa bb cc
ee ff gg
nn oo tt
AA HH

abcdefghijklmnopqrstuvwxyz
abcdefghijklmnopqrstuvwxyz
1 2 3 4 5 6 7 8 9 0
1 2 3 4 5 6 7 8 9 0
A B C D E F G H I J K L M N
A B C D E F G H I J K L M N
O P Q R S T U V W X Y Z
O P Q R S T U V W X Y Z

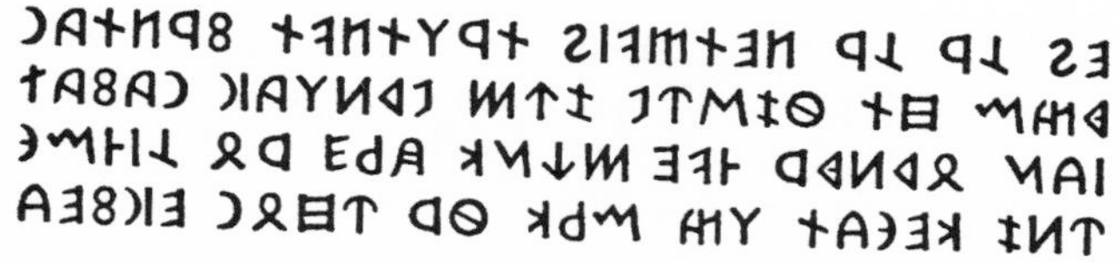

14 pt unserifed Etruscan cut by William Caslon for Oxford University Press, about 1746. Unserifed scripts are as old as writing itself, but this is one of the earliest unserifed *types*.

10.3 UNSERIFED TEXT FACES

Unserifed letters have a history at least as long, and quite as distinguished, as serifed letters. Unserifed capitals appear in the earliest Greek inscriptions. They reappear at Rome in the third and second centuries BC, and in Florence in the early Renaissance. Perhaps it is no more than an accident of history that the unserifed letters of fifteenth-century Florentine architects and sculptors were not translated into metal type in the 1470s.

At Athens and again at Rome, the modulated stroke and bilateral serif were the scribal trademarks and symbols of empire. Unserifed letters, with no modulation or, at most, a subtle taper in the stroke, were emblems of the Republic. This link between unserifed letterforms and populist or democratic movements recurs time and again, in Renaissance Italy and in the eighteenth and nineteenth centuries in northern Europe.

Many rotundas and Greek types cut in the 1460s and 1470s include sanserif forms, but none is consistently unserifed. (A recent example on similar lines is Karlgeorg Hoefer's San Marco, shown on page 252.)

Unserifed types were first cut in the eighteenth century, but they were cut at first cut for alphabets other than Latin. A sanserif Latin printing type was cut for Valentin Haüy, Paris, in 1786 – but Haüy's type was meant to be invisible. It was designed to be embossed, without ink, for the blind to read with their fingers. The first unserifed Latin type for the sighted – cut by William Caslon IV, London, about 1812 – was based on signwriters' letters and consisted of capitals only. Bicameral (upper- and lowercase) unserifed roman fonts were apparently first cut in Leipzig in the 1820s.

The importance of the Haüy italic was first pointed out by James Mosley. For more on the history of unserifed letters, see his essay "The Nymph and the Grot," *Typographica* n.s. 12 (1965), and Nicolete Gray, *A History of Lettering* (Oxford, 1986).

Most, though not all, of the unserifed types of the nineteenth century were dark, coarse and tightly closed. These characteristics are still obvious in faces like Helvetica and Franklin Gothic, despite the weight-reductions and other refinements worked on them over the years. These faces are cultural souvenirs of some of the bleakest days of the Industrial Revolution.

During the twentieth century, sanserifs have evolved toward

much greater subtlety, and in this evolution there seem to be three major factors. One is the study of archaic Greek inscriptions, with their light, limber stroke and large aperture. Another is the pursuit of pure geometry: typographic meditation first on the circle and the line, then on more complex geometric figures. The third is the study of Renaissance calligraphy and humanistic form – vitally important in the recent history of serifed and unserifed letters alike. But in retrospect it seems that both type designers and founders were for many years strangely reluctant to believe that one could simply write a humanist letter and *leave the serifs off*. When this is done, everything happens and nothing happens: if the stroke has width, the stroke-end too has shape and form; it takes the serif's place.

abcefghijop 123 AO *abcefghijop*

Caspari D Designed by Gerard Daniëls and issued by the Dutch Type Library in 1993. This is a subtly crafted and simple text face with the essential humanist attributes, including large aperture, a genuine italic with a modest slope of 6°, text figures, small caps and an impressive economy of form. It seems to me fully the equal of Gill Sans as a piece of design, and it is superior, in its present state, for text work, because its manufacturer has taken care to issue all the basic parts. (See also p 244.)

abcefghijop 123 AO *abcefghijop*

Charlotte Sans D This is the unserifed branch of the Charlotte family designed by Michael Gills and issued in 1992 in digital form by Esselte Letraset. The stroke, which may look monochrome at first, is full of subtle tapers, as in most sanserif faces built for text work. The italic has the artfully self-conscious air of its Neoclassical models, but italic it still is. Small caps and roman text figures have been issued. Italic text figures are present (though hidden) on the basic italic font.

A O *abcdefghijklmnopqrstuvwxyz*

Flora P/D Designed by Gerard Unger, released by Rudolf Hell in 1985 and licensed through ITC in 1989. Flora is a true sanserif italic – and it was, I believe, the first unserifed italic to approximate chancery form. It can be used very happily alone but is designed to function also as a companion to Unger's Praxis (unserifed roman) and Demos (serifed roman and italic). Because its slope is only 2.5°, Flora functions best with Praxis when it is used for setting separate blocks of text.

Unger has spoken persuasively about the importance of horizontals in his type designs. He associates the strong horizontal thrust of Hollander and Swift with the flat Dutch landscape in the midst of which he lives. But in most of his italics – Swift, Hollander and Flora included – it is verticals that seem to matter most. (See also p 244.)

See Gerard Unger, "Dutch Landscape with Letters," in issue 14 of the Dutch journal *Gravisie* (Utrecht, 1989): 29–52.

abcefghijop 123 AO *abcefghijop*

Frutiger P Designed in 1975 by Adrian Frutiger and issued by Mergenthaler. Frutiger was first designed for signage at the Paris-Roissy Airport but has prospered as a typeface. What it lacks in the way of humanist structure it makes up for in its open, fresh geometry, wide aperture and balance. It mates particularly well with the same designer's Méridien, though the families were never intended for joint use and do not match in body size. The so-called italic is a pure sloped roman. There are, however, two widths of Frutiger (normal and condensed) in an extensive range of weights. (See also pp 105, 244, 245.)

abcefghijop 123 AO *abcefghijop*

Futura H Designed by Paul Renner in 1924–26 and issued by the Bauer Foundry, Frankfurt, in 1927. Futura is a subtly crafted face, but many copies have been made in metal, film and digital form. By no means all these cuts are equally well made – and not all the weights added to the family in later years are Renner's own designs.

Geometric though it is, Futura is one of the most harmonious and rhythmical sanserifs ever made. Its proportions are graceful and humane, and it is suitable – like all the unserifed faces examined here – for setting extended text. (This is not, of course, to say that it is suitable for texts of every kind.) One barrier to its use for text, however, has always been the absence of text figures. These were included in Renner's original design, but Bauer never issued them in metal. New figures have been added, based on Renner's drawings, to make the font used here. (See also pp 14, 106, 133, 202, 244.)

abcefghijop 123 AO *abcefghijop*

Gill Sans M Designed by Eric Gill and issued by Monotype in 1927. Gill Sans is a distinctly British but highly readable sanserif, composed of latently humanist and overtly geometric forms. The aperture varies (it is large in *c*, moderate in roman *a* and *s*, small in roman *e*). The italic, like Fournier's, cut two centuries before, was a revolutionary achievement in its time. Books have been set successfully in Gill Sans, though it requires a sure sense of color and measure. Text figures – very useful when the face is used for setting text – have been privately produced but never issued by Monotype itself. (See also p 244.)

abcefghijop 123 AO *abcefghijop*

Goudy Sans M Designed by Frederic Goudy in 1929–30 and issued by Lanston Monotype. This was one of the first sanserifs to break from the Realist model by opening the aperture and implying a written more than a constructed form. Goudy Sans is the spiritual father of several recent sanserifs, including Erik Spiekermann's Meta and Officina – and like them it is not quite as sans as the name suggests. There are residual serifs in many of the forms. The digital version, issued in 1986 by ITC, is in some respects an improvement on the original. (See also p 244.)

18 pt Kabel

AO abcdefghijklmnopqrstuvwxyz 123

18 pt ITC Kabel

AO abcdefghijklmnopqrstuvwxyz

Kabel H Designed by Rudolf Koch and issued in several weights by the Klingspor Foundry, Offenbach, in 1927–30. In Koch's original design, the lighter weights of Kabel have a very small eye, while the eye in the black weight is large. The series was redrawn by ITC in 1986 with the eye uniformly large throughout. Both versions have now been digitized.

abcefghijop 123 AO *abcefghijop*

Laudatio P Designed by Friedrich Poppl and issued by Berthold in 1982. Laudatio, like Optima, lives on the borderline between serif and sanserif. The ends of the stems are flared, and in the lower case, at the upper ends of the strokes, where a head serif would occur on the left side in a normal roman or italic, the stroke end is canted and flared toward the left. The eye is very large but open. On a narrow measure, the face composes handsomely into text. The italic is a hybrid. There are several weights.

abcefghijop 123 AO *abcefghijop*

Legacy Sans D Designed by Ronald Arnholm and issued via ITC in 1992. To the best of my knowledge, this is the only published attempt to make an unserifed version of Nicolas Jenson's roman. Arnholm drew the serifed version first, and in the process made some drastic changes to Jenson's proportions, yet resemblances remain. The italic is based not on Arrighi but on Garamond's *gros romain*. There is more modulation of the stroke in Legacy Sans than in most unserifed types. Text figures and small caps are part of the design. (See also pp 223, 244.)

abcefghijop 123 AO *abcefghijop*

Lucida Sans D Lucida Sans – designed by Kris Holmes and Charles Bigelow – is part of the largest type family in the world. The Lucida tribe now includes not only serifed and unserifed roman and italic but also Greek, Cyrillic, Hebrew, a full phonetic character set, a multitude of mathematical symbol sets, swash italic, blackletter, script, a slightly rumpled series known as Lucida Casual, a higher-contrast series called Lucida Bright, a series designed for crude resolutions, known as Lucida Fax, a set of fixed-pitch typewriter fonts, and another fixed-pitch font, known as Lucida Console, designed for terminal emulation. Thai, Arabic and Vietnamese Lucida are also in the works.

The polylingual compass of the family makes it potentially very useful for specialized work in both humanities and sciences, but for ordinary text in the familiar Latin alphabet, the most useful branch of the family seems to me Lucida Sans. This is in fact one of the best sanserifs I know of for ordinary text. It has a poise, simplicity and energy that many serifed text faces lack. Lucida Sans has been issued by Y&Y in Concord, Massachusetts, as a Unicode font with over 1700 characters. Yet the basic text figures and small caps, long ago designed and needed for plain text work, have so far been omitted by every digital foundry that has merchandised the face. (See also p 244.)

abcdefghijklmnopqrstuvwxyz

FUTURA: Cursive characters: none — 0

abcdefghijklmnopqrstuvwxyz

FRUTIGER: Cursive characters: none — 0

abcdefghijklmnopqrstuvwxyz

OPTIMA: Cursive characters: none — 0

abcdefghijklmnopqrstuvwxyz

SYNTAX: Cursive characters: *bcdpq* — 5

abcdefghijklmnopqrstuvwxyz

GILL SANS: Cursive characters: *abcdfpq* — 7

abcdefghijklmnopqrstuvwxyz

MYRIAD: Cursive characters: *abcdegpq* — 8

abcdefghijklmnopqrstuvwxyz

CASPARI: Cursive characters: *abcdeghmnpq* — 11

*Flora is shown
here at 17 pt,
Lucida Sans at
16 pt, all other
samples at 18 pt.*

abcdefghijklmnopqrstuvwxyz

FLORA: Cursive characters: *abcdefghmnpqru* — 14

abcdefghijklmnopqrstuvwxyz

LUCIDA: Cursive characters: *abcdefghmnpqru* — 14

*Triplex italic and
Goudy Sans italic
get the highest
scores, but no
prize is being
given, and these
two faces get their
points by dubious
means. Both are
carrying several
residual serifs. If
we took these
serifs off, some
letters – i and l,
for instance –
would no longer
count as cursive.*

abcdefghijklmnopqrstuvwxyz

SCALA SANS: Cursive characters: *abcdefhmnpqtuvwy* — 16

abcdefghijklmnopqrstuvwxyz

LEGACY SANS: Cursive characters: *abcdefghkmnpqrtuy* — 17

abcdefghijklmnopqrstuvwxyz

GOUDY SANS: Cursive characters: *abcdefhiklmnpquvwxyz* — 20

abcdefghijklmnopqrstuvwxyz

TRIPLEX: Cursive characters: *abcdefghiklmnopqrtuvwxyz* — 24

SOME ITALICS are not italic at all – that is, they are not cursive. Others are very italic indeed. This is one of the salient differences among sanserif types. We can measure this aspect of a typeface, in a crude way, by counting how many letters in the basic lower case have visibly cursive characteristics. This tells us nothing whatsoever about how *good* or *bad* the typeface is. It tells us, instead, something about the *kind* of goodness it may or may not possess.

The same analysis can be performed on serifed italics too. But it is normal, in a serifed italic of humanist form, for every letter in the lower case to be noticeably cursive. There are no purely sanserif italics for which this seems to be true. (John Downer's Triplex italic lower case is close to 100% cursive in this sense, despite its highly geometric form – but it is not 100% unserifed.)

The features that mark an unserifed letter as cursive are often very subtle. In a letter such as *b, h, m, p* or *r*, for example, it is usually only the shape of the bowl, or the angle and the height at which the curved strokes enter or leave the stem, that reveals its cursive form.

bb pp rr · bb pp rr

In Frutiger (on the left, above), the oblique forms of *b, p* and *r* are no more cursive than the upright. In Legacy Sans (on the right, above), the oblique forms are visibly italic. They differ from the corresponding roman forms in structure as well as in slope.

The *g* can be cursive or noncursive, no matter whether it has the binocular form that is usual in serifed roman faces or the monocular form that is typical both of chancery italics such as Trinité and of Realist sanserifs such as Helvetica.

gg gg g · gg gg g
1   2   3   4   5   6

In Syntax (1), the oblique *g* keeps its essentially uncursive roman form. In Legacy Sans (2), the italic *g* differs more from the roman: it develops at least a little bit of swing as well as a slope. The *g* from DTL Elzevir italic (3) – a Baroque serifed face, based on the work of Christoffel van Dijck – provides a comparison. The *g* of Frutiger (4) is monocular but not cursive, even when it slopes. In Gerard Daniëls's Caspari (5), the italic *g* is cursive, like the *g* in Méridien italic (6).

245

abcefghijop 123 AO *abcefghijop*

Myriad D Designed by Robert Slimbach and Carol Twombly and issued by Adobe in 1991. Myriad, like Frutiger, is full of subtle and open geometric forms. Like Frutiger, it lacks text figures and small caps, but unlike Frutiger, it includes what might be called a real italic. In its multiple master form, it is continuously adjustable for weight and width. There are also playful versions of the face, known as Myriad Sketch and Myriad Tilt, useful for lightening the mood of oppressive technical perfection. (See also p 244.)

abcefghijop 123 AO *abcefghijop*

Optima H/M Designed by Hermann Zapf in 1952–55 and is-sued both by Stempel and by Linotype in 1958. The stroke weight is more variable in Optima than in Laudatio, but the degree of taper is less. Of the two, Optima is more purely a sanserif. The taper of the stroke derives from unserifed Greek inscriptions and the unserifed roman inscriptions of Renais-sance Florence, but in other respects the architecture of Optima is Neoclassical. Optima 'italic' is pure sloped roman. There is a range of weights and a matching text Greek, designed by Zapf and issued by Linotype in 1971. To the best of my knowledge, the Greek has never been digitized. Nor have Optima's text figures. (These, in fact, were never issued even in metal, though they were cut by August Rosenberger at the Stempel Foundry in at least one size and used by the designer in his *Manuale Typo-graphicum* of 1968. See also p 244.)

abcefghijop 123 AO *abcefghijopwy*

Scala Sans D A fine neohumanist sanserif designed by Martin Majoor and issued by FontShop International, Berlin, in 1994. This is as fully humanized as any sanserif I know. It has a crisp and very legible italic and small caps. Text figures and the full array of standard ligatures are present on the basic font. In the italic, even the geometric letters at the tail of the Latin alphabet (*v, w, y*) are cursive in their sharp and bony way. The relation-ship between the serifed and unserifed forms of Scala is studied in detail on pp 248–249. (Scala Sans is the unserifed face used throughout this book. See also pp 231, 244.)

abcefghijop 123 AO *abcefghijop*

Shannon **P** Designed by Kris Holmes and Janice Prescott Fishman, and issued first by Compugraphic as a photocomposition face in 1981. The axis of the letterforms (not to be confused with the axis of the *stroke*) is recognizably humanist, and the aperture is large. The face is further humanized by a slight flaring and bending of the stroke, and draws its architecture in part from semiserifed letterforms found in the Book of Kells. Text figures and small caps have been issued in digital form by Agfa. There is however a sloped roman in place of a true italic.

abcefghijop 123 AO *abcefghijop*

Stone Sans **D** Designed by Sumner Stone, issued by Adobe in 1987 and licensed through ITC in 1989. The axis varies, and the eye and aperture are large. This is part of the comprehensive Stone family, including serifed, unserifed, 'informal' and phonetic faces. Its primary value may lie in the typographic possibilities of this family relationship. The small caps and text figures have recently been issued by ITC itself. (See also p 232.)

abcefghijop 123 AO *abcefghijop*

Syntax **H** Designed by Hans Eduard Meier and issued by the Stempel foundry in 1969. The roman is a true neohumanist sanserif, in which Renaissance forms are clearly visible. The italic, however, is a hybrid, primarily sloped roman. Close scrutiny reveals that in Syntax the roman is sloped too. The italic slopes at 11° and the roman at something close to half a degree. Little as it is, half a degree is enough to add perceptible vitality and motion to the forms. The stroke is subtly modulated, and the stroke ends are trimmed at a variety of angles. There are several weights, but with this as with neohumanist faces generally, the weights above semibold are severely distorted. Syntax was the first sanserif of its kind and it remains in my opinion one of the best unserifed romans ever made. In the late 1990s Meier made it even better, by adding text figures and small caps, and subtly redesigning it throughout.

An extended Syntax character set, intended specifically for setting Native American languages, was produced in 1981 by Charles Bigelow and Kris Holmes. (See also p 244.)

For the Native American variant of Syntax, see Dell Hymes, "Victoria Howard's 'Gitskux and His Older Brother'," in Brian Swann, ed., *Smoothing the Ground: Essays on Native American Oral Literature* (Berkeley, 1983).

Martin Majoor's Scala and Scala Sans, shown here at 74 pt and 18 pt. The serifed and unserifed forms of Scala are closely related and highly compatible, but there are many subtle differences as well. Taking the serifs away from an alphabet changes the relative widths of the characters, which changes the rhythm of the face. In Scala roman, for example, the unserifed caps are uniformly narrower than the serifed caps. The unserifed lower case is slightly narrower too, but most of the difference comes in the straightlegged letters *h* through *n*.

aa bb cc
ee ff gg
nn oo tt
AA HH

abcdefghijklmnopqrstuvwxyz
abcdefghijklmnopqrstuvwxyz
1 2 3 4 5 6 7 8 9 0
1 2 3 4 5 6 7 8 9 0
A B C D E F G H I J K L M N
A B C D E F G H I J K L M N
O P Q R S T U V W X Y Z
O P Q R S T U V W X Y Z

248

aa bb cc
ee ff gg
nn oo tt
AA HH

abcdefghijklmnopqrstuvwxyz
abcdefghijklmnopqrstuvwxyz
1 2 3 4 5 6 7 8 9 0
1 2 3 4 5 6 7 8 9 0
A B C D E F G H I J K L M N
A B C D E F G H I J K L M N
O P Q R S T U V W X Y Z
O P Q R S T U V W X Y Z

In Scala italic, many lower-case letters are actually wider in the sans than in the serifed form, though the alphabet is narrower overall. And Scala Serif has a clearly modulated stroke, while Scala Sans is optically monochrome. Thinned and tapered strokes occur in the sans and serifed forms alike (in the brow of roman *a*, the bar of roman *e*, and in the roman and italic *g*, for example). But the unserifed stroke is never thinned *as much* as the stroke with serifs.

Blackletters

The first types cut in Europe, including all those used by Johann Gutenberg, were blackletters. Scripts and printing types of this kind were once used throughout Europe – in England, France, Hungary, Poland, Portugal, the Netherlands and Spain, as well as Germany – and some species thrived even in Italy. They are the typographic counterpart of the Gothic style in architecture, and like Gothic architecture, they are a prominent part of the European heritage, though they flourished longer and more vigorously in Germany than anywhere else.

> **de heeft hy ons gheuandet die vten hoghen opgegaenis Ⅰnlichte here denghenē die in dupfterniffe fitte eñ in die fcheme des doots. om te lepdē**

A 14-point textura cut by Henric Pieterszoon Lettersnider, probably at Antwerp in 1492. (Matrices for this font – likely the oldest set of matrices in existence – are now in the Enschedé Museum in Haarlem.)

Blackletter scripts, like roman scripts, exist in endless variety. Blackletter types are somewhat simpler, and not all of them need concern us here. But it is worth noting the presence of four major families: *textura, fraktur, bastarda* and *rotunda*. (Another variety of blackletter often listed in type catalogues is Schwabacher. This is bastarda by its domestic German name.) None of these families is confined to a particular historical period. All four of them have survived, like roman and italic, through many historical variations. Their differences are many and complex, but they can usually be distinguished by reference to the lowercase *o* alone. Though it is written with only two penstrokes, the *o* in a textura looks essentially hexagonal. In a fraktur, it is normally flat on the left side, curved on the right. In a bastarda, it is normally pointed at top and bottom and belled on both sides. In a rotunda, it is essentially oval or round.

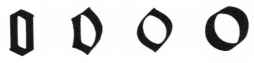

Typical lowercase forms in textura, fraktur, bastarda, and rotunda

Blackletters can be used in many contexts for emphasis or contrast – even in a world devoted to roman and italic – and need not be confined to the mastheads of newspapers or the titles of religious tracts. Type designers have also not abandoned them. Some excellent blackletters have been drawn in the twentieth century – by German artists such as Rudolf Koch and by the American Frederic Goudy.

A O ábçdèfghijklmnöpqrstûvwxyz ß

Clairvaux **D** The blackletter of the White Monks. The Cistercian abbey of Clairvaux, about half way from Paris to Basel, was founded by St Bernard in 1115 and thrived throughout the twelfth century. The typeface of the same name, designed by Herbert Maring and issued by Linotype in 1990, has much of the simplicity espoused by the old Cistercian order. It is also closer than any other bastarda to the forms of the Caroline minuscule, and thus more legible than most to modern eyes.

A O ábçdèfghijklmnöpqrstûvwxyz ß

Duc de Berry **D** A light French bastarda, designed by Gottfried Pott, issued in digital form by Linotype in 1991. Jean de France, the Duke of Berry (1340–1416) would, I think, have found these letterforms familiar, but they are not based on the script in any of the lavish Books of Hours he once owned.

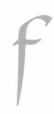

A O ábçdèfghijklmnöpqrstûvwxyz ß

Fette Fraktur **H** This heavy, Romantic fraktur was designed by Johann Christian Bauer and issued by his foundry at Frankfurt about 1850. It provides strong evidence that the Victorian 'fat face' is inherently more congenial to blackletter than to roman.

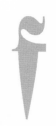

A O ábçdèfghijklmnöpqrstûvwxyz ß

Goudy Text **M** Designed by Frederic Goudy and issued by Monotype in 1928. A narrow, smooth, slightly ornamented textura, relatively legible in the upper as well as the lower case. There is a second set of capitals, known as Lombardic caps. In machine form and digital form alike, the type is poorly fitted, but it is worth the work of salvage.

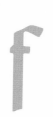

A O abcdefghijklmnopqrstuvwxyz

Goudy Thirty M This was one of Frederic Goudy's last type-faces, deliberately conceived as his memorial to himself. ('Thirty' is, of course, journalists' code for 'end of story.') It is a light and simple rotunda, designed in 1942, issued by Lanston Monotype in 1948 and now available from the Lanston Type Co. in digital form. There are two versions, differing in the forms of *a, s, w* and several of the capitals.

A O abcdefghijklmnopqrsstuvwxyz

Rhapsodie H This is an energetic, legible Schwabacher (German bastarda) designed by Ilse Schüle and issued by Ludwig & Mayer, Frankfurt, in 1951. There is an alternate set of ornamental capitals. I have not found a digital version of the face.

A O ábcdèfghíjklmnŏpqrstûvwxyz ß

San Marco D Designed by Karlgeorg Hoefer and issued by Linotype in 1991. This is the first digital blackletter inspired by the battery of rotundas cut at Venice in the 1470s by Nicolas Jenson. San Marco too is a rotunda – the genus of blackletter most closely connected to Italy and structurally closest to roman forms. It is named for the round-vaulted cathedral of San Marco, at the ceremonial center of Jenson's city. (See also p 105.)

A abcdefghijklmnopqrsstuvwxyz

Trump Deutsch H Designed by Georg Trump and issued in metal by the Berthold Foundry in 1936. This is a dark, wide, concave, unornamented and energetic textura. Both upper and lower case are open and easily legible forms. To the best of my knowledge, it has never yet been digitized.

A O ábçdèfghíjklmnŏpqrstûvwxyz ß

Wilhelm Klingspor Schrift H Rudolf Koch completed this narrow, ornamental textura in 1925, naming it in honor of the recently deceased co-owner of the Klingspor Bros. foundry in Offenbach, where Koch was chief designer. Not all the alternate glyphs in the handsome metal versions have been digitized.

Uncial letters were widely used by European scribes from the fourth through the ninth century AD, both for Latin and for Greek, but they had vanished from common use in the time of Gutenberg. Uncials were not cut into type until the nineteenth century, and then only for scholarly or antiquarian purposes. In the twentieth century, however, many designers – Sjoerd de Roos, William Addison Dwiggins, Frederic Goudy, Oldřich Menhart and Günter Gerhard Lange, among others – took an interest in uncial forms, and one artist and printer, Victor Hammer, devoted his life to them.

Historically, uncials are unicameral – they have only one case, as all European alphabets did until the late Middle Ages – but not all recent uncials are likewise. Early uncials, like recent ones, are sometimes serifed, sometimes not, and may be modulated or monochrome. They are now used chiefly for display, but some are quiet enough for extended texts.

It is often said that *uncial* (from Latin *uncia*) means 'inch,' but a better translation is simply 'small measure' or 'small standard.'

A O abcdefghijklmnopqrstuvwxyz

American Uncial H This is the fourth type Victor Hammer designed, the second for which he cut the punches, and the first he produced after moving to the USA from Austria in 1939. All Hammer's types are uncials, and two of them – this one and its predecessor Pindar – are bicameral. American Uncial was cast privately in Chicago in 1945, then commercially by Klingspor and sold in Europe as Neue Hammer Unziale. Digital versions exist – but digital copies of other Hammer types have also, confusingly, been marketed under the name American Uncial.

áßçdèfghijklmnôpqrstüvwxyz

Omnia D Lightly serifed, round, cursive uncials with a large aperture and humanist axis, designed by Karlgeorg Hoefer and issued by Linotype in 1991.

AbcdefghijklmnopqrstuvwxyZ

Solemnis H Serifed, square uncials with a humanist axis, designed by Günter Gerhard Lange and issued in metal by Berthold in 1953.

In ordinary usage, script is what is not type; it is writing: the mode of visual language used in public by calligraphers and in private by other literate humans, including typographers themselves. When script hardens, breaks and starts to look like type, we often call it printing – yet printing is what printers do with type, even type that looks like script, which we are likely to call script type. An innocent observer might conclude that English is an undernourished language, whose speakers cannot generate a new word even when they need one.

Script Types

At the root of this confusion is a portion of good sense. Type is writing edited or imitated, translated or paraphrased, honored or mocked – but writing itself is a fluid and linear version of more disconnected epigraphic signs. The difference between 'type' and 'script' reiterates the difference between *glyphic* and *graphic*, or carved and written, characters. That difference was established at least 1500 years before the printing press was born.

The craving to mate roman with italic appears to be an effort to have type and script, or glyphic and graphic, at once. This explains in part why it is difficult to classify a typeface like Poetica. Is it a script, or is it a solitary (romanless) italic?

On the early history of printed scripts, see Stanley Morison's essay "On Script Types," *The Fleuron* 4 (London, 1921): 1–42.

Scripts have thrived as foundry type, phototype and digital type, and several fine designers – Imre Reiner, for example – have focused as exclusively on scripts as others have on romans. But scripts had an importance in the world of commercial letterpress that they lack in the world of two-dimensional printing. Handwritten originals are expensive to photoengrave for reproduction on the letterpress. Specially commissioned calligraphy is easy to include, by way of scanning or photography, in artwork destined for the offset press. The best script to supplement a typographic page is now therefore more likely to be custom made.

Dozens of excellent script types are available. They include Arthur Baker's Marigold and Visigoth, Roger Excoffon's Choc and Mistral, Karlgeorg Hoefer's Salto and Saltino, Günter Gerhard Lange's Derby and El Greco, Michael Neugebauer's Squire, Friedrich Peter's Vivaldi, Imre Reiner's Matura and Pepita, Robert Slimbach's Caflisch and Sanvito, Georg Trump's Jaguar and Palomba, and Hermann Zapf's Venture and Zapf Chancery. I have chosen to illustrate here only a handful of the scripts that particularly interest me. Two of these – Eaglefeather and Tekton

– are architectural scripts and could have been included just as easily among the text types. I have put them here instead for what they reveal about the process of transition from writing to printing, script to type, and script type to roman and italic.

abcefghijop 123 ABDO *abcefghijop*

Eaglefeather D This is a family of type created in 1990 by David Siegel and Carol Toriumi-Lawrence, based on the architectural lettering of Frank Lloyd Wright (1867–1959). Eaglefeather is issued in two forms, called formal and informal, but only the roman lower case actually differs. The two share one italic, one set of roman caps, small caps, figures and analphabetics. Eaglefeather Informal (the version shown) is pure italic. The 'roman' is a crisp, unserifed italic with no slope. The 'italic' is the same set of letters with a slope of 10°.

A O abcdefghijklmnopqrstuvwxyz

Ex Ponto D This rough-edged, lyrical script was designed by Jovica Veljović and issued by Adobe in 1995. The design was completed in exile, and the name, Ex Ponto, alludes to the *Epistulae ex Ponto*, 'letters from the Black Sea,' written in exile before AD 13 by the Roman poet Ovid. Ex Ponto is issued as a multiple master face with a single axis (weight only), and interpolation is restricted, rightly, to a narrow range.

A O abcdefghijklmnopqrstuvwxyz

Legende H A wide, dark, disconnected script with a small eye but excellent legibility. It was designed by Ernst Schneidler and issued by the Bauer Foundry, Frankfurt, in 1937. This is one of the best modern exemplars of a class of Mannerist scripts inaugurated by Robert Granjon at Lyon in 1557. Typographers call them *civilités*.

abcdefghijklmnopqrstuvwxyz

Ondine H A dark but open, lucid, disconnected pen script designed by Adrian Frutiger and originally issued by Deberny & Peignot, Paris, in 1954. (An *ondine* is a sea-nymph, and this type is full of waves.)

The name *civilité* stems from the use of Granjon's script in an early French translation of one of Desiderius Erasmus's best-sellers, *De civilitate morum puerilium libellus*: 'A little book for children about civilized behavior.'

255

A O abcdefghijklmnopqrstuvwxyz

Present **H** A light, broad, disconnected brush script designed by Friedrich Sallwey and issued by the Stempel Foundry, Frankfurt, in 1974. In digital form, the family has been enlarged to include both regular and condensed versions in three weights.

m

The text is
handwritten
only in the first
two editions of
Ching's book.
The third edition
(1996) is set in
semicondensed
digital Tekton.

abcdefghijop 123 AO abcefghijop

Tekton **D** Designed by David Siegel, based on the lettering of architect Frank Ching, and issued by Adobe in 1989. A multiple master version (whose axes are width and weight) was released in 1992 and a GX version in 1995. In modest sizes, Tekton is functionally a sanserif. At larger sizes, its serifs are visible as tiny beads. It is fundamentally one alphabet, not two, because it has a pure oblique in place of an italic. The original script can be seen in Ching's book *Architectural Graphics* (New York, 1975; 2nd ed. 1985), which is printed from handwritten pages.

10.7 GREEKS

Greek type has a long and complex history peculiarly its own, yet closely entwined with the history of roman. The first full fonts of Greek were cut in Venice and Florence by Nicolas Jenson, Francesco Griffo and others who were simultaneously cutting the first roman and italic faces. Simon de Colines, Claude Garamond, Robert Granjon, Miklós Kis, Johann Fleischman and William Caslon cut good Greeks as well, and their type was widely used. Yet the first Greek book printed in Greece itself was the Mt Athos Psalter of 1759, and the first secular printing press in Greece was established during the War of Independence, with help from Ambroise Firmin-Didot, in 1821.

Greek adaptations of popular roman faces – Baskerville, Caledonia, Helvetica, Times New Roman, Univers and others – have been issued by Linotype, Monotype and other firms, and are widely used in Greece. But there, as in much of Eastern Europe, the more lyrical forms of modernism have been slower to arrive. Even in the multinational world of classical studies, where Greek types that will harmonize with neohumanist romans are perennially needed, they are in very short supply.

Three important classes of Greek type have been with us since the fifteenth century. These are the *orthotic,* the *cursive,* and the *chancery script*. Orthotic Greek is analogous to roman in the Latin alphabet. It is, in other words, *not cursive*. The letters are relatively self-contained, usually upright, and may or may not have serifs. Cursive Greek type – which exists in both sloped and vertical forms – is analogous to italic. Chancery Greeks are merely elaborate forms of the cursive, but they attained in Greek a level of typographic intricacy never yet approached by chancery italic type in the Latin alphabet.

μηχόμεμόμ Τε λέαμΔρομ ὁμοῦ καὶ λύχμο

Δράσαντι δ' αἰχρὰ, δεινὰ τἀπιτί μια

ϖϱὸς τὸν θεὸν, καὶ θεὸς ἦ ὁ λόγϘ.

Three early Greek types. *Above*: The Complutensian Greek, a 16 pt orthotic font cut by Arnaldo Guillén de Brocar at Alcalá de Henares, near Madrid, in 1510. *Center*: The 10 pt cursive cut by Francesco Griffo, Venice, in 1502 [here shown at twice actual size]. *Bottom*: An 18 pt chancery Greek cut by Robert Granjon in the 1560s.

The orthotic Greek types of the Renaissance resemble Renaissance romans yet differ from them too, in several interesting ways. The stroke is usually quite uniform in thickness, the stroke-ends are sharply rectangular, and the serifs, when present, are usually short, abrupt and unilateral. The geometric figures of triangle, circle and line are prominent in the underlying structure of these faces, though not to the exclusion of more complex curves. This is the oldest form of Greek type, first seen in the partial alphabets cut by Peter Schoeffer the Elder at Mainz and by Konrad Sweynheym at Subiaco, near Rome, in 1465. It is also the style of the first full-fledged and polytonic Greek type, cut by Nicolas Jenson at Venice in 1471.

The finest early example of orthotic Greek, in the opinion of many historians, is the Complutensian Greek of Arnaldo Guillén de Brocar, cut in Spain in 1510. A few years after that, orthotic Greeks completely disappeared. They were not revived until the end of the nineteenth century. The most widely used modern version is the New Hellenic type designed by Victor Scholderer in London in 1927.

The first cursive Greek font was cut by an unidentified

craftsman at Vicenza, west of Venice, in 1475. The second, cut at Venice by Francesco Griffo, did not appear for another twenty years – and it was not a simple cursive like the anonymous font from Vicenza but an elaborate chancery script. Griffo cut a simple Greek cursive in 1502, but chancery Greeks remained the fashion throughout Europe for the next two hundred years.

Greeks

A simple Greek cursive can be turned to a chancery script by the addition of ligatures, and a chancery script converted to simple cursive by leaving the ligatures out. But the battery of ligatures involved often runs to several hundred, and sometimes to more than a thousand.

Chancery Greeks were cut by many artists from Garamond to Caslon, but Neoclassical and Romantic designers – including Baskerville, Bodoni, Alexander Wilson and Ambroise Firmin-Didot – all returned to simpler cursive forms. Firmin-Didot's Greek is still in frequent use, in France and Greece alike, but in the English-speaking world the cursive Greek most often seen is the one designed in 1806 by Richard Porson.

Modernist Greeks, such as Jan van Krimpen's Antigone, Hermann Zapf's Heraklit, and Robert Slimbach's (still unfinished) Minion Greek, have opened a new chapter in the history of the Greek alphabet, by joining the humanist structure of Renaissance roman and italic to the forms of the Greek lower case. Ironically, these types evolved just as most paid custodians of European culture were abandoning the study of the classics.

Greek, like Latin, evolved into bicameral form in the late Middle Ages. The upper case in the two alphabets shares the same heritage, and more than half the uppercase forms remain identical. (The same is true of Greek and Latin uncials.) But the Greek lower case has evolved along a different path. There is a quiet and formal Greek hand, not dissimilar in spirit to the roman lower case, but the usual Greek minuscule is cursive. As a consequence, most Greek faces are like Renaissance italics: upright, formal capitals married to a flowing, often sloping, lower case. No real supporting face has developed in the Greek typographic tradition: no face that augments and contrasts with the primary alphabet as italic does with roman.

Twentieth-century designers have sometimes added bold and inclined variants to their Greeks, in imitation of Latin models. But most of the faces shown here are solitary. They are designed to be used alone or as supplementary faces themselves, for setting Greek intermixed with roman.

αβγδεζηθικλμνξοπρσςτυφχψω

Antigone H Designed by Jan van Krimpen and issued by Enschedé in 1927. This is a delicately sculpted neohumanist Greek, intended for the setting of lyric poetry. It was cut specifically to match the same designer's Lutetia roman and italic, but it composes well with his other Latin faces, including Romanée and Spectrum. There is no digital version of Antigone, but Chris Brand's Albertina Greek (expected soon in digital form from DTL) is Antigone's direct descendant.

*Prowling
the
Specimen
Books*

αβγδεζηθικλμνξοπρσςτυφχψω

Attika H/M An unserifed Greek designed by Hermann Zapf for the Stempel Foundry in 1953. A machine version was also issued by Linotype. Attika was designed as a Greek companion to Neuzeit, an unserifed roman drawn by Wilhelm Pischner. This is a rigorously Modernist, geometric face, larger in the eye and more purely sanserif than Gill Sans Greek. There is, however, still no digital version.

ἄβγδεζηθικλμνξοπρσςτυφχψω

Bodoni H Giambattista Bodoni designed and cut a large number of Greeks in the course of his career. Some are Neoclassical and some are Romantic in structure; some are sloped cursives, and some are inscriptional faces consisting of capitals only. The so-called Bodoni Greek of more recent typographic history represents none of Bodoni's originals though it looks as though it should be one of his designs. It is, in fact, an upright version of a font (the 18 pt Longus Greek) that Bodoni cut in sloped form in 1786. I do not know which founder cut the first commercial adaptation of Bodoni's Greek, but it was in use in Germany in the 1850s. Several German founders copied it, and it has served as the standard Greek type in German books for over a hundred years. The version shown here is a new digital interpretation, made in 1993 for the Greek Font Society, Athens, by Takis Katsoulides. It is Romantic in architecture but has been spared the exaggerated contrast found in many recent romans and italics that are advertised as Bodonis. The digital family as issued by GFS includes both sloped and upright forms, a bold, and Greek small caps. (See also p 113.)

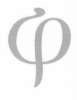

ἀβγδεζηθικλμνξοπρσςτυφχψω
Α Β Γ Δ Ε Ζ Η Θ Κ Λ Μ Χ

Didot H More than one typographer has wondered why Didot Greeks look so little like the Didot romans. The reason is that they were cut in different eras by father and son, and they embody the two punchcutters' different relationships to two distinct typographic traditions. The original Didot Greeks are the work of Ambroise Firmin-Didot, whose father, Firmin Didot, cut the best-known Didot romans and italics. The romans, cut in the thick of the French Revolution, have a strictly rationalist structure. They have left every vestige of Baroque variety behind. The Greeks have a lefthandedness learned from the Mannerist and Baroque Greeks of Granjon, Jannon, Kis, Caslon and Fleischman. The capitals are openly schizophrenic, with adnate, Neoclassical serifs on the thin strokes and abrupt, Romantic serifs on the thick ones. The digital version shown here was made for the Greek Font Society, Athens, by Takis Katsoulides in 1993. (See also p 113.)

ΑΒΓΔΕΙΗΘΙΚΛΜ
ΝΞΟΓΡΣΤΥΦΧΨΩ

Diogenes D An alphabet of pure archaic capitals, designed by Christopher Stinehour, Berkeley, in 1996. The face was commissioned by the printer Peter Rutledge Koch for use in an edition of the fragments of Parmenides. It is based on inscriptions of the fifth century BC from the old Greek city of Phokaia and its colony Elea, on the coast of Italy, where Parmenides was born.

αβγδεζηθικλμνξοπρστυφχψω

Gill Sans M This face was designed in the 1950s by Monotype draftsmen, not by Eric Gill himself, as a companion for the Gill Sans roman. Since the roman was itself much modified from Gill's drawings, Gill Sans Greek is twice removed from the artist for whom it is named. It is however a very clean piece of design. The lower case, like its roman counterpart, includes a few residual serifs. There are three useful weights (light, regular and bold) in both upright and oblique.

260

αβγδεζηθικλμνξοπϱσςτυφχψω

Heraklit **H/M** This face was designed by Hermann Zapf and issued both by Stempel and by Linotype in 1954. It is a neohumanist text Greek, intended to be used with the same designer's
Palatino and Aldus. There is a companion Greek titling face
called Phidias: the Greek counterpart to Zapf's Michelangelo.
Though the need for them seems obvious, no digital version of
either of these faces has appeared.

άβγδεζηθικλμνξοπρσςτυφχψω

δ / Δ · ζ / Ʒ · Ε / Є · Σ / C · Ω / ω

New Hellenic **M** Designed by Victor Scholderer and issued by
Monotype in 1927. This is an orthotic Greek, reasserting the
tradition of Nicolas Jenson, Antonio Miscomini and Arnaldo
Guillén de Brocar, instead of the cursive and chancery Greek
tradition of Francesco Griffo, Simon de Colines and Claude
Garamond. It is open, erect, gracious and stable, with minimal
modulation of the stroke and minimal serifs. There are well-
made variant forms of several letters. A digital version of the
face, shown here, was made in 1993 for the Greek Font Society
by Takis Katsoulides. (This is sold as *Neo* rather than *New* Hellenic. See also pp 108, 112.)

The digital New
Hellenic shown
here has been
modified as
follows: side
bearings of
several analpha-
betics have been
revised, a kerning
table has been
added, and five
alternate glyphs
(Δ, Ʒ, Є, C, ω)
have been resized.

άβγδεζηθικλμνξοπρσςτυφχψω

Porson **H** Designed by the English classicist Richard Porson for
Cambridge University and cut by Richard Austin beginning in
1806. The face was soon copied by several founders, and in 1912
an edited version was issued by Monotype. This has been the
standard Greek face for the Oxford Classical Texts for a full century. It is a calm yet energetic face of Neoclassical design that
composes well with many romans. During its long and fruitful
career, the Porson lower case has been fitted with several different series of caps, none of which quite matches Porson's original design. The digital version of the face shown here and elsewhere in this book is the one produced in 1996 by George
Matthiopoulos for the Greek Font Society, Athens. I have altered it, however, by reducing the size of the caps some 10%.
(See also pp 109, 113.)

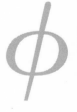

Cyrillics

The Cyrillic alphabet was adapted from Greek in the ninth century, and the first Cyrillic type was cut in Kraków by Ludolf Borchtorp in 1490. An improved Cyrillic was cut in Prague in 1517 by the Belorussian Frantsysk Skaryna, but the first Cyrillic cursive – corresponding to italic in the Latin alphabet – was not cut until 1583. The subsequent history of Cyrillic is largely parallel to that of Latin type, with the important exception that there is no humanist or Renaissance phase, and the intimate linkage between upright and italic which is now taken for granted in Western European typography did not develop in the context of Cyrillic. Slavic type, like Slavic literature, passed more or less directly from the medieval to the late Baroque. For this and for other, more overtly political reasons, the neohumanist movement in type design also came late to Cyrillic letters.

With minor variations, Cyrillic is now used by close to half a billion people, writing in Russian, Ukrainian, Belorussian, Bulgarian, Macedonian and other Slavic languages. In Serbia and Montenegro it is used for Serbo-Croatian, and in Moldova for Rumanian. It is also now the common alphabet for a host of unrelated languages, from Azerbaijani to Uzbek, spoken and written across what once was the Soviet Union.

Several excellent type designers have worked in Russia and the neighboring republics in the past century. The list includes Vadim Lazurski from Odessa, Galina Bannikova from Sarapul, Anatoli Shchukin from Moscow, Pavel Kuzanyan and Solomon Telingater from Tbilisi. Few of their designs have been available in the West; many, in fact, have yet to be produced in type at all.

Linotype, Monotype, ParaGraph and other digital foundries have issued Cyrillic versions of many well-known Latin faces, including Baskerville, Bodoni, Caslon, Frutiger, Futura, Helvetica, Jannon, Kabel, Officina, Plantin, Times and Univers. These have their uses, especially for multilingual work, when matching Latin and Cyrillic fonts may be required. But not all of these derivative Cyrillics can claim to be distinguished designs, and not all are suited to running text.

In its normal upright form – which is known in Russian as прямой (*pryamoi*) – Cyrillic is primarily an alphabet of small caps. There are fewer than half a dozen recognizably minuscule forms in the *pryamoi* lower case. Cursive Cyrillics, however, contain an abundance of minuscule forms and are structurally very close to Latin italic. Unserifed Cyrillics, like unserifed Latin faces, often come equipped with an oblique – a sloped *pryamoi* – in place of a true cursive.

абвгдежоф 1 2 3 АО *абвгдеж оф*

Baskerville м Baskerville himself did not design a Cyrillic, but Cyrillic adaptations of his roman and italic have been issued by Monotype, both in metal matrices and in digital form. For many Russian texts of the eighteenth century and later, a face of obviously Western origin and French Enlightenment spirit seems appropriate. Baskerville Cyrillic is one obvious choice for this purpose, especially if the text is bilingual and Baskerville roman and italic will suit the translation.

абвгдежофщ АЖО *абвгдежофщ*

Lazurski н This is a neohumanist Cyrillic designed by the Russian calligrapher Vadim Lazurski. It was produced in 1962 in two forms, under two names. As Lazurski, it was issued by the Polygraph Foundry, Moscow. Edited by Giovanni Mardersteig and cut under his direction by Ruggiero Olivieri, it is also known as Pushkin. In that form, it has been used only at Mardersteig's press, the Officina Bodoni in Verona. A bold weight was added in 1984 by Vladimir Efimov. Both the Cyrillic and its Latin companion were issued in digital form by ParaGraph International, Moscow, in 1991. (See also p 110.)

а б в г д е ж ф   А О Ф   *а б в г д е ж з ф*

Manuscript н A vigorous, expressionist Cyrillic designed in 1952 by Oldřich Menhart as a companion to his Manuscript roman and italic. It was issued by Grafotechna, Prague, in 1953 – but like its Latin companion face, it is apparently still waiting to be digitized.

абвгдежофщ АЖО *абвгдежофщ*

Minion D A neohumanist Cyrillic designed by Robert Slimbach as a companion to his Minion roman and italic. It was issued by Adobe in 1992. (This is the face used throughout this book where Cyrillic is required. See also p 107.)

абвгдежзийклмнопрстуфхцчшщъыьэюя

Trajanus м Upright and cursive Cyrillic companions to Warren Chappell's Trajanus were designed in 1957 by Hermann Zapf and issued by the Stempel Foundry. No other Cyrillic of Western origin comes so close to the proto-Renaissance spirit of much Slavic art and literature. Yet Trajanus Cyrillic is still waiting to be digitized.

Cyrillics

10.9 INSCRIPTIONAL & CALLIGRAPHIC CAPITALS

Every text begins at least once. Most stop and start again repeatedly before they run their course. These beginnings – of sentences, paragraphs, chapters or sections – are the doors and windows of the text. European scribes began to mark the major ones with large, sometimes ornate capital letters – versals – even before the Latin alphabet developed a lower case.

In many early printed books, space is left for such initials to be painted in by hand. Printers also began to print them, in multiple colors, as early as 1459. Many fine alphabets of capitals have sprung from this tradition: fonts of type designed for setting titles or short texts, or to be used one letter at a time. Some of these alphabets – Carol Twombly's Lithos and Gudrun Zapf-von Hesse's Smaragd, for example – are *glyphic* or inscriptional; others are purely calligraphic.

Because they are meant for use with other fonts of text size, many fonts of inscriptional initials are inlines: the interior of the stroke has been carved away to lighten the face. Jan van Krimpen's Romulus Open, for example, was made by hollowing out the capitals of his Romulus text face. But Cristal, designed by Rémy Peignot, and Castellar, designed by John Peters, were created from the start as inline types and exist in no other form.

Samples of many of these faces are shown on page 269.

The capitals from any text font can, of course, be enlarged for use as versals, but the proportions often suffer as a result, and specially proportioned titling capitals exist for only a few text faces. (Giovanni Mardersteig's Dante and Matthew Butterick's Wessex are two examples.) From time to time, however, the capitals from a bicameral titling face develop a separate life of their own. This has occurred with Berthold Wolpe's Albertus, Carl Dair's Cartier, Herb Lubalin's Avant Garde, and with Georg Trump's Codex and Delphin. The faces listed below were all designed, at least in the beginning, as capitals only.

A E G Q W

Ariadne **H** Calligraphic initials designed by Gudrun Zapf-von Hesse and issued by the Stempel Foundry, Frankfurt, in 1954. These initials combine especially well at text size with the same designer's Diotima, and at larger sizes with other neohumanist faces such as Nofret, Palatino and Aldus.

ABCDXYZ

Augustea **H/M** Sharply serifed, formal inscriptional capitals, designed by Aldo Novarese and Alessandro Butti, issued in metal by the Nebiolo Foundry, Torino, beginning in 1951. There is an inline version, known as Augustea Filettata or Augustea Inline. A lower case was also later added to the capitals. The result is known as Augustea Nova. (See also p 269.)

A B C D E F G H I J K L M N O P Q R S T U V W X Y Z

Castellar **M** Inline capitals, asymmetrically inscribed, so that the hollowed strokes are light on the left, dark on the right. The face was designed by John Peters and issued by Monotype in 1957. (See also pp 64, 160, 269.)

A B C D E F G H I J K L M N O P Q R S T U V W X Y Z

Charlemagne **D** Caroline capitals, based on the Carolingian titling scripts and versals of the ninth and tenth centuries, designed by Carol Twombly and issued in digital form by Adobe in 1989. (See also pp 120, 269.)

ABCDEFGHIJKLM
AKMNRUVXYZ
NOPQRSTUVWXYZ

Inscriptional and Calligraphic Capitals

Herculanum D Designed by Adrian Frutiger and issued by Linotype in 1990. There are many variant letters. Herculanum was a Roman city near present-day Naples, buried, like Pompeii, by the eruption of Vesuvius in AD 79. The face that bears its name is based on written and painted Roman letters of the first and second centuries AD. These unofficial and informal Roman inscriptions have been a source of inspiration to Frutiger for half a century. The capitals of his Ondine (p 255), designed in the early 1950s, derive from them as well. (See also p 118.)

ABCDEFGHIJKLM
NOPQRSTUVWXYZ

Lithos D Unserifed capitals with light stroke and large aperture, based on early Greek inscriptional letters. Designed by Carol Twombly and issued by Adobe in several weights. There are many subtle modulations in the stroke. An important precursor of this face is Robert Foster's now neglected Pericles, issued by ATF in 1934. (See also p 118.)

ABBAGGIIL&LLQQŒRRTTTT
ABCDEFGHIJKLM
NOPQRSTUVWXYZ
YYYLA MECVTTUPH&C

Mantinia D A complex face based on letterforms found in the work of the painter Andrea Mantegna (1431–1506). Andrea del Castagno, Fra Angelico and other fifteenth-century artists lavished as much care on their letterforms as on their human figures, but no Renaissance painter took the alphabet more seriously than Mantegna. The type that honors him was designed by Matthew Carter and issued by Carter & Cone in 1992.

ABCBCD

Michelangelo and *Sistina* H Two sets of serifed capitals designed by Hermann Zapf as complements to Palatino and Aldus. The original versions of both – the light, athletic Michelangelo and the darker, more ecclesiastical Sistina – were cut by August Rosenberger and issued by the Stempel Foundry in 1950–51. There is a third member of the series, Phidias, a Greek counterpart to Michelangelo. (See also p 269.)

ABCDPQR

Monument H Open inline capitals, designed by Oldřich Menhart and cast in 1950 by the Grafotechna Foundry, Prague. The imperial stillness typical of Roman inscriptional letters is transformed to a kind of stately folk dance under Menhart's hand.

ABCDEFGHIJKLMN OPQRSTUVWXYZ

Neuland H Dark, rugged, unserifed roman capitals, designed and cut by Rudolf Koch and issued in metal by the Klingspor Foundry, Offenbach, in 1923. Koch cut the original punches freehand, without pattern drawings. Each size in the foundry version therefore has many idiosyncracies of its own. These subtleties are lost in all the existing digital versions.

ABCDEFGHIJKLM NOPQRSTUVWXYZ

Rusticana D This is one of a group of three faces designed by Adrian Frutiger based on the more populist, less imperial varieties of Roman inscriptions. The other members of the family are Herculanum and Pompeijana. Rusticana owes its form to Roman inscriptional lettering of the fourth and fifth centuries AD. (See also p 118.)

A B C D E F G H I J K L M
N O P Q R S T U V W X Y Z

Smaragd D A set of light but powerful inline capitals designed by Gudrun Zapf-von Hesse and issued by the Stempel Foundry in 1952. Smaragd is, of course, emerald: the substance on which the secrets of Hermes Trismegistos – the Greek incarnation of Thoth, the inventor of writing – were reputedly engraved.

A A B C D E F G H I J K L M M
N O P Q R S T U V W X X Y Z

Sophia D Designed by Matthew Carter and issued by Carter & Cone in 1993. This complex face with its many variant glyphs is based primarily on the alphabet found on an inscribed cross, made in Constantinople in the mid sixth century and presented to the Bishop of Rome by the Byzantine Emperor Justin II and his wife – later also his regent – the Empress Sophia. (See also pp 182–184.)

A B C D E F G H I J K L M
N O P Q R S T U V W X Y Z

Trajan D Serifed capitals, based on the inscription at the base of Trajan's Column, Rome, carved at the beginning of the second century AD. Drawn by Carol Twombly and issued in digital form by Adobe. (See also p 120.)

A B C E E F A B C

Weiss Initials H There are three series of these initials, designed by Emil Rudolf Weiss in 1925 and cut by Louis Hoell at the Bauer Foundry as companions for Weiss's text face, Weiss Antiqua. Series 2 was cut in two weights and includes a number of alternate sorts.

Albertus
Augustea
Avant Garde

Cartier
Castellar
Charlemagne

Codex
Cristal
Delphin

Michelangelo
Monument
Neuland

Pericles
Romulus Open
Sistina

Visual Index of Analphabetic Characters

Single Stroke	Double Stroke	Letterforms and Modified Letters
˙ overdot	¨ umlaut/diaeresis	æ aesc
· midpoint	: colon	Æ aesc
. period	; semicolon	@ at
ˌ underdot	" " quotation	© copyright
• bullet	„ " quotation	¢ cent
' apostrophe	¡ ! exclamation	ð eth
' inverted comma	¿ ? question	đ dyet
, comma	" double prime	Đ eth/dyet
´ acute	˝ double acute	ə schwa
` grave	= equal	& ampersand
' prime	¦ pipe	⅋ ampersand
¯ macron	‖ double bar	ƒ guilder
- hyphen	+ addition	ħ barred н
- subtraction	× multiplication	Ħ barred н
_ lowline	« » guillemets	ı dotless ı
– en dash	⟦ ⟧ square brackets	ł barred ʟ
— em dash	♮ natural	Ł barred ʟ
‾ vinculum	♭ flat	£ sterling
∣ bar		μ mu
/ solidus		ŋ eng
⁄ virgule	**Multiple Stroke**	Ŋ eng
\ backslash		ø slashed o
¬ negation	… ellipsis	Ø slashed o
[ ] square brackets	÷ division	ơ horned o
⟨ ⟩ angle brackets	≠ unequal	œ ethel
‹ › guillemets	± plus-or-minus	Œ ethel
> greater than	# octothorp	¶ pilcrow
< less than	♯ sharp	® registration
ˇ caron	% per cent	§ section
ˆ circumflex	‰ per mil	ß eszett
∧ caret		$ dollar
˛ ogonek		þ thorn
¸ cedilla	**Pictograms**	Þ thorn
' hoi		ŧ barred т
˘ breve	* asterisk	Ŧ barred т
˜ tilde	† dagger	™ trademark
~ swung dash	‡ double dagger	ư horned ʋ
( ) parentheses	¤ currency	¥ yen
{ } braces	☞ fist	ȝ yogh
˚ ring	❧ hedera	
° degree		

There is, of course, no limit to the number of typographic characters. This appendix lists only those included on standard ISO Latin alphabet text fonts, and a tiny handful of additional characters of traditional typographic importance. (To date, ISO has defined at least nine separate official Latin character sets, but these differ little among themselves, and there is no impediment to putting all characters on a single font. Characters from all nine are therefore listed here together.) The hundreds of additional common characters required for mathematical and scientific work must generally be sought on specialized technical or pi fonts. These characters are subsumed in a more recent and extensive international standard known as Unicode.

acute An accent used on vowels – á é í ó ú ý – in Czech, French, Gaelic, Hungarian, Icelandic, Italian, Navajo, Spanish and other languages, and on consonants – ć ń ŕ ś ź – in Basque, Croatian, Polish and romanized Sanskrit. In romanized Chinese, it is used with vowels to mark the rising tone. It is also used with Cyrillic consonants – ŕ and ḱ – in Macedonian. The six acute vowels appear on normal ISO Latin fonts as composite characters.

á

aesc This ligature is a letter of the alphabet in Danish, Norwegian and Anglo-Saxon, corresponding to the Swedish *ä*. In English, words of Greek origin were formerly spelled with æ corresponding to Greek αι (alpha iota). Thus *aesthetics* in older texts is *æsthetics*. Deliberate archaism and pedantically correct quotation still, therefore, require the ligature even in English. *Aesc* (*æsc* in the older spelling) is pronounced *ash*.

æ

Æ

ampersand A scribal abbreviation for *and*. It takes many forms – *et* *&* & *&* &c – all derived from the Latin word *et*.

&

angle brackets These useful characters are missing from most text fonts, but they are readily found on pi fonts and on some fonts of blackletter and Greek. They serve many functions in mathematical and scientific writing. In the editing of classical texts, angle brackets are used to mark editorial *additions* while *braces* mark the editor's *deletions*. See also *square brackets*.

⟨a⟩

apostrophe Also called *raised comma* or *single close-quote*. A mark of elision in many languages. It grew from that use in English to become also a sign of the possessive. [*It's* = *it is*, but *John's* = *Johnes* = *John his* = belonging to John.] A superimposed apostrophe (not to be confused with the *acute*) is the standard symbol in linguistics for a glottalized consonant: ǩ m̓ p̓, etc. As a matter of convenience, these symbols are often converted to consonants followed by normal apostrophes: k' m' p', etc. Apostrophized consonants of this sort are frequent in typography. The apostrophized *d* and *t* (d' and t', whose capital forms are Ď and Ť) are letters of the alphabet in Czech; so are ľ and Ľ in Slovak, while ch', k', ḵ', l', s', t', tl', ts', x', x̱' and their corresponding capitals (written with apostrophes, not carons) are letters of the alphabet in Tlingit. Used alone, the apostrophe serves in many languages as a sign for the glottal stop. See also *glottal stop* and *quotation marks*.

arithmetical signs Only eight basic signs, + − ± × ÷ < = >, are in the standard ISO character set, and the subtraction sign and en dash are often identical. When other symbols, such as ≠ ≈ ∇ ≡ √ ≤ ≥, are required, it is generally best to take all signs, including the basic ones, from the same technical font so that all forms match in color and size.

asterisk A superscript, used primarily to mark referents and keywords. In European typography, it is widely used to mark a person's year of birth (as the dagger, substituting for a cross, is used to mark the year of death). In philology and other sciences, it is used to mark hypothetically reconstructed or fetal forms. The asterisk takes many forms (* * * * *, for example). It appears in the earliest Sumerian pictographic writing and has been in continuous typographic use for at least 5000 years.

at A commercial symbol meaning *at* or *at the rate of*. It has become essential in electronic mail addressing and computer coding but has no role in normal text.

backslash This is an unsolicited gift of the computer keyboard. Basic though it may be to elementary computer operations, it has no accepted function in typography.

bar The vertical bar is used in mathematics as a sign of absolute value, in prosodical studies to mark a caesura, and in propositional calculus (where it is called *Sheffer's stroke*) as a sign of nonconjunction. In bibliographical work, both single and double bars are used. Also called *caesura*.

barred H This is one of the ISO characters, but it is omitted from most fonts. It is a basic letter of the alphabet in Maltese, corresponding to the Arabic *ḥ*.

ħ Ħ

barred L A basic letter of the alphabet in Chipewyan, Navajo, Polish, and many other languages. The barred L (or *l-slash*, as it is known in PostScript) is now routinely included in standard text fonts. Henryk Mikołaj Górecki's Symphony N° 3, for example, is entitled *Symfonia Pieśni Żałosnych*, "Symphony of Sorrowful Songs." Also known by its Polish name, *ew*.

ł Ł

barred T This is a basic letter of the alphabet in Lapp and therefore one of the standard ISO characters. It is nevertheless absent from most text fonts.

t T

braces Braces are rarely required in text work, but they can function perfectly well as an extra and outer (or inner) set of parentheses: { ([–]) }. In mathematics they are used to mark phrases and sets. In editing classical papyri, braces are often used to mark editorial deletions.

{a}

brackets See *angle brackets* and *square brackets*.

breve An accent used on vowels and consonants – ă ĕ ğ – in Malay, Rumanian, Turkish, Vietnamese and romanized Korean. In English, it is used in informal phonetic transcriptions to mark lax (or so-called 'short') vowels. In writings on metrics and prosody, it is the sign of a quantitatively (genuinely) short vowel or syllable. It is also used on the Russian *i* (*й*, whose cursive form is *ŭ*) and on a second vowel, *ў*, in Belorussian. The breve is always rounded, and should not be confused with the angular caron. (*Breve* is two syllables, with the stress on the first, as in *brave, eh?*) Also called *short*.

ă

bullet A large version of the midpoint, used chiefly as a typographic flag. Bullets are commonly hung, like numbers, in the left margin to mark items in a list, or centered on the measure to separate blocks of text. See also *midpoint*.

•b

caret This is a stray, like the backslash, inherited from the standard ASCII keyboard. Along with the *dele* or delete sign, it is one of the most basic editorial symbols, but its only stock role in typography is as the sign of partial conjunction in symbolic logic. It is useless in that regard without the other standard logical operators, and with two exceptions (| and ¬) they are missing from the standard ISO character set.

caron An inverted circumflex. It is used on consonants and vowels – č ě ň ř š ž – in Croatian, Czech, Lapp, Lithuanian, Slovak, Slovene, Sorbian and other scripts. In romanized Thai, the caron indicates a rising tone. In romanized Chinese, it is used on vowels to mark the retroflexive third tone (falling/rising tone) of standard Mandarin, and it is often used in new scripts for Native American languages. For no apparent reason, most ISO fonts include a prefabricated upper- and lowercase š and ž, while other combinations, no less frequent in normal text, must be built with the floating accent. Typographers know the caron also by its Czech name, *háček,* pronounced *haa-check.*

cedilla An accent used with consonants – such as the ç in Catalan, French, Nahuatl and Portuguese, the ç and ş in Kurdish and Turkish, the ş and ţ in Rumanian, and the ŋ in Latvian. Not to be confused with the *ogonek* or nasal hook, which curves the other way and is used with vowels. The name means *little z.* Only Ç and ç appear on most fonts in prefabricated form.

circumflex An accent used on vowels – â ê î ô û ŵ ŷ –. in French, Portuguese, Rumanian, Turkish, Vietnamese, Welsh and many other languages. In transliterated texts (e.g., from Arabic, Greek, Hebrew and Sanskrit), it is sometimes used as a substitute for the macron, to mark long vowels. In romanized Thai, a circumflex signifies a falling tone. Normal ISO fonts include all the circumflexed vowels except the Welsh ŵ and ŷ in composite form.

colon A grammatical marker inherited from the medieval European scribes. It is also used in mathematics to indicate ratios and in linguistics as a mark of prolongation. The name is from Greek. In classical rhetoric and prosody, a *colon* (plural, *cola*) is a long clause, and a *comma* is a short one.

comma A grammatical marker, descended from early scribal practice. In German, and often in East European languages, the comma is used as an open quote. Throughout Europe, it is also used as a decimal point, where most North Americans expect a period. In North American usage, the comma separates thousands, while a space is preferred in Europe. Thus 10,000,000 = 10 000 000, but a number such as 10,001 is typographically ambiguous. In Europe it means ten and one one-thousandth; in North America, ten thousand and one.

copyright On poorly designed fonts, the copyright symbol sometimes appears as a superscript, but its rightful place in typography is on the baseline: ©.

curl See *hoi.*

currency symbols Standard ISO character sets include five real currency signs – $ £ ƒ ¥ ¢ – and one imaginary sign, ¤. The latter symbol, the so-called general currency sign, has no function except to hold a place on the font to which a real symbol for local currency (rupee, cruzeiro, peseta, etc) can be assigned. The cent sign (¢), now an American typographical heirloom, is equally irrelevant for most work. It remains in the character set chiefly out of nostalgia.

The dollar sign, a slashed *s*, is descended from an old symbol for the shilling. The same sign has come to be used for currencies with many other names: sol, peso, escudo, yuan, etc. The sign of the pound sterling is a stylized L, standing for the Latin *libra* (also the source of the abbreviation *lb*, used for the pound avoirdupois). This sign is now used not only for British currency but for the pound, lira or livre of many African and Middle Eastern states. The sign for Dutch guilders is *ƒ*, for *florin*, which is the old name for the currency. This *ƒ* is often cut shorter and wider than the normal italic lowercase *ƒ.*

dagger A reference mark, used chiefly with footnotes. In European typography, it is also a sign of mortality, used to mark the year of death or the names of deceased persons, and in lexicography to mark obsolete forms. In editing classical texts, daggers are used to flag passages judged to be corrupt. Also called *obelisk, obelus* or *long cross.*

dashes Latin text fonts include, at minimum, an em dash, en dash and hyphen. A figure dash and three-quarter em dash are often included as well, and a one-third em dash more rarely.

degree Used in mathematics and in normal text to give temperatures, inclinations, latitudes, longitudes and compass bearings. Not to be confused with the *superior o* used in abbreviations such as N°, nor with the *ring*, which is a diacritic.

diaeresis / umlaut An accent used with vowels – ä ë ï ö ü ẅ ÿ – in many languages, including Albanian, Breton, Estonian, Finnish, German, Swedish, Turkish and Welsh, and less frequently also in English, Spanish, Portuguese and French. Linguists distinguish between the *umlaut*, which marks a *change* in pronunciation of a single vowel (as in the German *Schön*) and the *diaeresis*, which marks the *separation* of adjacent vowels (as in naïve and Noël). The typographic symbol is the same, but in reference to English and the Romance languages, the correct term is diaeresis, while umlaut is correct in reference to most other languages in which the symbol is used. The umlauted or diaeretic vowels appear on normal fonts in composite form. Also called *tréma*, its French name. In Hungarian there are two forms of umlaut: this form, which is used for short vowels, and the *double acute* or long umlaut, used for long vowels. The ÿ is a vowel sometimes used in archaic French and still required in the modern form of a few personal names and place names. It is also an alternate form of the *ij* ligature in Flemish and Dutch.

diesis An alternate name for the *double dagger*.

dimension sign An unserifed x, identical to the multiplication sign. See *arithmetical signs*.

dotless ı A letter of the alphabet in Turkish. It is also used with floating accents to set í ì î ï ĭ ī. Only the first four of these are included in the ISO character sets in composite form.

double acute An accent used on the vowels ő and ű in Hungarian. Also called *long umlaut*. The name Hungarian umlaut should not be used, because the short umlauted vowels ö and ü also appear in Hungarian. Not to be confused with the double prime nor with the close quote.

double bar This is a standard symbol in bibliographical work and an old standard reference mark in European typography. It is nevertheless missing from the ISO character list. It is easily made by kerning two bars together.

‖

double dagger A reference mark for footnoting. Also called *diesis* or *double obelisk.*

‡

double prime An abbreviation for inches (1" = 2.54 cm) and for seconds of arc (360" = 1°). Not to be confused with quotation marks nor with the double acute. See also *prime.*

60"

dyet A basic letter of the alphabet in Croatian and Vietnamese. It is also required for romanized Macedonian and Serbian. The uppercase form of the letter is the same as the uppercase *eth.*

đ Đ

ellipsis The sign of elision and of rhetorical pause.

...

eng A basic letter of the alphabet in Lapp, and in its lowercase form, widely used in linguistics and lexicography. It represents the *ng* sound in the word *wing.* (Note the different sounds represented by the same letters in the words *wing, Wingate, singlet* and *singe.*) Though it is an ISO character, the eng is missing from most text fonts.

ŋ Ŋ

eszett The *ss* ligature, *long s* + *short s* (ſ + s). It was once essential for setting English and is still essential for German. Not to be confused with the Greek beta, β. Also known as *sharp s.*

ß ß

eth A basic letter of the alphabet in Anglo-Saxon, Faroese and Icelandic. The uppercase eth is the same as the uppercase *dyet,* but the lowercase forms are not interchangeable, and the letters represent quite different sounds. (The name *eth,* also spelled *edh,* is pronounced like the *eth* in *whether.*)

ð Đ

ethel A ligature formerly used in English and still essential for setting French. English words and names derived from Greek were formerly spelled with the ethel (or *æthel*) corresponding to the Greek οι (omicron iota). Thus the old form of *ecumenical* is *œcumenical,* and the Greek name Οἰδίπους (Oidípous), still disguised in English as Oedipus, was formerly written Œdipus. The ligature is required, therefore, for deliberate archaism and

œ

Œ

for academically correct quotation from older sources, as well as for the correct spelling of French words like *hors d'œuvre.*

ew See *barred L.*

exclamation In Spanish, the inverted exclamation mark is used at the beginning of the phrase and the upright mark at the end. In mathematics, the upright exclamation mark is the symbol for factorials ($4! = 4 \times 3 \times 2 \times 1$). It is also often used to represent the palatal clicks of the Khoisan languages of Africa. Thus, for example, the name !Kung. In England the exclamation mark is often called a *screamer.*

¡a!

figures A text font normally includes only one set of figures, which should usually be (but are usually not) text figures. The supporting fonts frequently include three further sets: titling figures, superior figures and inferior figures. The superiors are used for exponents, superscripts and the numerators of piece fractions. The inferiors are used for the denominators of fractions. For chemical formulae (H_2O etc) and mathematical subscripts, the inferior figures must usually be lowered.

1 2 3

4 5

fist The typographer's fist is not a blunt instrument but a silent, pointing hand. All too often, however, it is overdressed, with ruffles at the cuff. A Baroque invention, the fist is missing from the ISO character set and must be found on a supplementary font.

fractions Only three fractions – ¼, ½, ¾ – appear on standard ISO text fonts. For fractions beyond these three, whether prefabricated or custom-built from superior and inferior figures, a supplementary font is commonly required. See also *solidus.*

½

glottal stop The glottal stop is a sound, not a letter, but it is a typographic problem because it is a common and meaningful sound in human speech for which the Latin alphabet lacks a specific symbol. Linguists use the symbol ʔ – a gelded question mark – to represent this sound, but the best symbol to use in roman and italic text is usually the apostrophe. In romanized Arabic or Hebrew, the inverted comma or open quote (') is used to represent the letter *'ain,* whose phonetic symbol is ʕ, and the apostrophe (') is used to represent the *hamza* or glottal

a'a

stop. Thus, the Koran in Arabic is *al-Qur'ān*, but Arab is *'arab*, and the family is *al-'ā'ila*. See also *apostrophe, inverted comma* and *quotation marks*.

grave An accent used with vowels – à è ì ò ù – in French, Italian, Portuguese, Catalan, Vietnamese and many other languages. In romanized Chinese it signifies a falling tone. In Gaelic the grave is used to mark long vowels. Vowels with grave accents are included in the ISO character set in composite form.

à

guillemets Single and double guillemets are widely used as quotation marks with the Latin, Cyrillic and Greek alphabets in Europe, Asia and Africa. Attempts to introduce them into North America have, unfortunately, met with slight success. In French and Italian, the guillemets almost always point out, «thus» and ‹thus›, but in German they more frequently point in. Single guillemets should not be confused with angle brackets nor with the arithmetical operators meaning greater-than and less-than. Guillemet means Little Willy, in honor of the sixteenth-century French typecutter Guillaume [William] Le Bé, who may have invented them. Also called *chevrons, duck feet* and *angle quotes*.

‹ é ›
» ›ä‹ «
« é »

háček See *caron*.

hedera An ivy leaf: a type of fleuron. (*Hedera* is the Latin name for ivy.) This is one of the oldest of all typographic ornaments, present in many early Greek inscriptions.

hoi This is one of the five tonemarks used with vowels in the Vietnamese alphabet. It resembles a small question mark without the dot. The spelling in Vietnamese is, naturally, *hỏi* – and the name in Vietnamese does mean "question." In English it is also called a *curl*.

ỏ

horned o A letter of the alphabet in Vietnamese.

ơ

horned u A letter of the alphabet in Vietnamese.

ư

hyphen See *dashes*.

inverted comma Also called a single open-quote, and used for that purpose in English, Spanish and many other languages. In

'a

transliterated Arabic and Hebrew, it is also used to represent the letter *ain* or *ayin*, a pharyngeal continuant, while its opposite, the apostrophe, represents the glottal stop. Thus: King Ibn Saʿūd; the Beqaʿa Valley. By convention, the inverted comma and apostrophe used in transliterating Semitic languages must curve (' '). Rigid inverted commas and apostrophes (′ ′), also known as sloped primes, are unsuitable for this purpose. See also *glottal stop, quotation marks* and *reversed apostrophe*.

kroužek See *ring*.

letters Three varieties of letters appear on an ordinary font of type. There is normally a full alphabet in upper and lower case (or in full and small caps) and a partial alphabet of superior letters. The latter are used in numerical abbreviations such as 1st, 2nd, 3rd, the French 1e (*premier, première*) and the Spanish 2^a, 2° (*segunda, segundo*). They are also used in a few verbal abbreviations, such as 4° = quarto; 8° = octavo; M^r = mister; N^o = number, but in English most such forms are now archaic. The basic ISO alphabet includes only two superior letters, the *ordinal a* and *ordinal o*, which are essential for setting text in Romance languages. (They are called ordinals because they are used for ordinal numbers: first, second, third....) A fuller set – conventionally limited to $^{a\,b\,d\,e\,i\,l\,m\,n\,o\,r\,s\,t}$ – is usually to be found on a supplementary font. In some faces, the ordinal *a* and *o* are underlined while the superior letters are not.

A full superior and inferior italic alphabet is required for setting even simple mathematics. It must sometimes be created by resizing a regular or semibold italic.

ligatures Basic ISO fonts are limited to two rudimentary ligatures, fi and fl. Rigid definitions of the character set, leaving no provision for additional ligatures such as ff, ffi, ffl are a hazard to typography. Ligatures required by the design of the individual typeface should always be present on the basic font.

logical not See *negation*.

lowline This is a standard ISO character. On fonts intended for commercial work, it is sometimes positioned as a baseline rule. On text fonts, it is generally identical with the underscore.

macron A diacritic used to mark long vowels – ā ē ī ō ū – in many languages: Fijian, Hausa, Latvian and Lithuanian, among others. It is also used to mark long vowels in romanized Arabic, Greek, Hebrew, Japanese, Sanskrit and other Asian languages, and to mark level tones in romanized Chinese.

ā

midpoint An ancient European mark of punctuation, widely used in typography to flag items in a vertical list and to separate items in a horizontal line. A closely spaced midpoint is also often used to separate syllables or letters, especially in Catalan when one *l* adjoins another. (In Catalan as in Spanish, *ll* is treated as a single letter. When one *l* is adjacent to but separate from another, they are written *l·l*. Examples: the Catalan words *cel·les* [cells], *col·lecció* [collection] and *paral·lel*.) The same sign is used in mathematics for scalar multiplication and in symbolic logic for logical conjunction. Also called *small bullet.*.

(Upper- and lowercase *L + midpoint* [Ŀ & l·] are needlessly treated by ISO, and therefore by Unicode, as single characters.)

l·l

mu The Greek lowercase *m* represents the prefix *micro-* = 10⁻⁶. Thus milligrams is written *mg* and micrograms *µg*. (A millionth of a meter or *micron*, formerly written *µ*, is now written *µm*.)

µ

musical signs Three elementary musical symbols – ♭ ♯ ♮, the flat, sharp and natural – are needed for setting normal texts that make reference to standard European musical pitches and keys (Beethoven's Sonata Op. 110 in A♭, Ennemond Gaultier's Suite for Lute in F♯m, etc). These characters are, however, missing from standard ISO text fonts, and the octothorp is not a satisfactory substitute for the sharp.

♭ ♯ ♮

nang See *underdot*.

nasal hook See *ogonek*.

negation The negation sign used in the propositional calculus (symbolic logic) was formerly the swung dash (~). The usual form now is the angled dash (¬). It is part of the standard ISO Latin character set and included on most digital text fonts, even though it is useless without the other logical operators, such as ∪ ∩ ∧ ∨ ≡, which are usually missing from ISO fonts. Also called *logical not*.

¬ b

null A slashed or crossed zero, used to distinguish zero from the lowercase *o*. But the null in its commonest form, a slashed zero, is easily confused with the slashed *o* (ø, ø), which is a letter of the alphabet in Danish and Norwegian, and also with the phi (φ, φ), which is a letter of the alphabet in Greek. An alternate and sometimes less ambiguous form of the null is ⊖. The null is rarely found in text fonts, but either form is easy to build from existing components.

numeral sign See *octothorp*.

obelisk Also spelled *obelus* (plural, *obeli*). See *dagger*.

octothorp Otherwise known as the numeral sign. It has also been used as a symbol for the pound avoirdupois, but this usage is now archaic. In cartography, it is also a symbol for village: eight fields around a central square, and this is the source of its name. Octothorp means eight fields.

ogonek An accent used with vowels – ą ę į ǫ ų – in Lithuanian, Navajo, Polish, Tutchone and many other languages. Also called a *nasal hook*. Not to be confused with the cedilla, which is used with consonants and curves the other way. *Ogonek* is a Polish diminutive, meaning 'little tail.' It is also the Polish name for the stem of an apple.

ordinal a, ordinal o See *letters*.

overdot A diacritic used with consonants – ċ ġ ż – in Polish and Maltese, and with vowels – ė İ – in Lithuanian and Turkish. It is also required for several Native American languages, and for Sanskrit in romanized form.

paragraph See *pilcrow*.

parentheses Used as phrase markers in grammar and in mathematics, and sometimes to isolate figures or letters in a numerical or alphabetical list.

per cent Parts per hundred. Not to be confused with the symbol c/o, 'in care of,' which is not to be found in the iso Latin character set.

per mil Parts per thousand (61‰ = 6.1%). Though it is rarely required in text typography, this sign has been given a place in the ɪsᴏ Latin character sets.

%₀₀

period The normal sign for the end of a sentence in all the languages of Europe. But it is also a letter of the alphabet in Tlingit, pronounced as a glottal stop. In Catalan, it is sometimes used in the sequence *l.l*, as a poor substitute for the midpoint. Also called *full point* or *full stop*.

a.

pilcrow An old scribal mark used at the beginning of a paragraph or main text section. It is still used by typographers for that very purpose, and occasionally as a reference mark. Well-designed faces offer pilcrows with some character – ¶ ¶ ¶ ¶ (¶ ¶ – in preference to the over-used standard, ¶.

¶

pipe Despite its importance to programmers and its presence on the standard ᴀsᴄɪɪ keyboard, the pipe has no set function in typography. For drawing broken rules and boxes, a separate character from a specialized ruling font is commonly used. Also called a *broken bar* or *parted rule*.

|

prime An abbreviation for feet (1' = 12") and for minutes of arc (60' = 1°). Single and double primes may be sloped or vertical, but should not be confused with quotation marks, which in some faces (frakturs especially) also take the shape of sloped primes. See also *double prime*. Vertical primes are also known as *dumb quotes*, from their use in this capacity on typewriters.

60'

question In Spanish, the inverted question mark is used at the beginning of the phrase, in addition to the upright question mark at the end.

¿a?

quotation marks A standard ɪsᴏ font includes four forms of guillemet and six forms of Anglo-Germanic quotation mark – ' ' „ „ " " – but one of these is identical with the comma and one with the apostrophe. In English and Spanish, common usage is 'thus' and "thus"; in German, it is ‚thus' and „thus". This difference is parallel to the difference in usage of guillemets. In the Romance languages, guillemets point outward, and in German they point in. In French, "comme ça" and «comme ça»; in German, „auf diese Weise" and » diese Weise «. See also *prime*.

" ' X ' "

' » X « (

® registered trademark This is properly a superscript, though the otherwise similar copyright symbol is not.

‛ ‛‛ a reversed apostrophe(s) Mutant forms of the single and double open quote. They appear in many American advertising and text faces cut in the first years of the twentieth century and in some made at the end of that century as well.

ů ring Also called *kroužek*. A diacritic used in Arikara, Cheyenne, Czech, Danish, Norwegian and Swedish. The Scandanavian *round a* (Å and å) is included in the ISO character set, but Ů and ů (*u* with *kroužek*), just as common in Czech, must be built from the component parts. In Arikara and Cheyenne, the ring marks devoiced letters. The uppercase or small cap round A is the standard symbol for ångström units (10⁴ Å = 1 μm).

ə schwa An inverted *e*, used in phonetics to represent a short, bland vowel. Or in the technical jargon of phonetics, a mid central unrounded, unstressed vowel. It is not an ISO character and must be found on a phonetic font.

§ section A scribal form of double *s*, now used chiefly with reference to legal codes and statutes, when citing particular sections for reference. (The plural abbreviation, meaning sections, is written by doubling the symbol: §§.)

a; semicolon A grammatical marker, hybrid between colon and comma, derived from European scribal practice. But in classical Greek texts, the same symbol is used as a question mark.

ø Ø slashed o This is a basic letter of the alphabet in Norwegian and Danish, corresponding to the Swedish *ö*. Henrik Ibsen's last play, for example, was *Når vi døde vågner*, and one of his first was *Fru Inger til Østråt*. The letter is needed in English as well, for setting names such as Jørgen Moe and Søren Kierkegaard.

5/9 solidus The fraction bar. Used with superior and inferior numbers to construct ad hoc fractions. The solidus was a Roman imperial coin introduced by Constantine in AD 309. There were 72 solidi to the libra, the Roman pound, and 25 denarii to the solidus. The British based their own imperial coinage and its symbols – £/s/d, for pounds, shillings and pence – on the

Roman model, and *solidus* became in due course not only a by-word for shilling but also the name of the slash mark with which shillings and pence were written. (Given the design and fitting of the characters on most modern type fonts, the solidus is now best used for fractions alone. An italic virgule is usually the best character for setting references to British imperial money.) See also *virgule*, which is a separate character.

square brackets These essentials of text typography are used for interpolations into quoted matter and as a secondary and inner set of parentheses. In the editing of classical texts, square brackets normally mark editorial restorations, angle brackets mark editorial and conjectural insertions, and braces mark deletions. Double square brackets (rarely to be found except on technical fonts and fonts of polytonic Greek) are used by textual scholars to mark deletions made not by the editor but by the author or scribe. In editing manuscripts and papyri, square brackets also mark hiatuses caused by physical damage.

[a]

[[a]]

swung dash A stock keyboard character, used in mathematics as the sign of similarity ($a \sim b$) and in lexicography as a sign of repetition. The same sign has been used in symbolic logic to indicate negation, but to avoid confusion, the angular negation symbol ($\neg$) is preferred. Not to be confused with the *tilde*.

$a \sim b$

thorn A basic letter of the alphabet in Anglo-Saxon, Vietnamese, and of course in Icelandic: *Þótt þu langförull legðir....*

Þ þ

tilde Used on vowels – ã ĩ õ – in Estonian, Greenlandic, Portuguese and Vietnamese, and on consonants – g̃ ñ – in Quechua, Spanish, Tagalog and romanized Sanskrit, among other languages. The ñ and Ñ appear on standard text fonts in composite form. The remaining forms must usually be constructed.

ã

trademark A superscript, used in commercial work only.

TM

umlaut See *diaeresis.*

underdot An accent used especially with consonants – ḥ ṃ ṇ ṣ ṭ – in romanized Arabic, Hebrew, Sanskrit and other Asian languages, and often used in African and Native American scripts. In romanized Arabic and Hebrew, the underscore can be substi-

ạ

tuted, but the underdot is preferable. Editors of classical inscriptions and papyri routinely use the underdot to mark all letters whose reading is uncertain. The underdot is also one of the tone-marks used with vowels in Vietnamese. Its typographic nickname, *nang*, is a simplified form of its proper Vietnamese name, *nặng*. It is missing from the basic ISO character set.

underscore A diacritic required for many African and Native American languages, and useful for some purposes in English. It is also used as an alternative to the underdot in setting romanized Arabic and Hebrew. To clear descenders, a repositioned version of the character is required. See also *lowline*.

unequal A useful symbol missing from the ISO character sets. Apart from its importance in mathematics and general text, it has several more specialized uses. In writing the Khoisan languages of Africa, for example, it is used as a symbol for alveolar clicks.

vertical rule See *bar*.

vinculum An overbar, used in mathematics ($\sqrt{10}$) and in the sciences ($\overline{AB}$). *Vinculum* is Latin for *bond* or *chain*.

virgule An oblique stroke, used by medieval scribes and many later writers as a form of comma. It is also used to build *level* fractions, to represent a linebreak when verse is set as prose, and in dates, addresses and elsewhere as a sign of separation. In writing the Khoisan languages of western Africa, it is sometimes used to represent dental or lateral clicks. Compare *solidus*.

wedge Another name for the *caron*.

yen See *currency symbols*.

yogh A letter of the alphabet in Lapp. It was also part of the early English alphabet and is still therefore used in some editions of Anglo-Saxon and Middle English texts. It is absent from most text fonts, but the lowercase form can be found on any standard font of phonetic symbols, because the yogh is also part of the IPA (International Phonetic Association) alphabet. (The numeral 3 is not a suitable substitute.)

Names of individual characters and diacritics (circumflex, dyet, midpoint, virgule, etc) are not in this glossary. They appear in appendix A instead. For summary definitions of historical categories (Renaissance, Baroque, etc), see chapter 7.

10/12 × 18 Ten on twelve by eighteen, which is to say, ten-point (10 pt) type set with 12 pt leading (2 pt extra lead, in addition to the body size of 10 pt, for a total of 12 pt from baseline to baseline) on a measure of 18 picas.

Abrupt & Adnate Serifs are either *abrupt* – meaning they break from the stem suddenly at an angle – or they are *adnate*, meaning that they flow smoothly into or out of the stem. In the older typographic literature, adnate serifs are generally described as bracketed.

Aldine Relating to the publishing house operated in Venice by Aldus Manutius between 1494 and 1515. Most of Aldus's type – which included roman, italic and Greek – was cut by Francesco Griffo of Bologna. Type that resembles Griffo's, and typography that resembles Aldus's, is called Aldine. Monotype Poliphilus and Bembo roman are Aldine revivals, though their companion italics are not.

Analphabetic A typographic symbol used with the alphabet but lacking a place in the alphabetical order. Diacritics such as the acute, umlaut, circumflex and caron are analphabetics. So are the asterisk, the dagger, the pilcrow.

Aperture The openings of letters such as C, c, S, s, a and e. Humanist faces such as Bembo and Centaur have large apertures, while Romantic faces such as Bodoni and Realist faces such as Helvetica have small apertures. Very large apertures occur in archaic Greek inscriptions and in typefaces such as Lithos, which are derived from them.

Axis In typography, the axis of a letter generally means the axis of the stroke, which in turn reveals the axis of the pen or other tool used to make the letter. If a letter has thick strokes and thin ones, find the thick strokes and extend them into lines. These lines reveal the axis (or *axes*; there may be several) of the letter. Not to be confused with *slope.*

11

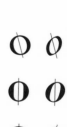

Ball Terminal A circular form at the end of the arm, leg or brow in letters such as a, c, f, j, r and y. Ball terminals are found in many romans and italics of the Romantic period, some Realist faces, and in many recent faces built on Romantic lines. Examples: Bodoni, Scotch Roman and Haas Clarendon. See also *beak terminal* and *teardrop terminal*.

Baseline Whether written by hand or set into type, the Latin lowercase alphabet implies an invisible staff consisting of at least four lines: topline, midline, baseline and beardline. The topline is the line reached by ascenders in letters like b, d, h, k, l. The midline marks the top of letters like a, c, e, m, x, and the top of the torso of letters like b, d, h. The baseline is the line on which all these letters rest. The beardline is the line reached by descenders in letters like p and q. The cap line, marking the top of uppercase letters like H, does not necessarily coincide with the topline of the lower case.

Round letters like e and o normally dent the baseline. Pointed letters like v and w normally pierce it, while the foot serifs of letters like h and m rest precisely upon it.

Bastarda A class of *blackletter* types. See page 250.

Beak Terminal A sharp spur, found particularly on the f, and also often on a, c, j, r and y, in many twentieth-century romans and, to a lesser degree, italics. Examples: Perpetua, Berling, Méridien, Pontifex, Veljović, Calisto.

Bicameral A bicameral alphabet is two alphabets joined. The modern Latin alphabet, which you are reading, is an example. It has an upper and a lower case, as closely linked and yet as easy to distinguish as the Senate and the House of Representatives. Unicameral alphabets (the Arabic, Hebrew and Devanagari alphabets, for example) have only one case. Tricameral alphabets have three – and a normal font of roman type can be described as tricameral, if you distinguish upper case, lower case and small caps.

Bilateral Extending to both sides. Bilateral serifs, which are always *reflexive*, are typical of roman faces, while unilateral serifs are typical of romans, Carolingians and italics.

Bitmap A digital image in unintelligent form. A letterform can be described morphologically, as a series of reference points and trajectories that mimic its perimeter, or embryologically, as the series of penstrokes that produce the form. Such descriptions are partially independent of size and position. The same image can also be described quite accurately

rately but superficially as the addresses of all the dots (or *bits*) in its digital representation. This sort of description, a bitmap, ties the image to one orientation and size.

Blackletter Blackletter is to typography what Gothic is to architecture: a general name for a wide variety of forms that stem predominantly from the north of Europe. Like Gothic buildings, blackletter types can be massive or light. They are often tall and pointed, but sometimes round instead. Compare *whiteletter*. The categories of blackletter include bastarda, fraktur, quadrata, rotunda and textura. See page 250.

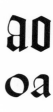

Bleed As a verb, to bleed means to reach to the edge of the page. As a noun, it means printed matter with no margin. If an image is printed so that it reaches beyond the trim line, it will bleed when the page is trimmed. Photographs, rules, solids and background screens or patterns are often allowed to bleed. Type can rarely do so.

Blind In letterpress work, printing blind means printing without ink, producing a colorless impression.

Blind Folio A page which is counted in the numbering sequence but carries no visible number.

Block Quotation A quotation set off from the main text, forming a paragraph of its own, often indented or set in a different face or smaller size than the main text. A *run-in quotation*, on the other hand, is run in with the main text and usually enclosed in quotation marks.

Body (1) In reference to foundry type: the actual block of typemetal from which the sculpted mirror-image of the printed letter protrudes. (2) In reference to phototype or digital type: the rectangular face of the metal block that the letter would be mounted on *if it were* three-dimensional metal instead of a two-dimensional image or bitmap. Retained as a fiction for use in sizing and spacing the type.

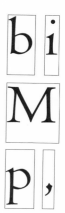

Body Size In graphic terms, the *height* of the *face* of the type, which in letterpress terms is the *depth* of the *body* of the type. Originally, this was the height of the face of the metal block on which each individual letter was cast. In digital type, it is the height of its imaginary equivalent, the rectangle defining the space owned by a given letter, and not the dimension of the letter itself. Body sizes are usually given in points – but European type sizes are often given in Didot points, which are 7% larger than the points used in Britain and North America.

Bowl The generally round or elliptical forms which are the basic bodyshape of letters such as C, G, O in the upper case, and b, c, e, o, p in the lower case. Also called *eye*.

Cap Height The distance from baseline to cap line of an alphabet, which is the approximate height of the uppercase letters. It is often less, but sometimes greater, than the height of the ascending lowercase letters. See also *baseline* and *x-height*.

Chancery A class of cursive letterforms, generally featuring extra ligatures and lengthened and curved extenders. Many, but not all, chancery letterforms are also *swash* forms.

Cicero A unit of measure equal to 12 Didot points. This is the continental European counterpart to the British and American *pica*, but the cicero is slightly larger than the pica. It is equivalent to 4.52 mm or 0.178 inch. See *point*.

Color The darkness of the type as set in mass, which is not the same as the *weight* of the face itself. The spacing of words and letters, the leading of lines, and the incidence of capitals, not to mention the color (i.e., darkness) of the ink and of the paper it is printed on, all affect the color of the type.

Contrast In the analysis of letterforms, this usually refers to the degree of contrast between the thick strokes and thin strokes of a given letter. In faces such as Gill Sans and Helvetica, there is no contrast. In Romantic faces such as Bulmer and Bodoni, the contrast is high.

Counter The white space enclosed by a letterform, whether wholly enclosed, as in *d* or *o*, or partially, as in *c* or *m*.

Crosshead A heading or subhead centered over the text. Compare *sidehead*.

Cursive Flowing. Often used as a synonym for *italic*.

Dingbat A typographic glyph or symbol subject to scorn because it has no apparent relation to the alphabet. Many dingbats are pictograms – tiny pictures of churches, airplanes, skiers, telephones, and the like, used in the tourist industry. Others are more abstract symbols – check marks, crosses, cartographic symbols, the emblems of the suits of playing cards, and so on.

Dot Leader A row of evenly spaced periods or midpoints, occasionally used to link flush-left text with flush-right numerals in a table of contents or similar context. (There are none in this book.)

DPI Dots per inch. The usual measure of output *resolution* in digital typography and in laser printing.

Drop Cap A large initial capital or *versal* mortised into the text. (See page 64 for examples.) Compare *elevated cap.*

Drop Folio A folio (page number) dropped to the foot of the page when the folios on other pages are carried near the top. Drop folios are often used on chapter openings.

Dropline Paragraph A paragraph marked by dropping directly down one line space from the end of the previous paragraph, without going back to the left margin. (See page 40 for an example.)

Elevated Cap A large initial capital or versal set on the same baseline as the first line of the text.

Em In linear measure, a distance equal to the type size, and in square measure, the square of the type size. Thus an em is 12 pt (or a 12 pt square) in 12 pt type, and 11 pt (or an 11 pt square) in 11 pt type. Also called *mutton.*

En Half an em. To avoid misunderstanding when instructions are given orally, typographers often speak of ems as *muttons* and ens as *nuts.*

Extenders Descenders and ascenders; i.e., the parts of the letterform that extend below the baseline, as in p and q, or above the midline, as in b and d.

Eye Synonym for bowl. But large eye means large *x-height*; open eye means large *aperture.*

FL Flush left, which means set with an even left margin. By implication, the right margin is ragged. To be more precise, one could write FL/RR, meaning flush left, ragged right.

FL&R Flush left and right, which is to say *justified.*

Fleuron A horticultural dingbat. That is to say, a typographic ornament ordinarily in the shape of a flower or leaf. Some fleurons are designed to be set in bulk and in combinations, to produce what amounts to typographic wallpaper.

Flush and Hung Set with the first line FL and subsequent lines indented, like the entries in this glossary.

Folio In bibliography, a page or leaf; but in typography, a folio is normally a typeset page *number*, not the page itself.

Font A set of sorts or glyphs. In the world of metal type, this means a given alphabet, with all its accessory characters, in a given size. In relation to phototype, it usually means the assortment of standard patterns forming the glyph palette, without regard to size, or the actual filmstrip or wheel on which these patterns are stored. In the world of digital type, the font is the glyph palette itself or the digital information encoding it. (The older British spelling, *fount*, has not only the same meaning but also the same pronunciation.)

Fore-edge The outside edge or margin of a book page; i.e., the edge or margin opposite the spine.

FR Flush right. With an even right margin. By implication, the left margin is ragged.

Fraktur A class of *blackletter* types. See page 250.

Glyph A version of a character. See *sort*.

Gutter The blank column between two columns of type or the margins at the spine between two facing textblocks.

Hanging Figures Text figures.

Hard Space A word space that will not translate into a line-break. Also called *no-break space.*

Hint The letterforms that make up a digital font are usually defined mathematically in terms of outlines or templates, which can be freely scaled, rotated and moved about. When pages are composed, these outlines are given specific locations and sizes. They must then be *rasterized*: converted into solid forms made up of dots at the resolution of the output device. If the size is very small or the resolution low, the raster or grid will be coarse, and the dots will fill the mathematical template very imperfectly. Hints are *the rules of compromise* applied in this process of rasterization. At large sizes and high resolutions, they are irrelevant. At smaller sizes and lower resolutions, where distortion is inevitable, they are crucial. Most, but not all, digital fonts are *hinted*. That is, they include hints as integral parts of the font definition. See also *bitmap.*

Humanist Humanist letterforms are letterforms originating among the humanists of the Italian Renaissance and persisting to the present day. They are of two primary kinds: roman and italic, both of which derive from Roman capitals and Carolingian minuscules. Humanist letterforms show the clear trace of a broadnib pen held by a right-handed scribe. They have a *modulated* stroke and a *humanist axis.*

Humanist Axis An oblique stroke axis reflecting the natural inclination of the writing hand. See pp 12–15.

Inline A letter in which the inner portions of the main strokes have been carved away, leaving the edges more or less intact. Inline faces lighten the color while preserving the shapes and proportions of the original face. *Outline* letters, on the other hand, are produced by drawing a line around the outsides of the letters and removing the entire original form. Outline letters, in consequence, are fatter than the originals and have less definition. Castellar, Smaragd and Romulus Open are examples of inline faces.

IPA International Phonetic Association. An organization of linguists founded in 1886. The IPA alphabet is a set of phonetic symbols, diacritics and tonemarks, widely used but – like any scientific system – subject to constant refinement and modification. (A widely used alternative is the phonetic system of the American Anthropological Association.)

ISO International Organization for Standardization, headquartered in Geneva. An agency for international cooperation on industrial and scientific standards. Its membership consists of the national standards organizations of more than one hundred countries.

Italic A class of letterforms more cursive than roman but less cursive than script, first developed in Italy during the fifteenth century.

Justify To adjust the length of the line so that it is flush left and right on the measure. Type in the Latin alphabet is commonly set either justified or FL/RR (flush left, ragged right).

Kern Part of a letter that extends into the space of another. In many alphabets, the roman *f* has a kern to the right, the roman *j* a kern to the left, and the italic *f* one of each. As a verb, to kern means to alter the fit of certain letter combinations – *To* or *VA*, for example – so that the limb of one projects over or under the body or limb of the other.

Lachrymal Terminal See *teardrop terminal.*

Lead [Rhyming with *red*] Originally a strip of soft metal (lead or brass) used for vertical spacing between lines of type. Now meaning the vertical distance from the baseline of one line to the baseline of the next. Also called *leading.*

Lettrine Literally, 'a large letter.' Synonym for *versal.*

Ligature Two or more letters tied into a single character. The sequence ffi, for example, forms a ligature in most Latin text faces.

Lining Figures Figures of even height. Usually synonymous with *titling figures,* but some lining figures are smaller and lighter than the uppercase letters.

Logogram A specific typographic form tied to a certain word. Example: the nonstandard capitalizations in the names e.e. cummings, ПараГраф, TrueType and WordPerfect.

Lowercase Figures Text figures.

ᴍ/3 A third of an em: e.g., 4 pt in 12 pt type; 8 pt in 24 pt type.

Measure The standard length of the line; i.e., column width or width of the overall textblock, usually measured in picas.

Mid Space A space measuring ᴍ/4, a fourth of an em.

Modulation In relation to typography, modulation means the usually cyclical and predictable variation in width of the stroke. In monochrome (unmodulated) letterforms like Frutiger, the stroke is always fundamentally the same width. In a face such as Bembo or Centaur, the stroke is based on the trace of a broadnib pen, which makes thin cross strokes and thicker pull strokes. When letters are written with such an instrument, modulation automatically occurs.

Monotonic Modern Greek orthography uses only one of the old tonic accent marks, the acute, along with an occasional di-aeresis. (Greek has often, in fact, been written and some-times typeset in this way, but the practice did not become official until 1982.) Fonts designed for setting only modern Greek are known as monotonic. Compare *polytonic*.

Mutton An *em*. Also called mutton quad.

Negative Leading Leading – that is to say, line space – smaller than the body size. Type set 16/14, for example, is set with negative leading.

Neohumanist Recent letterforms that revive and reassert *hu-manist* principles are called neohumanist.

Nut An *en*.

Old-Style Figures A poor but common synonym for *text figures*.

Orthotic A class of Greek scripts and types that flourished in Western Europe between 1200 and 1520, revived in the early twentieth century. Orthotic Greeks are noncursive and usu-ally bicameral. In other words, they are analogous to the ro-man form of Latin script. Both caps and lower case are usually upright. Serifs, when present, are usually short, abrupt and unilateral. The geometric figures of circle, line and triangle are usually prominent in their underlying struc-ture. Victor Scholderer's New Hellenic is an example.

Pi Font A font of assorted mathematical or other symbols, de-signed to be used as an adjunct to one or more text fonts.

Pica A unit of measure equal to 12 *points*. Two different picas are in common use. (1) In traditional printers' measure, the pica is 4.22 mm or 0.166 inch: close to, but not exactly, one sixth of an inch. This is the customary British and American unit for measuring the length of the line and the depth of the textblock. (2) The PostScript pica is precisely one sixth of an inch. (Note: the continental European counterpart to the pica is the *cicero,* which is 7% larger.)

Piece Fraction A fraction (such as 9/32) that is not included in the font and must therefore be made on the spot from separate components.

Point (1) In traditional British and American measure, a point is one twelfth of a *pica,* which makes it 0.3515 mm, or 0.01383 inch. In round numbers, there are 72 points per inch, or 28.5 points per centimeter. (2) In continental Europe a larger point, the Didot point, is used. The Didot point (one twelfth of a *cicero*) is 0.38 mm or 0.01483 inch. In round numbers, there are 26.5 Didot points per centimeter, or 67.5 per inch. (3) Many photosetters and most digital typesetting devices, as well as the PostScript and TrueType computer languages, round the point off to precisely 1/72 inch and the pica to precisely 1/6 inch.

Polytonic Classical Greek has been set since the fifteenth century with an array of tonic accents and other diacritics inherited from the Alexandrian scribes. These diacritics – acute, grave, circumflex, rough breathing, smooth breathing, diaeresis and iota subscript – are used singly and in a variety of combinations. Modern Greek retains only the acute and an occasional diaeresis. Greek fonts equipped with the full set of accents are accordingly known as polytonic Greeks, and modern Greek fonts as *monotonic.* Monotonic text can of course be set with a polytonic font, but not the other way around.

Quad An *em.* Also called *mutton quad.*

Ranging Figures Figures of even height. Synonymous with *lining figures.* Ranging figures are usually *titling figures,* but some ranging figures are smaller than the uppercase letters.

Raster Digital grid. See *hint.*

Rationalist Axis Vertical axis, typical of Neoclassical and Romantic letterforms. See pp 12–13. Compare *humanist axis.*

Reflexive A type of *serif* that concludes the stroke of the pen, but implies a continuation of the text. Reflexive serifs are typical of roman faces, including the face in which these words are set. They always involve a sudden, small stoppage and reversal of the pen's direction, and more often than not they are *bilateral.* See also *transitive.*

m

Resolution In digital typography, resolution is the fineness of the grain of the typeset image. It is usually measured in dots per inch (dpi). Laser printers, for example, generally have a resolution between 300 and 1200 dpi, and typesetting machines a resolution significantly greater than 1200 dpi. The resolution of the conventional television set is only about 50 dpi, and the resolution of most computer screens is less than 100 dpi. But other factors besides resolution affect the apparent roughness or fineness of the typeset image. These factors include the inherent design of the characters, the skill with which they are digitized, the *hinting* technology used to compensate for coarse *rasterization*, and the type of film or paper on which they are reproduced.

Rotunda A class of *blackletter* types. See page 250.

RR Ragged right, which is to say unjustified.

Sanserif From the earlier English forms *sans serif* and *sans surryphs*, without serifs: synonymous with *unserifed*.

Serif A stroke added to the beginning or end of one of the main strokes of a letter. In the roman alphabet, serifs are usually *reflexive* finishing strokes, forming unilateral or bilateral stops. (They are unilateral if they project only to one side of the main stroke, like the serifs at the head of T and the foot of L, and bilateral if they project to both sides, like the serifs at the foot of T and the head of L.) *Transitive* serifs – smooth entry or exit strokes – are usual in italic.

There are many descriptive terms for serifs, especially as they have developed in roman faces. They may be not only unilateral or bilateral, but also long or short, thick or thin, pointed or blunt, abrupt or adnate, horizontal or vertical or oblique, tapered, triangular, and so on. In texturas and some frakturs, they are usually *scutulate* (diamond-shaped), and in some architectural scripts, such as Eagle-feather and Tekton, the serifs are virtually round.

(Not all type historians agree that the word *serif* should be used in relation to italic letters. But some term is necessary to denote the difference between, for example, Bembo italic and Caspari italic. In this book, the former is described as a serifed italic, the latter as unserifed.)

Sidehead A heading or subhead set flush left (more rarely, flush right) or slightly indented. Compare *crosshead*.

Slab Serif An abrupt or adnate serif of the same thickness as the main stroke. Slab serifs are a hallmark of the so-called egyptian and clarendon types: two groups of Realist faces produced in substantial numbers since the early nineteenth century. Memphis, Rockwell and Serifa are examples. A more recent example is PMN Caecilia.

Slope The angle of inclination of the stems and extenders of letters. Most (but not all!) italics slope to the right at something between 2° and 20°. Not to be confused with *axis.*

Solid Set without additional *lead,* or with the line space equivalent to the type size. Type set 11/11 or 12/12, for example, is set solid.

Sort A single piece of metal type: therefore a letter in one particular style and size. In the world of digital type, where letters have no physical existence until printed, the word *sort* has been partially displaced by the word *glyph.* A glyph is a version – a conceptual, not material, incarnation – of the abstract symbol called a character. Thus, *z* and *ᴢ* are different glyphs (in the same face) for the same character.

Stem A main stroke that is more or less straight, not part of a bowl. The letter *o* has no stem; the letter *l* consists of stem and serifs alone.

Swash A letterform reveling in luxury. Some swash letters carry extra flourishes; others simply occupy an abnormally large ration of space. Swash letters are usually cursive and swash typefaces therefore usually italic. True italic capitals (as distinct from sloped roman capitals) are usually swash. (*The Capitals in this Sentence are Examples.*) Hermann Zapf's Zapf Renaissance italic and Robert Slimbach's Poetica are faces in which the swash can be extended to the lower case.

Teardrop Terminal A swelling, like a teardrop, at the end of the arm in letters such as a, c, f, g, j, r and y. This feature is typical of typefaces from the Late Renaissance, Baroque and Neoclassical periods, and is present in many recent faces built on Baroque or Neoclassical lines. Examples: Jannon, Van Dijck, Kis, Caslon, Fournier, Baskerville, Bell, Walbaum, Zapf International, Galliard. Also called *lachrymal terminal.* See also *ball terminal* and *beak terminal.*

Textblock The part of the page normally occupied by text, or the page minus its standard margins.

Text Figures Figures – 1 2 3 4 5 6 – designed to match the lowercase letters in size and color. Most text figures are ascending and descending forms. Compare *lining figures, ranging figures* and *titling figures.*

| $\dfrac{\text{M}}{3}$ | $\dfrac{\text{M}}{4}$ | $\dfrac{\text{M}}{5}$ |

Textura A class of *blackletter* types. See page 250.

Thick Space A space measuring M/3, a third of an em.

Thin Space In letterpress work, a space measuring M/5, a fifth of an em. In computer typesetting, sometimes understood as M/6. Compare *mid space* and *thick space*.

Three-to-em One-third em. Also written M/3.

Titling Figures Figures – 123456 – designed to match the up-percase letters in size and color. Compare *text figures*.

Transitive A type of serif which flows directly into or out of the main stroke without stopping to reverse direction, typical of many italics. Transitive serifs are usually unilateral: they extend only to one side of the stem. See also *reflexive*.

Type Size See *body size*.

U&lc Upper and lower case: the normal form for setting text in the Latin, Greek and Cyrillic alphabets, all of which are now *bicameral*.

Unicameral Having only one case – like the Hebrew alphabet and many roman titling faces. Compare *bicameral*.

Versal A large initial capital, either elevated or dropped. Also called *lettrine*.

Weight The darkness (blackness) of a typeface, independent of its size. See also *color*.

Whiteletter The generally light roman letterforms favored by humanist scribes and typographers in Italy in the fifteenth and sixteenth centuries, as distinct from the generally darker *blackletter* script and type used more persistently north of the Alps. Whiteletter is the typographic counter-part to Romanesque in architecture, as blackletter is the counterpart to Gothic.

White Line A line space.

Word Space The space between words. When type is set FL/RR, the word space may be of fixed size, but when the type is *justified*, the word space must usually be elastic.

x-height The distance between the baseline and the midline of an alphabet, which is normally the approximate height of the unextended lowercase letters – a, c, e, m, n, o, r, s, u, v, w, x, z – and of the torso of b, d, h, k, p, q, y. The relation of x-height to cap height, and the relation of x-height to length of *extenders*, are two important characteristics of any *bicam-eral* Latin typeface. See also *baseline, cap height* and *eye*.

APPENDIX C: TYPE DESIGNERS

A biographical index of designers important to typographic history, and of all those doing important work in the present day, would be a book in itself. The following list is little more than a cross-reference to important designers whose work is mentioned elsewhere in this book.

LUDOVICO DEGLI ARRIGHI (*c.* 1480–1527) Italian calligrapher and designer of at least six chancery italic fonts. Frederic Warde's Vicenza and Arrighi (the italic companion to Centaur) are based on one of his faces. Monotype Blado (the italic companion to Poliphilus) is a rough approximation of another.

ANTOINE AUGEREAU (*c.* 1490–1534) Parisian punchcutter and printer. Author of several text romans and at least one Greek. Along with his contemporary Simon de Colines, Augereau defined the style of French typography later identified with the name of his most famous apprentice, Claude Garamond. This activity came to an end when he was hanged and his corpse was publicly burnt, on Christmas Eve of 1534, for printing a psalm without permission.

RICHARD AUSTIN (*c.* 1765–1830) English punchcutter producing Neoclassical and Romantic faces. He cut the original Bell type, the first Scotch Roman, and the original version of Porson Greek. W. A. Dwiggins's Caledonia is based primarily on Austin's work.

JOHN BASKERVILLE (1706–1775) English calligrapher, printer and businessman. Designer of a series of Neoclassical romans, italics and one Greek. Most of the faces sold in his name are based on his work and some resemble it closely. His punches are now at the University Library, Cambridge, and the St Bride Printing Library, London. A set of original matrices, formerly in Paris, is now in the Frutiger Foundry, Münchenstein, Switzerland.

LUCIAN BERNHARD (1885–1972) German immigrant to the USA. Painter, poet, industrial designer and typographer. Author of a large number of roman faces, distinguished by their long extenders. These were cut and cast primarily by ATF and Bauer.

CHARLES BIGELOW (1945–) American typographer, scholar, linguist and artist. Codesigner, with Kris Holmes, of the Lucida family.

ARCHIBALD BINNEY (1762–1838) Scottish immigrant to the USA. He was trained as a punchcutter in Edinburgh. With James Ronaldson, another Scottish immigrant, he established the Binney & Ronaldson Foundry in Philadelphia, where he cut Baroque, Neoclassical and Romantic type.

FRANK BLOKLAND (1959–) Dutch typographer and founder of the Dutch Type Library in 's-Hertogenbosch. His faces include Berenice and Documenta.

GIAMBATTISTA BODONI (1740–1813) Italian punchcutter, printer and prolific designer of type, working at Rome and Parma. Bodoni is best known for his dark and razor-sharp Romantic romans, italics and sometimes wildly ornamental Greeks, but he also designed and cut a large number of Neoclassical fonts. Bauer Bodoni, Berthold Bodoni, and some of the other faces now sold in his name are based on his work. His punches are in the Bodoni Museum, Parma.

LUDOLF BORCHTORP (*c.* 1470– *c.* 1510) Polish mathematician and engraver. Author of the first fonts of Cyrillic type, which he cut in Kraków about 1490, for the printer Szwajpolt Fiol.

CHRIS BRAND (1921–1999) Dutch calligrapher, the designer of Albertina, Delta, Draguet Coptic and other faces.

MATTHEW CARTER (1937–) English type designer, punchcutter and scholar, working primarily in Europe and the USA. His text faces include Auriga, Charter and Galliard; his titling faces include Mantinia and Sophia.

WILLIAM CASLON (1692–1766) English engraver, punchcutter and typefounder; author of many Baroque romans, italics, Greeks and other non-Latin faces. ATF Caslon, Monotype Caslon, and Carol Twombly's Adobe Caslon are closely based on his work. A collection of his punches is now in the St Bride Printing Library, London.

WARREN CHAPPELL (1904–1991) American designer and scholar, trained in Germany, where he studied with Rudolf Koch. His typefaces include Trajanus, Lydian and the still unmanufactured Eichenauer.

SIMON DE COLINES (*c.* 1480–1547) French typecutter, master typographer and printer. Author of a dozen or more roman fonts, several italics, several blackletters and a fine cursive

Greek. Colines as much as any single person appears to be responsible for creating the typographic style of the French golden age. Garamond's romans derive directly from Colines, though his italics are quite different. None of Colines's faces has evidently yet been translated to digital form.

FRANÇOIS-AMBROISE DIDOT (1730–1804) Parisian printer and publisher. Designer of several Neoclassical romans and italics, cut under his supervision by Pierre-Louis Vafflard. Father of Firmin Didot and founder of the Didot dynasty in printing and typography.

FIRMIN DIDOT (1764–1836) Parisian printer and punchcutter; son of F.-A. Didot and student of Pierre-Louis Vafflard; father of Ambroise Firmin-Didot. Author of several Neoclassical faces as well as the Romantic fonts for which he is posthumously known. Monotype Didot and Linotype's digital Didot (drawn by Adrian Frutiger) are based on his work.

BRAM DE DOES (1934–) Dutch typographer, formerly chief designer at Joh. Enschedé en Zonen, Haarlem. Designer of the Trinité and Lexicon families.

WILLIAM ADDISON DWIGGINS (1880–1956) American designer and typographer. Dwiggins designed typefaces exclusively for the Linotype machine. In the 1930s and 1940s, he also created the typographic house style at Alfred Knopf, New York. His serifed faces include Caledonia, Eldorado, Electra and Falcon. His only completed sanserif is Metro. His uncial is Winchester. Many of his type drawings are now in the Boston Public Library.

ALFRED FAIRBANK (1895–1982) English calligrapher and designer of the Fairbank italic.

AMBROISE FIRMIN-DIDOT (1790–1876) French scholar, typecutter and printer. He was the son of Firmin Didot (whose full name he took as his own surname) and grandson of François-Ambroise Didot. Author of the Didot Greek fonts.

JOHANN MICHAEL FLEISCHMAN (1701–1768) German immigrant to the Netherlands. A prolific and skilled cutter of romans, italics and ornamental blackletters. Also the author of several Arabic and Greek fonts. Fleischman's early romans and italics are Baroque, but in the 1730s he cut a series of text fonts idiosyncratic and self-conscious enough to be called Rococo. Most of his surviving material is now at the Enschedé Museum in Haarlem.

KARL-ERIK FORSBERG (1914–1995) Swedish calligrapher and typographer, designer of the Berling text roman. His titling faces include Carolus, Ericus and Lunda.

PIERRE SIMON FOURNIER (1712–1768) French printer and punchcutter. Author of many French Neoclassical fonts and typographic ornaments. Nearly all of his original material has been damaged or lost. Monotype Fournier and Barbou are based on his work, and W. A. Dwiggins's Electra owes much to the study of it.

ADRIAN FRUTIGER (1928–) Swiss immigrant to France. A prolific and versatile designer of type. His serifed faces include Apollo, Breughel, Glypha, Iridium and Méridien. His sanserifs include Avenir, Frutiger and Univers. His titling and script types include Herculanum, Ondine, Pompeijana and Rusticana.

CLAUDE GARAMOND (*c.* 1490–1561) French punchcutter, working chiefly at Paris. Author of many roman fonts, at least two italics, and a full set of chancery Greeks. His surviving punches and matrices are now at the Plantin-Moretus Museum in Antwerp and at the Imprimerie Nationale, Paris. Stempel Garamond roman *and* italic, Linotype Granjon roman, Günter Gerhard Lange's Berthold Garamond roman, Robert Slimbach's Adobe Garamond roman and Ronald Arnholm's Legacy *italic* are all based on his designs. Monotype Garamond is not. (See also pp 218–220.)

ERIC GILL (1882–1940) English engraver and stonecutter, working in England and Wales. His serifed faces include Joanna, Perpetua and Pilgrim. His one unserifed face is Gill Sans. Perpetua Greek is also his, but Gill Sans Greek is by other hands. Gill's type drawings are now in the St Bride Library, London. Some of his matrices and punches are at the University Library, Cambridge; others are in the Clark Library, Los Angeles – but none of these punches were cut by Gill himself.

FREDERIC GOUDY (1865–1947) American type designer and founder. His serifed faces include University of California Old Style (later adapted for machine composition as Californian), Deepdene, Italian Old Style, Kaatskill, Kennerley, Village Nº 1 and Village Nº 2. His blackletters include Franciscan, Goudy Text and Goudy Thirty. His titling faces include Forum, Goudy Old Style and Hadriano. Goudy Sans is his only unserifed face. His only uncial is Friar. Most of

Type Designers

The spelling *Garamont* is now customary in France. The English spelling *Garamond* is derived from the Latin *Garamondius*, often used by Garamont himself.

Goudy's original material was destroyed by fire in 1939. What survives is at the Rochester Institute of Technology.

ROBERT GRANJON (c. 1513–1590) French typecutter working at Paris, Lyon, Antwerp, Frankfurt and Rome. Author of many Renaissance and Mannerist romans, italics, scripts, several Greeks, a Cyrillic, some Hebrews, and the first successful fonts of Arabic type. Some of his punches and matrices survive at the Plantin-Moretus Museum, Antwerp and the Nordiska Museet, Stockholm. Matthew Carter's Galliard is based primarily on Granjon's Ascendonica roman and italic.

FRANCESCO GRIFFO (c. 1450–1518) Bolognese punchcutter, working in Venice, Bologna and elsewhere in Italy. Author of at least seven romans, three italics, four Greeks and a Hebrew. None of Griffo's actual punches or matrices are known to survive, and the house of Aldus Manutius in Venice, where he did most of his work, has vanished. (The site is now occupied by a bank.) Griffo's letterforms have nonetheless been patiently reconstructed from the printed books in which his type appears. Giovanni Mardersteig's Griffo type is an exacting replica of one of Griffo's fonts. Monotype Bembo roman is based more loosely on the same font. Monotype Poliphilus is a rough reproduction of another. Mardersteig's Dante roman and italic are also based on a close study of Griffo's work. The italics, overall, have received far less attention than the romans.

ARNALDO GUILLÉN DE BROCAR (c. 1460–1524) Spanish printer and typographer working at Alcalá de Henares, near Madrid. Author of several romans and at least two Greek fonts, notably the Complutensian Greek type of 1510.

FRANÇOIS GUYOT (c. 1510–1570) Punchcutter and typefounder, born at Paris. He moved to Antwerp in the 1530s and spent most of the rest of his life there, cutting type for the printer Christophe Plantin and others.

VICTOR HAMMER (1882–1967) Austrian immigrant to the USA. All of Hammer's types are uncials. These include American Uncial, Andromache, Hammer Uncial, Pindar and Samson. His type drawings and punches are now at the University of Kentucky, Lexington.

KRIS HOLMES (1950–) American calligrapher. Designer of Isadora and Sierra; codesigner with Janice Fishman of Shannon, and with Charles Bigelow of the Lucida family.

Type Designers

For an excellent introduction to Griffo's roman types and their derivatives, see Giovanni Mardersteig's postscript to Pietro Bembo, *De Aetna* (Verona: Officina Bodoni, 1969): 136–149.

Complutensian means 'from Complutum,' which is the old Roman name for Alcalá.

JEAN JANNON (1580–1658) French punchcutter and printer. Author of a series of Baroque romans and italics. Much of his material survives at the Imprimerie Nationale, Paris, where his type is known as the *caractères de l'université*. Monotype 'Garamond,' Linotype 'Garamond' 3, ATF 'Garamond,' Lanston 'Garamont,' and Simoncini 'Garamond' are all based on his work. (See pp 218–220.)

NICOLAS JENSON (*c.* 1420–1480) French punchcutter and printer, working in Venice. Author of at least one roman, one Greek and five rotundas. Jenson's punches have vanished, but his type has often been copied from his printed books. Bruce Rogers's Centaur, Ronald Arnholm's Legacy roman and Robert Slimbach's Adobe Jenson roman are based on his. Karlgeorg Hoefer's San Marco is based in large part on Jenson's rotundas.

In addition to his 16 pt roman, Jenson cut at least the caps for a 12 pt font. In addition to his five rotundas (ranging from 12 to 21 pt), he also cut at least the lower case for a sixth and smaller font.

GEORGE WILLIAM JONES (1860–1942) English printer and type designer. Author of Linotype Estienne, Linotype Granjon, and the Venezia roman, which was later mated with an italic by Frederic Goudy. All Jones's faces are historical reconstructions. Granjon was the first commercial adaptation of a Garamond roman, mated with a Granjon italic.

MIKLÓS TÓTFALUSI KIS (1650–1702) Hungarian scholar, printer and typecutter. Kis was trained in Amsterdam and worked there and in Kolozsvár (now Cluj, Romania). Stempel Janson is cast from his surviving punches. Linotype Janson Text and Monotype Erhardt are based on his work.

RUDOLF KOCH (1876–1934) German calligrapher and artist. His titling faces include Koch Antiqua and Neuland. His blackletters include Claudius, Jessen, Wallau and Wilhelm Klingspor Schrift. Kabel is his only sanserif. Much of his material, formerly in the Klingspor Archive, Offenbach, is now in the Haus für Industriekultur, Darmstadt.

GÜNTER GERHARD LANGE (1921–) German typographer. Formerly art director at the Berthold Foundry, Berlin. His titling faces and scripts include Derby and El Greco. Solemnis is his uncial face.

VADIM VLADIMIROVICH LAZURSKI (1909–1994) Russian master calligrapher and typographer. His Lazurski family includes both Cyrillic and Latin alphabets. The Cyrillic also exists in a foundry version known as Pushkin.

HENRIC PIETERSZOON LETTERSNIDER (*fl.* 1492–1511) Dutch punchcutter working at Gouda, Antwerp, Rotterdam and

Delft. Author of a substantial number of blackletter types and fonts of large initials.

ZUZANA LIČKO (1961–) Slovakian immigrant to the USA. Cofounder of *Emigre* magazine and its offshoot, the Emigre digital foundry. Designer of Journal, Electrix, Modula and other faces. With John Downer, codesigner of Triplex.

MARTIN MAJOOR (1960–) Dutch graphic artist. Designer of the Scala family.

GIOVANNI MARDERSTEIG (1892–1977) German immigrant to Italy. A master printer, scholar, typographer and type designer. Author of Dante, Fontana, Griffo and Zeno. His material is at the Officina Bodoni, Verona.

HANS EDUARD MEIER (1922–) Swiss typographer. Designer of Barbedor, Syndor and the Syntax sanserif.

JOSÉ MENDOZA Y ALMEIDA (1926–) French graphic artist. His faces include Mendoza, Photina, Pascal, Fidelio (a chancery script), Sully Jonquières (an upright italic) and Convention.

OLDŘICH MENHART (1897–1962) Czech designer. His serifed Latin faces include Figural, Menhart and Parliament. His Manuscript family includes both Latin and Cyrillic faces. His titling faces include Czech Uncial and Monument.

ANTONIO DI BARTOLOMEO MISCOMINI (c. 1445–c. 1495) Italian punchcutter and printer. He was probably born in Bologna but did most of his work in Venice, Modena and Florence, where he printed during the early 1490s and brought his roman and orthotic Greek types to final form.

PETER MATTHIAS NOORDZIJ (1961–) Dutch typographer. Designer of PMN Caecilia and proprietor of the Enschedé Font Foundry.

ALEXANDER PHEMISTER (1829–1894) Scottish punchcutter. Author of the Old Style Antique issued by Miller & Richard, Edinburgh, beginning in 1858. In 1861 he moved to Boston where he worked for the Dickenson Foundry.

FRIEDRICH POPPL (1923–1982) German calligrapher. His serifed faces include Pontifex and Poppl Antiqua. His sanserif is Laudatio. His titling faces include Nero and Saladin. His script types include Poppl Exquisit and Residenz.

RICHARD PORSON (1759–1808) English classical scholar. Designer of the original Porson Greek, first cut by Richard Austin. Monotype Porson and the digital GFS Porson are based closely on his work.

VOJTĚCH PREISSIG (1873–1944) Czech artist, typographer and teacher, working in Czechoslovakia and in New York City. Preissig designed several text and titling faces, including the one that bears his name. His surviving drawings are in the Strahov Abbey, Prague.

ERHARD RATDOLT (1447–1528) German punchcutter and printer working at Augsburg and Venice. Author of at least ten blackletters, three romans and one Greek. In 1486 he issued the first known type specimen.

IMRE REINER (1900–1987) Hungarian artist and designer working in Germany, the USA and Switzerland. He was a skilled wood engraver and book illustrator. Author of several Expressionist script faces.

PAUL RENNER (1878–1956) German typographer. Designer of Futura, Topic and Renner Antiqua. His drawings for Futura are now in the Fundición Tipográfica Bauer, Barcelona.

BRUCE ROGERS (1870–1957) American typographer, working chiefly in Boston, London and Oxford. Designer of Montaigne and Centaur. The original drawings for Centaur are now in the Newberry Library, Chicago.

SJOERD HENDRIK DE ROOS (1877–1962) Dutch designer, typographer and printer. Author of many faces, include the uncials Libra and Simplex, the Nobel sanserif, and De Roos roman and italic.

RUDOLPH RŮŽIČKA (1883–1978) Czech immigrant to the USA. Designer of Linotype Fairfield and Primer.

VICTOR SCHOLDERER (1880–1971) English classical scholar and librarian. Designer of the New Hellenic Greek.

FRANTSYSK HEORHII SKARYNA (*c.* 1488–*c.* 1540) Belorussian physician, translator and printer, educated at Kraków and Padova. Author of several fonts of Cyrillic type, with which he printed at Prague and Vilnius.

ROBERT SLIMBACH (1956–) American. His serifed faces include Giovanni, Minion, Poetica, Slimbach, Utopia and Adobe Garamond. The sanserif Myriad is a joint design by Slimbach and Carol Twombly.

ERIK SPIEKERMANN (1947–) German graphic artist and one of the founders of the FontShop digital foundry. Designer of Meta and of the Officina family.

SUMNER STONE (1945–) American. Author of Silica, Cycles, Stone Print, and of the Stone typeface family, which includes both serifed and unserifed forms.

KONRAD SWEYNHEYM (c. 1415–1477) German monk and printer, working in central Italy. Probably the author of the two romans and one Greek which he and his partner Arnold Pannartz used at Subiaco and Rome between 1464 and 1473.

GIOVANANTONIO TAGLIENTE (fl. 1500–1525) Italian calligrapher and designer of at least one chancery italic type. Monotype Bembo italic is derived from this font.

AMEET TAVERNIER (c. 1522–1570) Flemish typecutter and printer working primarily at Antwerp. Author of many romans, italics, blackletters and civilité script types.

GEORG TRUMP (1896–1985) German artist. Trump studied lettering with Ernst Schneidler. His serifed text faces include Mauritius, Schadow and Trump Mediäval. His blackletters include Trump Deutsch. His titling faces and scripts include Codex, Delphin, Jaguar and Time.

JAN TSCHICHOLD (1902–1974) German immigrant to Switzerland. A number of Tschichold's phototype designs were destroyed in the Second World War. Designer of the Sabon family and the Saskia script.

CAROL TWOMBLY (1959–) American. Designer of Charlemagne, Lithos, Nueva, Trajan and Viva. Adobe Caslon is also her work, based on William Caslon's originals. With Robert Slimbach, she is codesigner of the Myriad sanserif.

GERARD UNGER (1942–) Dutch designer and teacher. His serifed faces include Amerigo, Demos, Hollander, Oranda and Swift, and his unserifed, Argo, Flora and Praxis.

HENDRIK VAN DEN KEERE (c. 1540–1580) Belgian typecutter, working at Ghent and Antwerp. He cut many romans and blackletters, at least one script type (a civilité) and several fonts of music type. DTL Van den Keere is a digital roman based on his work.

CHRISTOFFEL VAN DIJCK (1606–1669) Dutch punchcutter. Author of several Baroque romans, italics and blackletters. Monotype Van Dijck and DTL Elzevir are based on his work. Jan van Krimpen's Romanée and Gerard Unger's Hollander echo it in various ways. Most of Van Dijck's material has perished. The surviving punches and matrices are at the Enschedé Museum, Haarlem.

JAN VAN KRIMPEN (1892–1958) Dutch typographer. His serifed faces include Lutetia, Romanée, Romulus, Spectrum, Haarlemmer and the chancery italic called Cancelleresca

Bastarda. His only sanserif is Romulus Sans. His Greek is Antigone. His titling faces include Double Augustin Open Capitals, Lutetia Open Capitals and Romulus Open Capitals. Except for Haarlemmer, all these faces were first cut at Enschedé by Paul Helmuth Rädisch.

JOVICA VELJOVIĆ (1954–) Serbian immigrant to Germany. A gifted calligrapher and author of many Latin and Cyrillic faces. Esprit, Gamma, Veljović and Ex Ponto are his work.

JUSTUS ERICH WALBAUM (1768–1837) German typefounder and printer, author of several Neoclassical and Romantic faces. Both Berthold Walbaum and Monotype Walbaum are based on his surviving punches and matrices.

FREDERIC WARDE (1894–1939) American, working chiefly in France, Italy and England. Designer of the Arrighi italic. Some of Warde's drawings are in the Newberry Library, Chicago. Punches and matrices for the early (handcut) Arrighi are now at the Rochester Institute of Technology.

EMIL RUDOLF WEISS (1875–1942) German poet, painter, calligrapher and type designer. Author of a fraktur, a textura (Weiss Gotisch), a rotunda (Weiss Rundgotisch), a roman and italic known as Weiss Antiqua, a suite of typographic ornaments, and three series of titling caps or initials. All these fonts were cut by Louis Hoell and issued by the Bauer Foundry, Frankfurt.

BERTHOLD WOLPE (1905–1989) German immigrant to England. Pegasus is his text face. His titling faces include Albertus and Hyperion.

HERMANN ZAPF (1918–) German calligrapher, type designer, artist and teacher. His serifed faces include Aldus, Comenius, Euler, Marconi, Melior, Orion, Palatino, Zapf Book and Zapf Renaissance. His sanserifs include Optima, and his blackletters include Gilgengart, Winchester and Stratford. His titling faces and scripts include Kompakt, Michelangelo, Sistina, Venture, Zapf Chancery, Zapf Civilité and Zapf International. His Greeks include Attika, Euler, Heraklit, Optima and Phidias.

GUDRUN ZAPF-VON HESSE (1918–) German calligrapher and book artist. Her text and titling faces include Alcuin, Carmina, Diotima, Nofret, Ariadne and Smaragd.

APPENDIX D: TYPEFOUNDRIES

A reliable encyclopedia of the world's typefoundries – metal, photographic and digital; present and past – would be a very useful document. It would also be a thick one. This brief list is limited to metal and digital foundries and matrix engravers that have issued or preserved original designs that seem to me of lasting value for setting Latin, Greek or Cyrillic text.

Many of the type designers listed in appendix C (e.g., Robert Granjon, William Caslon, Frederic Goudy) also cast and sold their own type. Their foundries are listed again here only if (1) they outlived their founders and developed into independent entities or (2) they are currently active.

The phone numbers, fax numbers and postal addresses of foundries are subject to frequent change. Under present conditions, so is their financial health and consequent legal status. Current information is obtainable from websites and the trade press. For digital type, other useful references include the consolidated catalogues issued by FontShop International and by Precision Type, Commack, New York.

Adobe Systems, Mountain View, Calif. Originally a software company, founded in 1982 by John Warnock and Charles Geschke. Adobe was the original developer of the PostScript computer language used for the electronic storage and manipulation of typographic information. The firm now issues digital versions of many historical types as well as original designs by Robert Slimbach, Sumner Stone, Carol Twombly, Jovica Veljović and many others.

Agfa, Wilmington, Mass. In 1988 Agfa-Gevaert absorbed the Compugraphic Corporation, a manufacturer of photosetting machines and film matrices. A digital foundry known as Agfa-Compugraphic was subsequently formed. The firm has since been bought and sold repeatedly by people with no knowledge of or interest in typography. As of 1996 it was the Agfa Division of the Bayer Corporation. Agfa has issued new designs by Otl Aicher, Cynthia Hollandsworth, David Siegel and others.

Amsterdam Foundry, Amsterdam. A metal foundry established in Rotterdam in 1851 by Nicolaas Tetterode with stock from the Broese Foundry in Breda. The firm moved to Amsterdam in 1856 and in 1892 changed its name from Lettergieterij N. Tetterode to Lettergieterij Amsterdam. Typecasting operations waned in the 1970s and ceased altogether in 1988. During the twentieth century it issued new designs by S.H. de Roos and Dick Dooijes.

ATF (*American Type Founders*), Elizabeth, New Jersey. This was the largest metal typefoundry in North America, formed in 1892 by amalgamating a number of smaller firms. In its best days, it issued original designs by M.F. Benton, Lucian Bernhard, Frederic Goudy and many others. Though the company began to falter in the 1920s, it clung to life until 1993. Its library is now at Columbia University, New York, and most of the older typographic material is in the Smithsonian Institution, Washington, DC.

Bauer Foundry, Frankfurt. A metal foundry established in 1837 by Johann Christian Bauer. It expanded into an international network toward the end of the nineteenth century. The Bauer foundry as such ceased to exist in 1972, but one branch of the old empire – now called the Fundición Tipografica Bauer in Barcelona – remains in operation. Bauer issued original faces by its founder and later by Lucian Bernhard, Imre Reiner, Paul Renner, E.R. Weiss and others. The surviving punches and matrices are now at FTB in Barcelona and at WMD in Leipzig.

Berlingska Stilgjuteriet, Lund, Sweden. A metal typefoundry and printing house important for its castings, during the twentieth century, of original faces by Karl-Erik Forsberg.

H. Berthold, Berlin. Hermann Berthold's metalworks entered the typefounding business in 1893. It acquired the original punches and matrices of J.E. Walbaum and later issued original faces by G.G. Lange, Herbert Post, Imre Reiner and others. Berthold was involved in the creation of phototype as early as 1935. It ceased casting metal type in 1978 and turned to producing digital fonts in the 1980s. This activity all but ceased in 1993. The foundry's collection of punches and matrices is now in the care of the Museum für Verkehr und Technik, Berlin. Its extensive library of digital faces is now distributed in part by FontShop International and by Adobe.

Bitstream, Cambridge, Mass. A digital foundry established in 1981 by Matthew Carter and Mike Parker, both of whom later left the company. Bitstream has issued digital revivals of many earlier faces and new designs by Carter, Richard Lipton, Gerard Unger, Gudrun Zapf-von Hesse and others.

Carter & Cone, Cambridge, Mass. A digital foundry established in 1992 by Matthew Carter and Cherie Cone. It issues original designs and historical revivals by Carter.

Caslon Foundry, London. A metal typefoundry established by William Caslon about 1723 and maintained as a family business for four generations. It remained in operation as H.W. Caslon until 1936. Most of the older surviving punches are now in the St Bride Printing Library, London. The newer material passed to Stephenson Blake.

Deberny & Peignot, Paris. Joseph Gaspard Gillé the elder, one of Fournier's apprentices, opened his own foundry in Paris in 1748 and left the business to his son in 1789. In 1827, the novelist Honoré de Balzac acquired this foundry as part of his intended writing, printing and publishing empire. The scheme failed at once, but the foundry was rescued by its manager and bought by Alexandre de Berny. Gustave Peignot entered separately into the typefounding business in 1865. His own foundry entered its first creative phase under his son and grandson Georges and Charles Peignot, who issued historical revivals of the work of Jean Jannon and created a series of types based on the lettering of the eighteenth-century engraver Nicolas Cochin. The De Berny and Peignot foundries merged in 1923. Under the guidance of Charles Peignot, the enlarged firm issued new designs by Adolphe Cassandre, Adrian Frutiger and others. When D&P ceased production in 1975, the type drawings and company library went to the Bibliothèque Forney, Paris, and most of the typographic material – including a set of original Baskerville matrices – to the Haas (now Frutiger) Foundry, Münchenstein. Baskerville's punches, also formerly held by D&P, are now at the University Library, Cambridge.

DTL (*Dutch Type Library*), 's-Hertogenbosch, Netherlands. A digital foundry established by Frank Blokland in 1990. It has issued original faces by Blokland, Chris Brand, Gerard Daniëls, Sjoerd de Roos, Gerard Unger and others, and historical revivals of types by Christoffel van Dijck, Jan van Krimpen, J.M. Fleischman and Hendrik van den Keere.

EETS (Εταιρεία Ελληνικών Τυπογραφικών Στοιχείων). See *Greek Font Society*.

Elsner + Flake, Hamburg. A digital foundry established in 1989 by Günther Flake and Veronika Elsner. The firm has produced a large number of digital revivals and made the original digital versions of a number of ITC faces.

Emigre, Sacramento. A digital foundry established in Berkeley in 1985 by Rudy VanderLans and Zuzana Ličko. In 1992, the office moved to Sacramento. The firm issues original faces by Ličko, VanderLans, John Downer and others.

Joh. Enschedé en Zonen (Johann Enschedé & Sons), Haarlem, Netherlands. A printing plant and typefoundry operating from 1743 to 1990. In two and a half centuries of operation, the firm acquired material from many sources, including some of the punches and matrices of J.M. Fleischman and Christoffel van Dijck. During the early twentieth century, it issued in foundry form the types of its artistic director, Jan van Krimpen. In 1990, its stock of matrices and punches was transferred to the Enschedé Museum.

The Enschedé Font Foundry, Hurwenen, Netherlands. A digital foundry established in 1991 under the direction of Peter Matthias Noordzij. It has issued original designs by Bram de Does and a digital version of Jan van Krimpen's Romanée.

Esselte Letraset, London. Letraset Ltd. was founded in 1959 as a manufacturer of dry transfer lettering. It was acquired by the Swiss firm Esselte in 1981 and a few years later began to issue its faces in digital form. The digital library now includes both historical revivals and original designs by Michael Gills, Michael Neugebauer and others.

Fann Street Foundry, London. A metal foundry established in 1802 by Robert Thorne. Its creative period came in the 1850s, when it was owned by Robert Besley and issued original designs cut by Benjamin Fox. The surviving material was acquired by Stephenson Blake in 1905.

Font Bureau, Boston. A digital foundry established in 1989 by David Berlow and Roger Black. It has issued both historical revivals and original designs by John Downer, Tobias Frere-Jones, Richard Lipton, Greg Thompson and others.

FontShop International, Berlin. A digital foundry established in 1989 by Erik Spiekermann. It has issued original designs by Spiekermann, Erik van Blokland, Martin Majoor, Just van Rossum, Fred Smeijers and many others.

The Foundry, London. A digital foundry established by David Quay and Freda Sack. It has issued original designs by the

Type-foundries

proprietors and historical revivals of work by Max Bill, Paul Renner, Jan Tschichold and others.

Walter Fruttiger, Münchenstein, Switzerland. The new Fruttiger Foundry traces its roots to an operation founded by Jean Exertier in 1580 and can accordingly claim to be the world's oldest surviving foundry. For more than two centuries it was known as the Haas Foundry, after Johann Wilhelm Haas, who acquired the company in 1740. It possesses little material from before the eighteenth century, and during its long life it has not been the source of many original designs. In the first half of the twentieth century, however, Haas issued new designs by Walter Diethelm and, in 1951, the first versions of Max Miedinger's Helvetica.

FTB (*Fundición Tipográfica Bauer*), Barcelona. A metal foundry established in 1885. It is the last surviving branch of the old Bauer network and now holds much of the Bauer Foundry's surviving typographic material. Until 1995 it was known as FTN, the Fundición Tipográfica Neufville.

Golgonooza Letter Foundry, Ashuelot, New Hampshire. Established in 1980 by Dan Carr and Julia Ferrari, who cast type from Monotype matrices and issue Carr's own faces, some cut by hand in steel and others created in digital form.

Grafotechna, Prague. A metal typefoundry important for its castings of the work of Miloslav Fulín, Oldřich Menhart, Vojtěch Preissig and other Czech designers.

GFS (*Greek Font Society*), Athens. A digital foundry established in 1992. It has issued digital versions of historically important Greek types designed by Ambroise Firmin-Didot, Richard Porson and Victor Scholderer, as well as new Greek designs by Takis Katsoulides.

Haas Foundry. See *Walter Frutiger*.

Rudolf Hell. See *Linotype-Hell*.

Imprimerie Nationale, Paris. A printing house and foundry established by Louis XIII in 1640 as the Imprimerie Royale. With the French Revolution (1789), the Imprimerie Royale became first l'Imprimerie Nationale and then l'Imprimerie de la République. With the coronation of Napoleon I in 1804, it became l'Imprimerie Impériale. After the Restoration of 1815, it was again l'Imprimerie Royale. In 1848, after two more revolutions, it was l'Imprimerie Nationale again, and so it has remained – except for the hiatus, 1852–1870, under Napoleon III, when it was again called l'Imprimerie

Impériale. It owns the surviving punches and matrices of Jean Jannon (the source of most of the world's 'Gara-monds') and a large quantity of historically important material for the typography of Asian languages. It has sponsored original designs by many hands, including Firmin Didot, Philippe Grandjean, Marcellin Legrand, Louis-René Luce and José Mendoza y Almeida.

Intertype (International Typesetting Machine Co.), New York. When the basic Mergenthaler Linotype patents expired in 1912, a group of investors had assembled in New York, ready to build a competing machine. The matrices issued for Intertype machines included new adaptations of foundry faces designed by Dick Dooijes and S. H. de Roos. Intertype was involved in phototypesetting as early as 1947. After a merger in the 1950s, the firm was known as the Harris Intertype Corporation and became a principal manufacturer of photographic matrices.

ITC (*International Typeface Corporation*), New York. Founded by Aaron Burns and Herb Lubalin in 1969 as a typeface licensing and distribution agency. The original domain was limited to phototype. In the 1980s, ITC began to license digital designs as well. Not until 1994 did it start to produce and market its faces directly. For more than a decade, there was a readily identifiable ITC style: a standardized large torso with interchangeable serifs that reduced the alphabet and its history to superficial costume. This Procrustean approach to type design faded in the 1980s. Coincidentally, the company was bought in 1986 by Esselte Letraset. The list includes original designs by Ronald Arnholm, Matthew Carter, Erik Spiekermann, Hermann Zapf and many others.

Klingspor Brothers, Offenbach. A metal foundry established in 1842 and operated under several different names before its acquisition in 1892 by Karl Klingspor. It issued original faces by Peter Behrens, Rudolf Koch and Walter Tiemann. After its closure in 1953, the library and drawings were transferred to the Klingspor Museum, Offenbach, and most of the matrices to the Stempel Foundry, Frankfurt.

Lanston Monotype Machine Co., Philadelphia. The Monotype machine as we know it was devised by John Sellers Bancroft of Philadelphia in 1900. It grew, however, from a series of earlier machines invented by Tolbert Lanston of Washington, DC, beginning in 1887. The American company created to manufacture and sell these devices started slowly and was soon outdistanced by its English counterpart, formed a decade later with the same objective and almost the same name (see below: *The Monotype Corporation*). The American firm nevertheless remained in business, moving to Philadelphia in 1901 and pursuing on a smaller scale its own design agenda. This included cutting mats for historical revivals and original designs by Frederic Goudy, Sol Hess and others. The surviving material was dispersed in 1983.

Lanston Type Co., Mt Stewart, Prince Edward Island. In 1983 Gerald Giampa acquired a collection of patterns and drawings from the Lanston Monotype Company of Philadelphia. With this foundation, he established a digital foundry in Vancouver, moving to PEI in 1994. The library consists almost entirely of digitized versions of American Monotype faces, especially work by Frederic Goudy.

Linotype Library, Frankfurt. Founded as the Mergenthaler Printing Co., Brooklyn, in 1886 by Ottmar Mergenthaler, to sell his newly invented Linotype machine. Many of the early matrices were produced under contract by the Stempel Foundry, Frankfurt, from designs by artists such as Warren Chappell, Georg Trump and Hermann Zapf. Others were produced in England from the designs of George W. Jones, and in the USA from designs by W.A. Dwiggins, Rudolph Růžička and others. The company began to produce photosetting equipment and film matrices in the 1950s, CRT (cathode ray tube) photosetters in the 1960s, and high-resolution laser setters in the 1980s. In 1990, Linotype merged with Dr.-Ing. Rudolf Hell GmbH of Kiel. In 1998, it became the Linotype Library. The firm has issued many of the old Linotype faces in digital form, and new designs by Adrian Frutiger, Karlgeorg Hoefer and others. Large collections of earlier material from the American branch of the company are now at the Rochester Institute of Technology, Rochester, New York, and the University of Kentucky, Lexington.

The Ludlow Typograph Co., Chicago. Washington Ludlow of Chicago began making typecasting machinery in 1906, but the Ludlow caster which his company sold throughout the early twentieth century was a later device, designed and built by William Reade in 1909. The machine casts slugs from handset proprietary matrices and was therefore used for little except display type, but several Ludlow faces have been successfully adapted for digital text composition. The company issued both historical revivals and original designs, chiefly by its director of typography, R.H. Middleton. It ceased operation in North America in 1986. The English arm, founded in the early 1970s, closed in 1990.

Ludwig & Mayer, Frankfurt. A metal foundry that ceased operation in 1985. The surviving material was transferred to FTB in Barcelona. During its heyday, the firm issued original designs by Jakob Erbar, Helmut Matheis and others.

Mergenthaler. See *Linotype-Hell.*

Miller & Richard, Edinburgh. A metal foundry established in 1809 by George Miller, joined by Walter Richard in 1832. The foundry issued original designs by Richard Austin, Alexander Phemister and others. When it ceased operation in 1952, the surviving material went to Stephenson Blake.

The Monotype Corporation, Redhill, Surrey, England. An entity called the Lanston Monotype *Company* was first formed in the USA in 1887. Another, called the Lanston Monotype *Corporation* (later simply the Monotype Corporation) was formed in England a decade later. For the American firm, see *Lanston Monotype.* The typographically creative phase of the English firm began in 1922 with the appointment of Stanley Morison as typographic advisor. Over the next few decades, English Monotype cut a number of meticulously researched historical revivals as well as new designs by Eric Gill, Giovanni Mardersteig, José Mendoza y Almeida, Victor Scholderer, Jan van Krimpen, Berthold Wolpe and others. The firm began producing photosetting equipment and photographic matrices in the 1950s, and laser typesetting machines in the 1970s. Its fortunes then slumped, and in the early 1990s a new and smaller company, Monotype Typography Inc., was formed to produce and market digital type, including digital reincarnations of the faces originally cut in metal for the Monotype machine. Metal matrices are still made on demand by the Monotype Trust.

Nebiolo Foundry, Torino. A metal typefoundry established in 1878 by Giovanni Nebiolo through the amalgamation of several older and smaller firms. It is important for its castings of original designs by Alessandro Butti and Aldo Novarese. Nebiolo ceased operation about 1990.

Norstedt Foundry, Stockholm. A metal foundry, formerly supplied with matrices by Robert Granjon, François Guyot,

Ameet Tavernier and others. The surviving material is now in the Nordiska Museet, Stockholm.

Fonderie Olive, Marseilles. A metal foundry which ceased operation in 1978. It issued a number of original designs by Roger Excoffon, François Ganeau and others. The surviving material is now at the Fruttiger Foundry, Münchenstein.

ParaGraph International (ПараГраф Интернэшнл), Moscow. A digital foundry established in 1989. It issues original designs and historical revivals of Cyrillic, Latin, Georgian, Arabic, Hebrew and Greek faces.

Plantin-Moretus Museum, Antwerp. The printing house and foundry established by Christophe Plantin about 1555 was conserved for nearly three centuries by descendants of Plantin's son-in-law, Jan Moretus. It was converted to a museum in 1877 but still possesses the resources required for casting type. It includes a rich collection of original material by Claude Garamond, Robert Granjon, Hendrik van den Keere, Ameet Tavernier and other early artists.

Polygraph (НПО Полиграфмаш), Moscow. A manufacturer of typesetting machines and matrices. It has issued original designs, especially Cyrillics, by Vadim Lazurski, Svetlana Ermolaeva and others.

Scangraphic, Hamburg. Formerly Mannesmann Scangraphic, a manufacturer of photosetting equipment. In the 1980s it began to issue digital fonts, including new designs by Volker Küster and Hermann Zapf.

D. Stempel, Frankfurt. After its foundation by David Stempel in 1895, this firm absorbed the holdings of many other German foundries. It also issued many original faces by Hermann Zapf, Gudrun Zapf-von Hesse and others, and sold type cast from the original matrices of Miklós Kis. After the foundry closed in 1986, the typographic material was transferred to a museum known as the Haus für Industriekultur in Darmstadt. The tools of Stempel's last master punchcutter, August Rosenberger (who cut the original versions of Zapf's Palatino) are now in the Gutenberg Museum, Mainz.

Stephenson Blake & Co., Sheffield, England. A metal foundry established in 1819 by John Stephenson, James Blake and William Garnet, using materials acquired chiefly from William Caslon IV. Over time, the firm has added further material from the Fann Street Foundry, the original Caslon Foundry, and other operations. It continues to cast type.

Stone Type Foundry, Palo Alto. A digital foundry established in 1991 by Sumner Stone. It issues faces designed by the proprietor.

Tetterode. See *Amsterdam Foundry*.

Typoart, Dresden. A metal foundry formed in the 1950s by nationalizing the existing operations of Schelter & Giesecke and Schriftguss. It is important also for its castings, during the twentieth century, of original designs by its artistic director, Albert Kapr. The surviving typographic material is now at WMD, Leipzig.

URW (*Unternehmensberatung Karow Rubow Weber*), Hamburg. Established as a software firm in 1971, URW was diverted into digital typography by Peter Karow, a physicist excited by typography, who joined it in 1972. It was the original developer of the Ikarus system (a predecessor of PostScript) for digitizing type. It issued a large number of historical revivals as well as original faces by Hermann Zapf, Gudrun Zapf-von Hesse, and others. The firm entered receivership in 1995. Its library has since been distributed by a corporate successor known as 'URW++.'

Victoria Foundry, Koropi, Attika. A metal foundry, still in operation, casting chiefly nineteenth- and early twentieth-century Greek faces.

Johannes Wagner, Ingolstadt. A metal foundry established at Leipzig in 1902 by Ludwig Wagner and relocated to Ingolstadt in 1949 by his son Johannes. It has acquired matrices from Berthold, Johns, Weber and other foundries, and continues to cast type.

Weber Foundry, Stuttgart. A metal foundry that issued original faces by Georg Trump and others. In 1971 it was absorbed by the Wagner Foundry, Ingolstadt.

WMD (*Werkstätten und Museum für Druckkunst*), Leipzig. A working typographic museum founded in 1994 by Eckehart Schumacher-Gebler. Its large stock of typographic material includes original punches and matrices by Johann Christian Bauer, Lucian Bernhard, Jakob Erbar, Albert Kapr, Paul Renner, Jacques Sabon and many others.

Y&Y, Concord, Mass. A digital foundry specializing in fonts and system software for the setting of mathematics and scientific texts. It has issued original designs by Charles Bigelow, Kris Holmes and Hermann Zapf.

APPENDIX E: RECAPITULATION

Page

APPENDIX F: FURTHER READING

Typography is an ancient and polylingual enterprise, and the recent literature on digital typography is vast. Much of that literature is, however, highly technical, and much is quite remarkably superficial. This short list includes only a selection of the more important works available in English.

F.1 GENERAL HISTORY & PRINCIPLES

Anderson, Donald M. *The Art of Written Forms.* New York. 1969.

Bennett, Paul A., ed. *Books and Printing: A Treasury for Typophiles.* Cleveland. 1951.

DeFrancis, John. *Visible Speech: The Diverse Oneness of Writing Systems.* Honolulu. 1989.

Degering, Hermann. *Lettering.* New York. 1965.

Gaur, Albertine. *A History of Writing.* London. 1984.

Gelb, I. J. *A Study of Writing.* 2nd ed. Chicago. 1963.

Gray, Nicolete. *A History of Lettering.* Oxford. 1986.

———. *Lettering as Drawing.* 2 vols. Oxford. 1970. Reprinted as one vol., 1971.

Kenney, E. J. *The Classical Text: Aspects of Editing in the Age of the Printed Book.* Berkeley. 1974.

Knuttel, Gerard. *The Letter as a Work of Art.* Amsterdam. 1951.

Meggs, Philip B. *A History of Graphic Design.* New York. 1983.

Morison, Stanley. *Politics and Script.* Oxford. 1972.

———. *Selected Essays on the History of Letter-forms.* 2 vols. Cambridge, UK. 1981.

Vervliet, H. D. L., ed. *The Book through 5000 Years.* London. 1972.

F.2 SCRIBAL ROOTS

Avrin, Leila. *Scribes, Script and Books: The Book Arts from Antiquity to the Renaissance.* Chicago & London. 1991.

Diringer, David. *The Hand-Produced Book.* London. 1953. Reprinted as *The Book Before Printing,* New York. 1982.

Jeffery, Lillian K. *The Local Scripts of Archaic Greece.* 2nd ed. Oxford. 1990.

Knight, Stan. *Historical Scripts*. London. 1984.
Noordzij, Gerrit. *The Stroke of the Pen*. The Hague. 1982.
Parkes, M.B. *Pause and Effect*. Berkeley. 1993.
Stevick, Robert D. *The Earliest Irish and English Bookarts*.
    Philadelphia. 1994.
Wardrop, James. *The Script of Humanism*. Oxford. 1963.

F.3 TYPOGRAPHIC HISTORY

Barker, Nicolas. *Aldus Manutius and the Development of Greek
    Script and Type in the Fifteenth Century*. 2nd ed. New York.
    1992.
Blumenthal, Joseph. *Art of the Printed Book, 1455–1955*. New
    York. 1973.
Carter, Harry. *A View of Early Typography*. Oxford. 1969.
*Catalogue of Books Printed in the xvth Century Now in the
    British Museum*. 12 vols to date. London. 1908–85.
Chappell, Warren. *A Short History of the Printed Word*. New
    York. 1970.
Day, Kenneth, ed. *Book Typography 1815–1965*. London. 1966.
Dreyfus, John, ed. *Type Specimen Facsimiles*. 2 vols. London.
    1963–72.
Enschedé, Charles. *Typefoundries in the Netherlands*. Translated
    with revisions and notes by Harry Carter. Haarlem,
    Netherlands. 1978.
*Fine Print on Type: The Best of Fine Print Magazine on Type and
    Typography*. San Francisco. 1988.
Huss, Richard E. *The Development of Printers' Mechanical
    Typesetting Methods, 1822–1925*. Charlottesville, Virginia.
    1973.
Johnson, A.F. *Selected Essays on Books and Printing*.
    Amsterdam. 1970.
———. *Type Designs*. 3rd ed. London. 1966.
Lawson, Alexander. *Anatomy of a Typeface*. Boston. 1990.
Layton, Evro. *The Sixteenth Century Greek Book in Italy*. Venice.
    1994.
Morison, Stanley. *Letter Forms: Typographic and Scriptorial*.
    New York. 1968. Reissued, Vancouver, 1996.
Morison, Stanley, & Kenneth Day. *The Typographic Book,
    1450–1935*. London. 1963.
Proctor, Robert. *The Printing of Greek in the Fifteenth Century*.
    Oxford. 1900.

Scholderer, Victor. *Greek Printing Types 1465–1927*. London. 1927.

Steinberg, S.H. *Five Hundred Years of Printing*. 3rd ed., rev. by James Moran. London. 1974. 4th ed., rev. by John Trevitt, New Castle, Delaware, 1996.

Updike, Daniel Berkeley. *Printing Types: Their History, Forms and Use*. 2nd ed. 2 vols. Cambridge, Mass. 1937.

Vervliet, H. D. L. *Cyrillic and Oriental Typography in Rome at the End of the Sixteenth Century: An Inquiry into the Work of Robert Granjon*. Berkeley. 1981.

Zimmer, Szczepan K. *The Beginning of Cyrillic Printing*. New York. 1983.

F.4 TYPOGRAPHY IN RECENT TIME

André, Jacques, & Roger Hersch, ed. *Raster Imaging and Digital Typography*. Cambridge, UK. 1989.

Carter, Sebastian. *Twentieth-Century Type Designers*. London & New York. 1987.

Dreyfus, John. *The Work of Jan van Krimpen*. The Hague. 1952.

Goudy, Frederic W. *Goudy's Type Designs*. 2nd ed. New Rochelle, NY. 1978.

———. *Typologia: Studies in Type Design & Type Making*. Berkeley & Los Angeles. 1940.

McLean, Ruari. *Jan Tschichold: Typographer*. London. 1975.

Morison, Stanley, et al. *A Tally of Types*. 2nd ed. Cambridge, UK. 1973.

Raster Imaging and Digital Typography: Proceedings of the Third International Conference. New York. 1994.

Snyder, Gertrude, & Alan Peckolick. *Herb Lubalin*. New York. 1985.

Spencer, Herbert. *Pioneers of Modern Typography*. Rev. ed., Cambridge, Mass. 1982.

Tracy, Walter. *Letters of Credit*. London. 1986.

Zapf, Hermann. *Hermann Zapf and His Design Philosophy*. Chicago. 1987.

———. *Manuale Typographicum*. Frankfurt. 1954. Rev. ed., Cambridge, Mass. 1970.

———. *Manuale Typographicum 1968*. Frankfurt & New York. 1968.

———. *Typographic Variations*. New York. 1963. Reissued, New Rochelle, NY, 1978.

Benjamin, Walter. "The Work of Art in the Age of Mechanical Reproduction," in *Illuminations*. London. 1970.

Davids, Betsy, & Jim Petrillo. "The Artist as Book Printer." In Joan Lyons, ed., *Artists' Books*. New York. 1985.

Dowding, Geoffrey. *Finer Points in the Spacing and Arrangement of Type*. 3rd ed. London. 1966.

Duncan, Harry. *Doors of Perception*. Austin, Texas. 1987.

Gill, Eric. *An Essay on Typography*. 2nd ed. London. 1936. Reissued, Boston, 1993.

Huntley, H.E. *The Divine Proportion: A Study in Mathematical Beauty*. New York. 1970.

Le Corbusier. *The Modulor*. 2nd ed. Cambridge, Mass. 1954.

Massin, [Robert]. *Letter and Image*. London. 1970.

Morison, Stanley. *First Principles of Typography*. New York. 1936.

Mumford, Lewis. *Art and Technics*. New York. 1952.

Pye, David. *The Nature and Art of Workmanship*. Cambridge, UK. 1968.

Stevens, Peter S. *Patterns in Nature*. Boston. 1974.

Thompson, D'Arcy. *On Growth and Form*. Cambridge, UK. 1917. Rev. ed., 1942; abridged by J.T. Bonner, 1961.

Tschichold, Jan. *Asymmetric Typography*. New York. 1967.

———. *The Form of the Book*, ed. Robert Bringhurst. Vancouver. 1991.

Warde, Beatrice. *The Crystal Goblet*. London. 1955.

Washburn, Dorothy K., & Donald W. Crowe. *Symmetries of Culture: Theory and Practice of Plane Pattern Analysis*. Seattle. 1988.

F.6 MANUALS & TEXTBOOKS

Adobe Systems Incorporated. *PostScript Language Program Design*. Reading, Mass. 1988.

———. *PostScript Language Reference Manual*. 2nd ed. Reading, Mass. 1990.

———. *PostScript Language Tutorial and Cookbook*. Reading, Mass. 1986.

Dair, Carl. *Design with Type*. 2nd ed. Toronto. 1967.

Itten, Johannes. *The Art of Color*, trans. Ernst von Haagen. New York. 1961.

Karow, Peter. *Digital Typefaces: Description and Formats.* 2nd
    ed. Berlin. 1994.
————. *Font Technology: Methods and Tools.* Berlin. 1994.
Legros, L.A., & J.C. Grant. *Typographical Printing Surfaces.*
    London. 1916. Reissued, New York, 1980.
McLean, Ruari. *Thames and Hudson Manual of Typography.*
    London. 1980.
Martin, Douglas. *Book Design: A Practical Introduction.* New
    York. 1989.
Roth, Stephen F., ed. *Real World PostScript.* Reading, Mass.
    1988.
Smith, Ross. *PostScript: A Visual Approach.* Berkeley, Calif.
    1990.
Tufte, Edward R. *Envisioning Information.* Cheshire,
    Connecticut. 1990.
————. *The Visual Display of Quantitative Information.*
    Cheshire, Connecticut. 1983.
West, Martin L. *Textual Criticism and Editorial Technique
    Applicable to Greek and Latin Texts.* Stuttgart. 1973.
Wick, Karl. *Rules for Typesetting Mathematics.* Prague. 1965.
Williamson, Hugh. *Methods of Book Design.* London. 1983.
Wilson, Adrian. *The Design of Books.* New York. 1967.
    Reprinted, Salt Lake City, 1974.

F.7 WORKS OF REFERENCE

Chicago Manual of Style. 14th ed. Chicago. 1993.
Coulmas, Florian. *The Writing Systems of the World.* Oxford.
    1989.
Daniels, Peter T., & William Bright, ed. *The World's Writing
    Systems.* New York. 1996.
Eckersley, Richard, et al. *Glossary of Typesetting Terms.* Chicago.
    1994.
Hart's Rules for Compositors and Readers. 39th ed. Oxford.
    1983.
Hlavsa, Oldřich. *A Book of Type and Design.* New York. 1961.
International Organization for Standardization. *Information
    Technology: Coded Graphic Character Set for Text
    Communication.* ISO 6937. 2nd ed. Geneva. 1994.
————. *Information Processing: 8-bit Single-byte Coded
    Graphic Character Sets.* ISO 8859. Parts 1–9. Geneva.
    1987–89.

————. *Information Technology: Universal Multiple Octet Coded Character Set.* ISO 10646-1: *Architecture and Basic Multilingual Plane.* [Rev. ed.] Geneva. 2000.

Jaspert, W. P., et al. *Encyclopedia of Typefaces.* 5th ed. London. 1983.

McGrew, Mac. *American Metal Typefaces of the Twentieth Century.* New Castle, Delaware. 1993.

Pullum, Geoffrey K., & William A. Ladusaw. *Phonetic Symbol Guide.* 2nd ed. Chicago. 1998.

Sutton, James, & Alan Bartram. *An Atlas of Typeforms.* London. 1968.

Unicode Consortium. *The Unicode Standard.* Version 3.0. Reading, Mass. 2000.

F.8 PERIODICALS

Fine Print. Quarterly. San Francisco. 16 vols, 1975–90.

The Fleuron. Annual. Cambridge, UK. 7 vols, 1923–30.

Journal of the Printing Historical Society. London. Annual, 1965– .

Letterletter. Journal of the Association Typographique Internationale. Münchenstein, Switzerland. Semiannual through 1990, then biennial. 15 issues in all, 1985–96. Issued in book form, 2001.

Matrix. Andoversford, Glos. Irregular, 1981– .

Printing History. Journal of the American Printing History Association. New York. Semiannual, 1979– .

Serif. Claremont, California. Irregular. 5 issues, 1994–97.

Typografische Monatsblätter. St Gallen, Switzerland. Monthly, then bimonthly, 1881– .

Typographica. London. Irregular, then semiannual. 13 + 16 issues. 1949–59; new series, 1960–67.

Visible Language. Published 1967–70 as the *Journal of Typographic Research.* Cleveland. Quarterly, 1967– .

AFTERWORD TO VERSION 2.4

The first edition of this book contained erroneous statements about the form of Baskerville's parentheses, the abandonment of the typographic long *s*, the etymology of the word *sanserif*, and the date of birth of the American designer Frederic Warde. It is a privilege to be able to correct these mistakes and to try my luck at making more.

Though not quite every page has changed, the second edition has been reset from beginning to end by Susanne Gilbert, for whose skill, patience and impatience I have the very highest admiration. Glenn Woodsworth also recreated all the drawings.

A few old friends and typographic mentors are mentioned in the foreword. I owe thanks to many others – among them Charles Bigelow, Frank Blokland, Fred Brady, Dan Carr, Matthew Carter, Sebastiano Cossia Castiglioni, Mary Conibear, Burwell Davis, James Do, Bram de Does, John Dreyfus, Paul Hayden Duensing, Richard Eckersley, Veronika Elsner, Günther Flake, Richard Hendel, Sjaak Hubregtse, Susan Juby, Peter Karow, Peter Rutledge Koch, John Lane, David Lemon, Ken Lunde, Linnea Lundquist, Michael Macrakis, Russell Maret, David Michaelides, Brenda Newman, Gerrit Noordzij, Peter Matthias Noordzij, Ilya Poluektov, Will Powers, Robert Slimbach, Jack Stauffacher, Carol Twombly, Gerard Unger, Glenda Wilshire, Ken Whistler, Doyald Young and Maxim Zhukov – who have made this a better book, and its author a less ignorant human being, in a variety of ways.

The book has involved the use of a great many fonts of type – most of them digital, some of them metal – and the inspection and close testing of still more. These fonts were kindly supplied by Adobe Systems Inc. in San Jose, California; the Agfa Division of the Bayer Corporation, in Wilmington, Massachusetts; Barbarian Press in Mission, British Columbia; Carter & Cone Type in Cambridge, Massachusetts; the Dutch Type Library in 's-Hertogenbosch; Elsner + Flake in Hamburg; Emigre, Inc., in Sacramento; Esselte Letraset in London; The Font Bureau, Inc., in Boston; FontShop International in Berlin and FontShop Canada in Toronto; The Foundry, London; the Golgonooza Letter Foundry in Ashuelot, New Hampshire; the Greek Font Society (Εταιρεία Ελληνικών Τυπογραφικών Στοιχείων) in Athens;

the International Typeface Corporation in New York; the Lanston Type Company in Mount Stewart, Prince Edward Island; Linotype-Hell AG in Frankfurt and the Linotype-Hell Company in Hauppauge, New York; Scangraphic PrePress Technology in Hamburg; Monotype Typography Ltd in Redhill, Surrey, and Monotype Typography, Inc., in Chicago; ParaGraph International in Moscow and in Campbell, California; Precision Type in Commack, New York; the Stone Type Foundry in Palo Alto, California; and URW Software and Type GmbH in Hamburg. Additional artwork was kindly supplied by Peter Matthias Noordzij at the Enschedé Font Foundry in Hurwenen, Netherlands, and by Christopher Stinehour in Berkeley.

I owe particular thanks to Fred Brady, Bur Davis and Robert Slimbach of Adobe Systems, and to Michael Macrakis and George Matthiopoulos of the Greek Font Society, who permitted me to test and use draft versions of several fonts well in advance of their public release.

*Afterword
to the Second
Edition*

INDEX

The names of typefaces are italicized in this index, but no distinction is made between generic names, like *Garamond* or *Bodoni*, and specific ones, like *Aldus*.

This book was designed by Robert Bringhurst,
set into type by Robert Bringhurst and Susanne Gilbert
at The Typeworks in Vancouver, and
printed and bound by Friesens in Altona, Manitoba.

The text face is Minion,
designed by Robert Slimbach,
issued in digital form by Adobe Systems,
Mountain View, California, in 1989.

It is supplemented here with Minion Cyrillic
and a trial version of Minion Greek,
used with the kind permission
of Robert Slimbach and Adobe Systems.

The captions are set in Scala Sans,
designed in the Netherlands by Martin Majoor
and issued in digital form by FontShop International,
Berlin, and its affiliates in 1994.

The paper is Cougar Opaque Smooth
made by Weyerhauser and
is of archival quality and acid-free.